Praise for *Bright Ligh*

"Karen Grassle's new memoir is breath and unvarnished account of the life bad, and the ugly. Karen encapsulates both the joys found and the sacrifices made in the name of our beloved craft. I will happily recommend the book to all the women I care about."

—BETTY BUCKLEY, actress and singer

"I've always loved Karen Grassle. My respect and admiration for her are even better informed now, thanks to her excellent new book. Karen shares a joyous, searching, and sometimes devastating personal and artistic life driven by her commitment to artistic excellence. As we all witnessed for ourselves on TV, Karen's craft transformed her turmoil into touchstones of serenity and strength that audiences have always adored."

—DEAN BUTLER, actor and producer

"Bravo to my fellow TV mom! What a fascinating journey. The book is so well written . . . I couldn't put it down."

—MARION ROSS, actor

"Karen weaves a fascinating story of her life and of her experiences, first as a developing artist in the theatre and later as a star in in Hollywood. This book strikes me as a work of courage and hard-earned wisdom as she artfully bares her soul with eyes wide open."

—DIRK BLOCKER, actor

"In this unique portrait of an artist, Karen Grassle details the good, the bad, and the ugly aspects of her life in theatre, television, and film. From a scrappy beginning in the theatre in '60s New York to the not-so-pretty behind-the-scenes of a favorite American show, Karen shares her experience, strength, and hope with us in her battle with alcoholism and showbiz with courageous honesty."

—JEAN LOUISA KELLY, actress (*Uncle Buck,*
Mr. Holland's Opus, Top Gun 2)

"A touching, honest, and powerful memoir. By the end, we feel great affection and respect for Karen Grassle, the person—a role she struggled with through much of her life but eventually fulfilled in fine style. She found acting and feminism at Berkeley in the '60s, and they never let her down."

—PETER GLAZER, playwright, director, associate professor, TDPS, UC Berkeley

"I started to read this book as a favor to my friend Karen, and soon realized that the favor came from her to me! This is a story about a woman who has shared her heart, soul, and humor. It is a beautiful story from childhood to stardom. I couldn't put it down."

—MICHAEL LEARNED, Emmy Award–winning actress (*The Waltons*)

"Behind the 'Ma' we adored on our screens lies a gritty story of perseverance and heartache—both on and off the prairie. Karen's book will surprise the *Little House* fan in all of us."

—WENDI LOU LEE, author and actress on *Little House on the Prairie*

"If you think you know Karen Grassle, you don't. If you think she's simply 'Ma,' she isn't. I was fascinated and intrigued and astonished reading this book. I couldn't put it down. Do yourself a favor and go on her life journey with her. It will make yours better!"

—DEE WALLACE, actress

"Karen Grassle's brilliant, painful, and passionate memoir is both heartbreaking and downright fun. Fans of her beloved, iconic 'Caroline Ingalls' from *Little House on the Prairie* will be thrilled with the personal and private backstage details, though I'd recommend the book to anyone looking for an entertaining and immersive read."

—BETH GRANT, actress (*Rain Man, No Country for Old Men, Little Miss Sunshine, Speed*)

"Karen has lived a fascinating life which she recounts with heart-breaking honesty. I'm so proud of my TV 'Ma' for her take on our *Little House* adventure and so much more!"

—MELISSA ANDERSON, Emmy Award–winning actress
and author

"Part coming-of-age story, part Hollywood tell-all, part chronicle of American history, part guidebook to being a great actor, all told with warmth and humor and brutal honesty, Karen Grassle's *Bright Lights, Prairie Dust* is a thrilling memoir of a life both extraordinary in its adventures and achievements and ordinary in its commonality with the experiences of women everywhere."

—RINNE B. GROFF, playwright

"As a Religious Science Minister, I read everything through my metaphysical filter in order to better serve my spiritual community and the world. Karen's transparent sharing of her life left me moved—I laughed, cried, and felt my own heart and mind shift and expand. I am grateful!

—REV. DR. RAYMONT ANDERSON, Sr. Minister, CSL,
Greater Baltimore

"Brace yourselves! She is nothing like Ma! Hear it all from the woman behind the petticoats."

—ALISON ARNGRIM, actor and *New York Times* best-selling
author *Confessions of a Prairie Bitch*

"Karen Grassle's arresting memoir is a gift to the millions of fans of *Little House*. She shares an ongoing spiritual journey as she dedicates herself to a life in the theatre while untangling the knots along the way. It's a highly honest, detailed, and fast-paced voyage that's sure to make a proper prairie woman blush! Be swept away reading about the radical '60s of Berkeley, Broadway, and Hollywood, and of becoming the iconic 'Ma Ingalls' while always being committed to women's rights. This is a brave book; I was truly enthralled."

—LUCY LEE FLIPPEN, actress

"Karen Grassle's transformation from edgy Good Girl into formidable Big Girl, in her own voice: 'a chance to make a difference revved my motor.' It's all here—navigating ruthless *Little House* contract negotiations, debating the ERA with Phyllis Shlafly, helping build a battered women's shelters network . . . while relentlessly pursuing the most demanding lover of all: her acting Muse."

—MARGIE ADAM, feminist singer-songwriter

"Every beginning actor should read this book. Karen's journey intimately guides the reader both through immersive actor training and the professional industry and what it takes to be an actor. Fearlessly and rigorously authentic, Karen's memoir makes you feel your own heartbeat, see your own shadow, and begin to rediscover what it is that makes life, with all its ache and glory, worth living."

—LAUREN ENGLISH, casting director and performance coach

"Karen is beloved by *Little House* fans for her portrayal of Ma, strong matriarch of a family beginning a difficult journey to a new life. Reading about her life before she was my TV Ma shows how that strength and resiliency developed. It gives us a look into a rich life and the struggles that shape us, beyond what America saw each week watching TV's favorite family."

—MATTHEW LABYORTEAUX, actor

"An absorbing and compelling memoir that traces a true hero's journey from growing up in an alcoholic home through the terrain of mental illness and addiction to hard-won recovery. Karen gives us a master class in acting, an intimate glimpse behind the scenes of a successful television series, and a clarion call from the frontlines of the fight for women's rights. All told with a storyteller's gift, and the authentic voice of a close and reliable friend."

—DIANA GOULD, producer, screenwriter, and author of award-winning *Coldwater*

"Karen Grassle's memoir, written with passion and candor, is a delightful, intimate portrait of an actor's life. I think it is a valuable book for students preparing for a career in theater, film, or television. Karen has practical advice about auditions, rehearsals, and working on a television set. An inspiration!"

—CHRISTINE ADAIRE, Head of Voice, American Conservatory Theatre, and Linklater Voice Teacher

Bright Lights,
Prairie Dust

Bright Lights, Prairie Dust

Reflections on Life, Loss, and Love from *Little House*'s Ma

KAREN GRASSLE

SHE WRITES PRESS

Published 2021
Printed in the United States of America
Print ISBN: 978-1-64742-313-1
E-ISBN: 978-1-64742-314-8
Library of Congress Control Number: 2021912225

For information, address:
She Writes Press
1569 Solano Ave #546
Berkeley, CA 94707

Interior design by Tabitha Lahr

She Writes Press is a division of SparkPoint Studio, LLC.

For my son, Zach

And for my mother, Frae Ella Grassle
And my father, Gene F. Grassle

"Tell him . . . tell him you saw me and that . . . that you saw me. You're sure you saw me, you won't come and tell me tomorrow that you never saw me!"

—*Waiting for Godot*, SAMUEL BECKETT

"You take everything in your life, you put it into your work, and it transcends and transforms."

—*Cyndi Lauper: A Memoir*, CYNDI LAUPER

Contents

Prologue

SMILING AND SIGNING, NODDING AND SIGNING, smiling again; escaping now from the crowd, one more public appearance, one more drop-off exhausted at some airport—*Where the heck am I anyway? A telethon in Tennessee? A mall in Missouri? Why? This has nothing to do with acting.* I traveled after work Friday night, worked through Sunday, then boarded a flight back to California to film on Monday. *God, I need a drink! Careful, can't miss my plane to San Francisco.* There I would catch my ride to the location.

In first class, the stewardesses were pouring the wine before takeoff. My polite "Oh just a little please" kept me humming after what I gulped down at the airport. Sitting in the rear aisle next to some guy, I reached for my cigarettes before the No Smoking light blinked off. He lit my cigarette. Banalities about the beauty of San Francisco. Staying long? No, just one night. All was dark and shadowy, but the next thing I knew my new friend and I were making out while the other passengers watched a movie or slept. He invited me to his apartment for the night. I agreed.

Stuffed my swollen feet back into high heels. We deplaned together. In the hallway after baggage claim, bright lights smacked me awake. *What am I doing? Oh no. Think fast: there—a ladies' room.* He started for the men's. I dashed in, made a U, looked out— no guy—and ran crazily for the curb. There—a taxi. Bouncing my heavy bag against my thigh, I jumped in and gave the driver the name of the hotel. He wouldn't take my traveler's check and insulted my—what? my hair? It needed washing. I was belligerent, knew I was a mess. I hid my shame by calling him provincial, scrawled a check, scrammed. Tried to stand tall at the desk—*just give me the key, if I can just get to the room. Hold on. Solitude soon.* But when I closed the door, loneliness whacked like a wall of ice. Hungry. No food. Just bathe and get to bed.

Gasp. Splash. *Oh. Fell asleep in the tub.* The water tepid, I dragged the body out and into bed, called someone, someone who cared, soothed. I didn't tell about the guy on the plane, just the mean cabbie. Rambling... keeping the black hole at bay, telephone receiver growing heavy. I knew to ask for two wake-up calls and set the travel clock across the room. Gathering darkness of unconsciousness, slack-jawed, I held the small rag doll I called Sunny in the hollow by my shoulder . . . and out.

Morning. Oh God, this is bad. I struggled to standing, got into my jeans and warm sweater for the trip to Sonora. Coming up: winter scenes. I was sick. Entire bloodstream felt poisoned. My usually cast-iron stomach queasy. Couldn't make it down the hall for ice to cool the hot, red coals that were my eyes. Splashed cold water on my face to revive. I retrieved yesterday's celebrity outfit from the chair and the floor, grabbed panty hose, packed heels, then tucked the little doll into my suitcase. *The guy!* Adrenaline shot to my fingertips. Almost didn't make it here. Close call. *How did I get like this?*

Gary was fresh and ready for the journey. The Gold Country would be a welcome change from the office at Paramount, where he crunched the numbers. Breakfast? No. No time. He'd eaten. I swallowed my need. As we crossed the Bay Bridge, my head twisted toward Berkeley, dear birthplace—I discovered my calling and awakened as a citizen there. I lamented silently my losses: idealism, Shakespeare, like-minded friends, aspirations to make a difference. What happened? I had been so dedicated. My love of work I thought would protect me. Bankrupt. To distract myself from myself, I asked Gary questions about the economy—What makes it work? It seemed it ran on faith. Faith that people believed it was working made it work. Interesting notion. Long time since I felt any faith.

We passed Sonora and climbed up the steep mountain to the snowy location. I greeted everybody, and they were glad to see me. Freezing air was a welcome tonic. Deep breath. I got a coffee and trudged to the makeup trailer, where Larry and Whitey put me back together, and I emerged from their caring cocoon with the head of Ma. Then the wool skirt and Ma's boots and I'd be back in the saddle. Playing strength of character, integrity, kindness, fortitude. Acting.

Part One

Growing Up Absurd

"This little light of mine, I'm gonna let it shine."
—"This Little Light of Mine,"
Harry Dixon Loes

1. Miracle Baby

"But the real things haven't changed. It is still best to be honest and truthful; to make the most of what we have; to be happy with simple pleasures and to be cheerful and have courage when things go wrong."
— *The Selected Letters of Laura Ingalls Wilder*,
WILLIAM ANDERSON, EDITOR

FROM 1973 THROUGH 1984, I WAS IN my thirties, playing Ma in *Little House on the Prairie*. I based Ma's character as much on my own mother as I did on the actual Caroline Ingalls. I grew up with the living embodiment of the kind of strength, devotion, and intelligence Laura Ingalls Wilder described in her books. Like Caroline, my mother, Frae Ella Berry, rode barefoot on horseback to school, worked as a one-room-schoolhouse teacher, and, like Caroline, chose a husband who was a devoted partner but whose restlessness also challenged all her strength.

My mother was born in 1909, and when she was still a baby, her sharecropper father, Charles Berry, and housekeeper mother, Winifred, fled the hopelessness of Oklahoma for a new start in Idaho. Like Pa, my grandfather was looking for "greener pastures." My grandmother "couldn't settle for Oklahoma." The Berrys had ambitions to make a better life.

I CAN STILL SEE MY MAMA on Saturday mornings—the way she strode into the bedroom I shared with my little sister, Janey. She would open the curtains energetically.

"Rise 'n' shine! Rise 'n' shine!" but unlike Mary and Laura in *Little House*, Janey and I did not spring into smiling obedience. The sun seemed too bright. Her voice too loud. We barely stirred.

"C'mon, you slug-a-beds, I've already done a load of wash. I need these sheets next—" and we could hear that machine chugging underneath us in the basement.

I was never a bright early morning person. As an adolescent, at night I hid the radio under the covers to listen to the pop music. As a teenager, I read late and slept in on weekends. Once I began to work in the theatre, I was right on schedule. Television was another story; early morning calls a challenge that evolved into a torture once I began to have hangovers. But back then Mama didn't let us sleep the day away.

She was a tough critic and saw the flaw in anything we did. But she was hardest on herself. Like a pioneer woman, she did it all because she had to. She not only made all our clothes (swearing at the Singer when it didn't cooperate), she created a garden where we all worked, remodeled our house, and meanwhile earned a real estate license. She was forever improving our lives. She worked out her frustration and anger with Daddy on the house—scouring, polishing, and organizing. When the last task was completed, she protected her pin curls with a plastic shower cap, relished her hot shower, patted herself dry, and puffed powder onto her personal parts. In the fragrant bathroom, she "put on her face." Dressed in fresh clothes, she poured a cold beer, amber bubbles streaking to the light layer of foam. Finally, feet bare, she sank into her chair, lit up a Kent cigarette, and opened the *Ventura Star Free Press*. She inhaled.

That's when the rest of us could finally breathe.

Prompted by a particular food or activity, Mama shared stories of her childhood, her family who lived in Idaho where Charles

Berry, my grandfather, worked another man's fields, and Winnie, my grandmother who she called Mamam, pronounced M'am M'am, kept another woman's house. But one day Winnie ran, taking her two little girls and boarding a train. Mama and her sister Edith were surprised to be met at the station in California by Mr. Fullerton from the big house. Mamam and her girls settled in an apartment in San Jose. I guess Mr. Fullerton went back to Idaho to take care of business and maybe to get a divorce. And for years my grandfather pursued his family.

Mama's childhood stories came out in pieces, vivid but disconnected in my mind like the pieces of my grandmother's quilt, bright hexagons of calico, that lay unfinished on the high shelf in Mama's closet. Mama told me and Janey how often she and her sister returned from school to find the family trunk packed—their father had been asking around for them. Mamam scooped them up, and they fled up to the Russian River, then to Fort Bragg. I can't hear the names of these places even now without wondering where they might have landed. They thought their luck had changed when Mamam married the successful Mr. Fullerton from Idaho, and they all moved back there. But soon his behavior became erratic, and when my mother was just thirteen, after her prowling stepfather tried to fondle her, she escaped by moving into the nearby town to work for her board and room. Already a rock, she chose not to say a word for fear of spoiling Mamam's chance at security. I thought she was very brave.

About the time they were ready for high school, Mamam and the girls returned alone to San Jose, beginning again.

Mama's big sister, Edith, my aunt, grew into a curvaceous, highstrung blonde. Mama said Edie was "the pretty one" and she was "the smart one," auburn-haired and the spitting image of her own mother. She worked her way through San Jose State in three years, and at the age of twenty-one, she started teaching in a one-room schoolhouse. Her principal preyed upon her in the cloak room, but she minimized how much it bothered her.

I was lucky that both my parents were storytellers, and Janey and I asked to hear the tale of Daddy and Mama's first meeting again and again. Frae and her girlfriend were at a take-out stand when her friend noticed a "blond fella" really giving her the "once over." Frae glanced over, laughed, and she and her friend got their fried chicken, jumped back in her pal's car, and headed down the two-lane country road between the lettuce fields outside Hollister. The blond and his friend followed in hot pursuit. The girls sped up; the boys did, too. The girls howled and stepped on it. The fellows pulled up alongside and gently edged them onto the grassy shoulder. Gene Grassle introduced himself, his blue eyes full of laughter. He was well-spoken and determined to get Frae's number. Flattered, she gave it to him. That evening he called for a date. Mama was flattered all over again in remembering and Daddy looked proud of himself, though shaking his head at his bold behavior. I could feel their love, and at that moment it was clear they belonged together. I wanted my life to be exciting and romantic, too.

My father was the youngest of ten children, who grew up on his father's homestead on the most desirable rolling hill above the little town of Kirksville, Missouri. My grandfather, whom we all called Dad Grassle, had done so well building wagons and buggies that he had retired at fifty, built the first indoor plumbing in the whole town. He was a strict Germanic papa, but by the time my father came along, he'd mellowed. They left Missouri after his mother died—he and his brother Bill finished high school in California where their oldest brother, Harry, had moved. He made us laugh when he described the Ferris wheel the brothers built alongside the pond, situated so that the person in the bottom seat would land *under* the water.

He had a wonderful dark sense of humor, and moved Mama with his concern over social ills, but there was a dark underside to their life together I would not fully understand until much later. In those days, I just pictured them full of love and optimism as they celebrated their marriage on the boardwalk in Santa Cruz with a small gang of friends and family, dancing joyfully, gracefully to big band music my father adored in the ballroom before heading to their best friends' apartment for bathtub gin and laughter.

My parents married into the Depression and found their living where they could. My father burned up his fair skin and his idealism growing cotton in the blistering heat of the San Joaquin Valley, only to be docked by the government for his too-successful crop. He remained forever bitter about that. They migrated to Laguna with Dad Grassle and my uncle Harry. My mother turned out chicken pot pies as fast as she could in a little shop. They survived.

Just before World War II, they settled in Berkeley and got jobs, Daddy managing a service station and Mama cooking and running the White Kitchen Café. Chastened by the Depression, all they wanted was to have a family, give their kids a good education, and be able to "tell anyone to go to hell."

Fulfilling their dream had not been easy. I eventually understood that they had suffered trying to have children. At first, I only heard about the baby, Karl, who had died after twenty-four hours, but when I was about thirteen and Mama's dear friend lost a baby, I began to learn about the miscarriages Mama had had. Sadness permeated the house, and Mama was softer. During ten years of marriage, there had been four miscarriages, the lost baby boy, endless doctors and lab tests. My mother was ready to give up when they heard about Dr. Penland, who told them he didn't see any reason my mother couldn't have a baby.

Mama told me Dr. Penland's tone was so reassuring, she felt a deep hope rise inside. My father feared the risk to Mama, but Dr. Penland told them it wouldn't be any worse than what she'd already been through and they decided to try again. He was so different from the many self-important "scientists" they had seen, and his attitude gave them confidence. Nine months later the doctor told them their baby was positioned and ready.

But I wasn't quite ready! I turned around and stayed where it was safe and warm until the February false spring called me forth. Often Berkeley is drenched in rain for days but suddenly, sun warms shoulders, and people shed jackets, and uncertainty. It was then and forever has remained a rapture the way pink petals bloom suddenly on bare branches, and soon after white apple blossoms appear. The fragrance lifts the nose to sniff the scent, like a wild thing that senses dinner on the wind. Daily the show of blossoms increases, like hundreds of Rockettes tap dancing onto the stage: the double cherries so thick with rich pink petals you wonder how the bees—yes! a big bumblebee hovers—can get in. Red plum leaves like tiny mouse ears prick up and, in a crescendo, the brightest yellow smothers old acacias, inviting early daffodils to join the show.

Who could resist? Earth's miraculous renewal called to me with this song of abundance. A month late, my mother's labor began. I often wonder if my struggle for punctuality is congenital.

On the way to the hospital, my parents heard a radio report that a factory in San Francisco had been bombed. Just two months earlier, Pearl Harbor had been hit. But they had no time to check reports: They had a baby about to make her entrance, feet first, and the next morning, their "miracle baby" was born, and I don't suppose any baby has ever been more welcome. They called me their "miracle baby," and yet, when I was a child, Mama seemed determined to teach me that I was not special. Still, this story of my birth made me feel that maybe I was, and certainly that I was wanted and loved.

Daddy went to work in the shipyards. On the swing shift, he arrived home in the morning while the radio played Strauss waltzes. My earliest memory is of being lifted, swayed and swooped, balanced in his large hands, spinning in the circling force field, gravity-free, my first high: Turning and turning as he waltzed, his Austro-Germanic blood rising like sap in a big tree.

My parents' optimism persisted, and two and a half years later, the doctor delivered my sister, Jane Ellen, and soon after, my parents managed to swing a down payment on a small house in Oakland. They cleaned and polished the wooden stairs and banister and carried the second baby girl up to the girls' room. Settled.

My aunt Edith, Mama's sister, and her husband, Bill Hall, drove up from Gilroy in their new Packard. Doctors had told Bill, the driven money man, if he didn't cut back on his work, he would die, so Edith pleaded with Daddy to come and manage their booming business. My parents, Mama told me, felt trapped. But to help her sister, they sold our home and moved to Gilroy, a one-horse town adjacent to Steinbeck's fertile valley full of crops. There was nothing else nearby—no San Francisco, no university, no opportunities—just a main street six blocks long. My father took over the management of Hall's Levi's, which made a fortune selling jeans to the itinerant workers who flooded into the Valley and picked crops. Mama took a job teaching fourth grade.

Things did not go well in Gilroy. It seemed to me the house was dark. Baby Janey was sick, couldn't seem to get better, and my folks were worried. She finally needed a tonsillectomy. With both of them working and a neighbor caring for Janey, they were under pressure, even before Dad Grassle came to live with us, and he had dementia. My job became following him on my trike so if he got lost, I could bring him home. We sometimes had a stolen pleasure when he went to the drugstore fountain and ordered a milkshake and poured some for me in my own glass. We were happy sitting together, sucking up shakes. I cherished him and was proud that he was, at ninety-four, one of the oldest grandparents in my kindergarten.

Mama relied on me more and more to help her. I tried to learn everything so I wouldn't be a burden, but when I got fed up with her requests, I tried yelling, "Shut up!" and after she gave me a good spanking, I never tried that again.

My Daddy had painful talks with his brothers about putting Dad Grassle in a home, but they accused Daddy of not caring and it was terribly upsetting. Dad Grassle died without anything having been worked out in the family. I was four and sad, and I wanted to go to his funeral, but my parents wouldn't let me.

They seemed to be worn down, and I felt lonely. I dreamed of a girl named Karen who was sick but if she told anyone she was, she would die. I never told anyone about that dream.

When Daddy's oldest brother, Uncle Harry, came to visit, there was more laughter and talk in the evenings. He brought three boxes of See's chocolates—one for Mama, one for me, and one for Janey. I was allowed one piece after dinner—the most divine thing I had ever tasted. After Uncle Harry went home, Mama put the candy boxes in the hall closet and forgot about them. But I didn't forget. The candy boxes called to me and I went back again and again. Day after day. When I complained to Mama that my bottom hurt, she discovered a bad rash of boils, and when she checked the candy and discovered how much I had eaten, she was shocked.

After that, they hid chocolate from me. I would hear Daddy say, as they were putting the groceries away, "I'm putting the C-A-N-D-Y up high, with the glasses." My attention was riveted and I quickly learned to spell *candy*. Years later, I learned that a chocolate addiction often prefigures alcoholism. As a child, though, all I knew was that *I wanted more*.

At Hall's Levis, blue jeans were wall-to-wall, stacked to the ceiling. Daddy spoke Spanish to the customers. I thought the fact that he could speak Spanish was impressive, but he said it was only *poca, poca*, a little bit. He kept things shipshape, monitored inventory, and closed out the register. One day, as he climbed up on a stool to retrieve a special size from a top shelf, the stool tipped, and down he went, breaking his arm. Uncle Bill's reaction was to point to the fine print in Daddy's contract. "That's the thanks we get for leaving everything to help them!" Mother was furious, and they agreed that was the end of Gilroy. When the school year was over, we'd be moving on. But where?

Uncle Harry lived in Ventura. I was excited to take the train overnight with Daddy. We traveled the California train tracks, sitting up, side by side all night. I felt grown-up being able to go with him, and loved leaning against him, falling asleep to the rumble and sway of the train. Then he was lifting me up in the dark early morning, exiting the train, and out of a thick gray fog, Uncle Harry emerged in a rough wool overcoat and hat.

We stayed several days while he and Daddy discussed the options. Uncle Harry criticized me for using too much toilet paper. The Grassle boys had been trained to be thrifty, some would say "tight," but mostly the visit was a happy one, and the two men decided my father would manage Harry's real estate office. That year, Daddy moved ahead of the rest of us to Ventura to begin working and find us a house while I finished kindergarten and Mama completed her contract in Gilroy.

Mama was glad to be going. In Gilroy, a place my mother started to hate, a pattern had begun of her dragging me and baby Janey to the bar to tell Daddy to come home. Later, I learned, it was Uncle Bill coming to check the day's receipts and suggesting to my father to have "just one" across the street at the hotel that precipitated those hours of drinking. When he saw us walk into the bar, my father was, honestly, surprised—and chastened, and said, "Christ, Frae, I'm sorry. I had no idea it was so late." This had added to the tension in the house, where the mood was already dark. It would be good to leave.

2. Saved!

"Remember well, and bear in mind, a constant friend is
hard to find."
—Childhood Poem, LAURA INGALLS WILDER

DESPITE THE FACT THAT ONCE IN Ventura Mama looked
up and down Prospect Street, muttered about "Okies," and called
our little stucco house a "cracker box," and despite my seeing, even
at five, how that pained Daddy, I was excited about our move.
The neighborhood was full of kids, and Janey, whose health had
improved and was full of spunk, and I joined those kids who spilled
out onto the streets to play.

· Thanks to the California public school system, we also both
had opportunities for music lessons and I joined the Brownies. In
summer the Red Cross gave free swimming lessons, and the city
Recreation Department kept the school playgrounds open for
supervised play, sports, and crafts. I liked everything.

On my first day of first grade in Ventura, I experienced my first
moment of stage fright. I wore a brand-new, dark cotton print dress
Mama made special for this day, and when my teacher asked, "Does
anyone know 'School Days,'" my hand shot up. I knew it because
Mama sang that song to me many times. When the teacher told me

13

to stand in front of the class and sing it, I went to the front where she was standing and looked out at the faces staring at me and froze. The teacher helped me to begin and I sang it, but quite timidly I think, and when it was over, suddenly, I felt hot, sat down, and told myself not to do *that* again. Before too long, I forgot my fright and my embarrassment and, eager to show off what I knew, would throw up my arm, wiggle my hand, volunteer to read out loud, perform in the play, dance in the assembly—that was Karen.

Our neighbors, Ella Mae and Freddy, invited us to go with them to Sunday school. Their parents were driving. That sounded good to me, and I loved the Bible stories—Jesus letting the little children come unto him—and songs and prayers promising peace. I didn't need any convincing about original sin. I felt it.

One day I came home and told my parents I'd been saved. I had found my first answer. Jesus could fix anything. It didn't take long before I began to wake in the night, screaming. Mama rushed to me, and I told her "Jesus doesn't love me and I am going to hell." She sat with me, calmed me and I slept again. What I didn't know then was that she made a visit to the First Baptist Church and gave them a piece of her mind for scaring little children.

Still, I was hooked on Jesus and when Daddy came home "tight" from Harry's office, and when dinner hour was thickly silent, I comforted myself knowing I could turn to Jesus. I didn't know then that our family already was living in hell—the hell of alcoholism—and it would take me years to understand what that even meant.

One summer afternoon, I walked over to my friend Kay's house to see if she wanted to play, only to find a sign on the fence: "Quarantine. Keep Out." It was polio, a plague that crippled children, closed the swimming pool, and hung in the air all around us that summer, like an imminent storm. I knew it was "catching," and you could *die*, and at night I prayed for Kay. When she recovered with no lasting paralysis, I thanked Jesus. Life went on. Polio was still there. And that tension in the house.

Janey and I were crazy about our daddy. He was fun. He could wiggle his ears, draw funny looking cows, and tell jokes. Mama didn't swim and didn't like the beach (too sandy!), but Daddy loved it. He carried me on his shoulders into the surf. Janey and I became capable swimmers and spent countless hours riding the waves. At six feet two, with his spontaneous guffaw, his patience seemed endless, and I was proud when relatives said I took after him.

When I was seven, in 1950, I met Toni, who would forever be an important part of my life. We met at Brownie Day Camp in the summer. She became my hero. We were chasing butterflies and putting them in a wire cage. She showed me how that would kill them, their fine white powder damaged by the wires. She was so wise. And she also looked like no one else I'd ever known. She had long brown braids, soulful dark eyes, and she dressed like a boy in jeans and a shirt. She seemed less gawky than I felt. When we hiked together, she showed me lichen on the oaks. Toni seemed to know everything about nature. And she respected me because when she told me we were killing the butterflies, I was the one who insisted the counselor make us stop, and we freed them.

But Toni lived in a different part of town from our family, and on the last day of camp, I felt forlorn and panicky. I only knew to tell her I hoped I would see her the next summer because I knew something important had happened to me. Playdates were not common, and Mama had no car to drive us around, so we could only say goodbye.

MAYBE A YEAR LATER, DADDY WAS excited about a new house listing—"Helluva nice duplex on Main Street, lotta potential, good price, too," he said, as Mama washed dishes and he polished two pairs of white little girls' shoes and set them to air on the window sill. The next day we went to see the place. Two rows of tall skinny palms stood like exclamation points on either side of Main Street. I liked it at once. And my church was somewhere close by. We stopped at a solid duplex with a double front porch, a front yard, a big backyard, a garden, and a little ivy-covered cottage. We looked all around, and Daddy drove us by the Lincoln School, only two blocks up Main. I could see Mama's wheels turning: With the money they had saved and the two rentals to help pay the mortgage, they could do it. That decade was a decade of optimism in America, and no one was more optimistic than my folks. They would work hard as a team and be honest and fulfill their dream of sending us kids to college. Ventura County was booming—its population would grow by 75 percent by the time I graduated from high school ten years later.

On Main Street the town opened up for us—the soft rolling hills, like a cape around the shoulders of Ventura, were only two blocks from our house. The white sand beaches were but a swift bike ride away. I could walk to the big Victorian Library set back by a green lawn where shelves promised endless other worlds, and there I read especially biographies of brave young women like Clara Barton, and I read *Little Women* over and over. The Taylor Ranch at the northwest end of town spread wide with green grass. Only occasionally did the wind blow those manure fumes straight down Main and own us all.

Our lives became a rhythm of school and work, rounded out by family dinners and long summers at home—the busiest time in the real estate business since families had to get settled before school started. As a small-town Realtor, Daddy was the first person many people encountered in Ventura, and he'd drive them up to the cross on the hill and from there he enthusiastically laid out the neighborhoods and assets of his town, from the oil fields inland to the pier to the developing east end, where the orange groves were rapidly being overtaken by homes. He was American through and through. His enthusiasm for Ventura never waned—even on gray days, he'd grin and exclaim, "Isn't that fog great?"

The end of summer was marked by Labor Day, so we packed all the fun we could into that long weekend, riding waves with unrestrained vigor, getting sunburned again—preposterously as if this time would be different—and the family picnic on Monday. The night before, Mama fried up her chicken and chilled it in the ice box, whipped up potato salad and chopped the pimentos and black olives into the macaroni salad. And Monday off we went for a hot day at Camp Comfort, with its little creek that danced with water spiders and pollywogs. On our hikes we knew to be on the lookout for rattlers, and Daddy showed us how to play horseshoes that thudded in the soft dirt. At the end of that weekend, on the way home, we sang "Down by the old mill streeeam . . . " and I eagerly anticipated the first day of school.

The east wind always seemed to blow in during the night, chasing away fog and cutting out the world in stark relief. The weeds grew crisp. The skinny trunks of the tall palms swayed, their dry fronds rustling, blown clear of dust by desert wind. I recall the pleasure I felt seeing the world tremble with light, beams bouncing every which way. My skin prickled with dry alertness, and static electricity pulled my fine hair out into wild strands. As I walked to school, Janey beside me, I felt like a small boat floating on dazzling air. We both had new dresses Mama sewed on the Singer.

Into the new classroom I walked, and there was a great surprise—Toni in a pretty plaid dress with tiny gold rings in her ears and the same long braids and warm brown eyes. I discovered she lived just a few blocks from us, up the hill. Her parents, Mr. and Mrs. Clark, ran the Ventura Theatre, and they let us jump on the bed in Toni's room. She and I did scarf dances—skinny kids wafting bright silk scarves into the air, and on Saturdays we helped make the popcorn at the theatre, then hid in the balcony and tried to see who could stuff more Red Hots into her mouth at once.

Toni had a gentle mare called Bobbi, and although I felt nervous as I climbed up on the fence to get on her back while Toni held her, I also found it thrilling. Toni hopped on in front of me and we took off up the hill on a dirt path into what felt like our private wonderland. The sweet brown nag carried us bareback, and the smell of wild weeds tickled. We dismounted to the toasted grass and wildflower stems, and Toni showed me how to crunch and rub their seed pods and save the dried flowers and pods in brown paper bags. Foxtails clinging to my socks, we climbed on Bobbi's warm back and rode to Toni's house, where her father, who was fascinated by the natural world, helped her collect caterpillars, and she taught me to let them crawl on my hands. Her father also had built a boat, and sometimes Janey and I joined the family to water-ski up the coast off Santa Barbara.

My father wasn't like Toni's father. He had neither time nor money for such pursuits. When friends stayed overnight, he made pancakes, and he was fun, but he was also in a hurry. Whenever he picked us up from a lesson or Sunday School, almost before the car door closed, he was off and running back to the house, with too much to do—on Sundays, helping his wife with the gardening. When churchgoers walked past our front yard, I was mortified they could tell he and Mama didn't go, seeing him in his sweaty undershirt. I didn't know it was unusual to work in an undershirt—it was natural to me—and Daddy laughed a brusque snort at my self-consciousness, exclaiming, "Jesus Christ!" while I dead-headed the petunias and kept my head bowed and worried for his soul.

More often than not, the phone rang, and he had to quickly shower and dress in a clean shirt and tie. A bit of tissue often stuck to the spot where he cut himself shaving, but he was rushing again, out the door to meet a client because Sunday was an important day in the real estate business. Everybody liked him.

But those who didn't live with him didn't actually know him. Along with his high-performance ebullience came irritability and impatience. He sweated over making money, although he gave me plenty for the collection plate. He sweated from rushing but never slowed down. He sweated from nerves over the development he had put their savings in just before a downturn in the housing market. He had a bad back that caused him agony.

And he drank.

Often Mama joined him for a drink at the end of the day, but other days we waited and waited for him to come home. He forgot about our lessons and everything else. On those days we sat down glumly for dinner without him, nervously anticipating the angry outburst that would erupt when he arrived home lit up and his chagrin when he realized that he had let us down.

Mama's compulsion for order after her turbulent childhood was frustrated by trying to manage Daddy's drinking. Family dinners, an absolute ritual, could combust into flames. Sometimes his razor-sharp sarcasm cut into my being, and I'd sit there wondering who he was, what had happened, why he had suddenly changed. When he was soaked with drink, I could see but couldn't stop the dark pool of his depression overflowing and swamping us all. At those times he conked out in his chair, often his cigarette still burning.

And still, whenever Mama got mad at him, I took his part, silently thinking about how hard he tried and wondering why she couldn't see that. I sensed how hard he was on himself. Sure, there were skid marks on my heart when his personality changed abruptly; sure, Mama's neck and shoulders turned to rock worrying, feinting, and parrying to keep it all going; sure, when he didn't show up for dinner, I was disappointed and worried.

But I always forgave him, and it would be years and years before I understood that the worm of disappointment and hurt and anger was quietly, privately eating at my core, at my ability to trust.

I don't know how soon Mama began to confide in me, but surely by the time I was nine she began to wonder out loud, to me, if she should leave him. She tried drinking with him. She tried not drinking at all. Nothing helped. She agonized and shared her agony, rationalizing by noting his strong points—he went to work every day, remembered every birthday and holiday, didn't beat anyone. When I was older and understood that there are many ways of beating someone, I wondered about that. Now I think his shutting down into vodka-steeped silences was punishment. Whether he intended it or not. And holding the blade. The threat—just out of sight.

AT OUR HOUSE, WE "LIKED IKE" and knew that Communism was bad. The McCarthy hearings on our new television paraded movie stars and famous writers, asking, "Are you now or have you ever been a member of the Communist Party?" I felt loyal to these actors, wondered how it could be possible that all of those accused were Communists. Judy Holliday? Charlie Chaplin? Lucy? Mama's favorite. But Daddy said, "If you're innocent, why not answer?" I didn't know. Just to be accused was to be considered possibly disloyal.

As a young actress, I shared outrage with my friends over the blacklists, the lost careers, the talented who fled the country. I learned later that my own father had been a youthful socialist, full of ideals about sharing the wealth. But he had become disillusioned and by the time they were raising us, he and Mother were both firm Republicans.

At school, we stood dutifully with our classmates, hands on hearts, to recite the Pledge of Allegiance. Often during those early post-war years, the placid atmosphere of our little classroom was ripped apart with a horrific crack when jets flying out of the nearby naval base broke the sound barrier. We were "war babies," and I understood that all of us had to be vigilant and keep perfecting the stuff of war. My classmates and I all paid close attention to Miss Davis, our sixth-grade teacher, when she led us through air raid drills. She read from the government guidelines: "What to Do in the Event of a Nuclear Attack."

Miss Davis was not afraid to question the guidelines nor was she reluctant to point out that colors that supposedly didn't "go together" like green and blue looked beautiful together in nature—trees and sky. Toni and I were glad she questioned our assumptions. But we dutifully climbed under our desks and shielded our eyes from the "bright flash of light." We knew nothing of Hiroshima, zip of Nagasaki. No one talked about nuclear fallout, and we all took war planes and possible atom bomb attacks for granted. We knew we'd better stay alert and felt that the clear blue sky held terrifying possibilities.

3. Baptism and Blood

"You could buy a suckling pig with it, if you want to. You could raise it, and it would raise a litter of pigs, worth four, five dollars apiece. Or you can trade that half-dollar for lemonade and drink it up. You do as you want, it's your money."

—*Farmer Boy*, LAURA INGALLS WILDER

ALONG WITH THE MOVE TO MAIN STREET when I was eight came the promise of ballet lessons for me and Janey. When my parents told me, I burst into tears of happiness. The new teacher in town, Barbara Brent, had a taut dancer's body, wore glamorous eye makeup and black leotards and tights set off by a scarlet scarf holding her long black hair. She was like no one else in our town. She had been in *vaudeville*, had worked in *Hollywood*, and she taught it all: ballet, tap, Hawaiian, acrobatics.

Barbara Brent's Spring Shows were big events, with lighting and professional costumes that attracted a full house—everyone, not just the loyal family members of us kids. Barbara also booked us into every local institution that would have us: The Girls' School (for wayward girls), Camarillo State Hospital for the Mentally Ill, and we even traveled in our parents' cars to the Troopers' Club in

Hollywood where eccentric old show biz folks lavishly praised our performances. Barbara always arrived looking stunning in royal blue and turquoise that set off her intense blue eyes. At school the next day, if I had traces of lipstick on my lips, I got a secret kick out of an excusable scandal.

Before I was to perform my first solo, I was assaulted by the worst stage fright—far worse than what I felt in front of my class. Mama was working in the wings, and when I looked to her for help, she instructed me to take deep breaths, and she hugged me, and when my cue came, I entered in the dark, and as soon as "Waltz of the Flowers" began, I was dancing and fine. From the audience, I could hear Daddy's robust cigarette cough, and I was overjoyed because he'd made it, and I knew the surprise that was coming— black light that would make my flower garland glow in neon colors and seem to dance magically in the dark—would make Daddy and everyone else gasp.

Dancing absorbed me completely, gave me a way to express what I couldn't say out loud. I was the skinny one with lank hair and pointy elbows near the end of the line, but I was dancing with the big girls.

Our tiniest star was Millie, and her mom, Ruby, sewed beautifully. She and Mama became pals. Our mothers made this all work for us. They drove us to Hollywood to the Capezio store for shoes and to the Home Silk Shop for the right color satin. They sewed our elaborate costumes, and although Mama worked backstage at dress rehearsals and performances, she was determined not to be a "stage mother." When all the girls in their taffeta and tutus thronged around her with needs and questions, she wouldn't even look at me until I tricked her by saying, "Mrs. Grassle?"

The first time I saw the movie *The Red Shoes* I became obsessed. In the movie, Moira Shearer plays a ballerina who is to star in a new ballet. In her off-stage life, she falls in love with a young composer who doesn't want her to keep dancing. While her fiancé is away working, her teacher persuades her to take the starring role in his new ballet, *The Red Shoes*. When her fiancé returns, he insists she must choose between him or dancing. Broken-hearted and unable to choose, she dances, frenzied, off a balcony to her death.

Every day, after school, I tried to persuade one girlfriend or another to go with me to the library and re-create *The Red Shoes*. Over and over, I danced the conflict, breaking my own heart, exhausting my passion. The myth of *The Red Shoes* took root in me and later, in my twenties when I was a struggling actress in New York and beginning to explore my psyche in Jungian analysis, I named my issue—the conflict between love and work—the Red Shoes Complex. Whenever I met women who seemed to do both with ease, I studied them closely, hoping I could learn their secret.

AT SUNDAY SCHOOL, I LEARNED THERE was a weeklong, sleepaway camp in the summer, but my parents said we couldn't afford it. But one day, when I came in from school, a cardboard box had come for me. Mama asked me if I knew what it was.

I did. It was my Christmas card samples, and we opened the box while I explained to her that they sent me free samples so I could sell door-to-door to make money for camp.

"Gene F. Grassle, Realtor" was my first customer. Mama was my second. Mama then drove me to the Avenue where I walked up and down pulling my samples in my red wagon. She helped to check my order sheets and took me to the Bank of America to open my own bank account. And year after year, until I was twelve, I made enough money to go to camp where I deepened my commitment to Jesus, swam in the lake, prayed in the pine woods, and flirted with a boy from Texas by the last year. I had proved to myself that I could find a way to get what I wanted.

ONE MORNING MAMA FOUND BLOOD IN my PJs, and she dressed hurriedly and came to school. She spoke to Miss Davis, and I had to go with her to girls' room down the hall. I never went there, a dank cement room with high windows, it was like a dungeon. She explained to me that I may have gotten my period. We'd never discussed this. I was still so undeveloped. I knew she had one and sometimes the pain put her to bed for a day.

She steered me into a gray stall to check my panties. No blood. Still, she said, I should wear a pad for today "just in case." She explained this would be a monthly occurrence. Bleed every month?! Well, I cried and exclaimed this was the worst thing that could happen, why did I have to be a girl, why did we have to bleed every month? It wasn't fair. She said it was so I could have babies. Oh. Well, I did want to have babies.

"C'mon, let's get this on so you can get back to class." Back into the stall. Mama threaded the ends of the pad through the metal clasps of the elastic belt and I was caught, it was on. You couldn't see it under my full skirt. She was firm now. "Here, wash your face." Cold water, some of her sweet-smelling powder to cover my blotchy face. "We'll talk more later," she said, as I tried to drag out the conversation, dreading returning to the class. But she led me back to the classroom door and left.

That afternoon, she was prepared with a pamphlet that explained it all in straightforward language with fascinating drawings of my insides. I read it over and over and put it in my bedside drawer, where I'd hide my cigarettes later on. My period first came when I was getting ready to go to my first dance convention in Hollywood and stay at a hotel with Millie, her mom, and this *boy*, Bobby, from our dance class. I was about to spend five full days in leotards and tights dancing with strangers and a boy was to share our quarters. Mama was in her bedroom ironing. With a half-smirk, I walked in and told her the news, and we shared a meaningful shake of the head. She helped to suit me up, and when she dropped me at Ruby and Millie's, she discreetly filled Ruby in on the developments. I never for a moment considered canceling—it was the event of the year; but all week I was sure everyone could smell that rank, earthy, unmistakably itself smell. From that day on, my "visitor" made a habit of appearing whenever I wanted to be at my best—for swim meets, special dates, and of course, later on, for opening nights.

FROM EARLY ON I WANTED TO BE baptized, to become a full-fledged member of my church, but Mama and Daddy decided I had to wait until I was thirteen. I wonder if they hoped that by then my passion for the church would wane, and later we laughed about it. But when I turned thirteen and still insisted, they could no longer say no, so I took weeks of classes with two adults, and Pastor Parks prepared us for our day of commitment. He called me his "little theologian."

The baptismal font was above the choir loft, its height appropriate to my aspirations for redemption and ascension to the spiritual life. It was like a big bathtub hidden on a small stage. The congregation was singing as we walked to the back of the choir loft and, in privacy, took off our clothes and put on white robes. The choir hummed as we climbed the narrow steps to the entrance of the font. I was last because I was youngest. The first of our group reappeared, dripping. I stepped up one step. The second person I heard say, "I do." A splash, and he bobbed out, blinking. I stepped down into the water. Pastor Parks, whom I idolized, opened his arms and smiled, and as rehearsed, I turned around and crossed my arms over my chest. He asked me if I believed in the Lord Jesus Christ as my personal savior. I answered meekly, "I do," held my breath, leaned into his arms, and he submerged me in the water. Lifted me up again. I felt nothing special. Was I supposed to? I walked back down to the spot where the kind women handed us towels, and we changed back into our clothes. I had done what I felt compelled to do.

Mrs. Parks came over and whispered to me my folks had gone forward. This was an amazing surprise, and I wondered if I had helped to "save" them? I was sure all I needed was faith, that now Dad's drinking, his "going on the wagon," raising our hopes only to fall off and crush them, again and again was going to stop.

Just at this time, Barbara announced ballroom classes on Friday nights. She made it into a social event, with etiquette and punch and cookies. Although I knew the Baptists didn't approve of dancing, I hung on, practicing separation of church and dance. I knew I wasn't going to sacrifice dancing with boys on the Baptist altar.

Every summer, just before school was to start, Mama and Daddy checked the bank account. When escrows had closed, clients were settled, and there was a little surplus, we took our Labor Day trip. Mama and Daddy liked Las Vegas best: Nice rooms were cheap, the lavish brunch at the Riviera was a dollar a person, and they liked to gamble. During the day, Janey and I swam and worked on our tans and in the evenings, we all went to a show together. Mama played the slot machines, and sometimes even managed to pay for the trip with her winnings. Daddy's game was craps. More exciting. And drinks in the casino were free.

The years they could afford these trips, we usually took off at the end of the day, so they could work all day. We packed a cooler full of tuna sandwiches, hard boiled eggs, and milk in the backseat with me and Janey, and we drove through the desert in the cool night air. The road to Las Vegas was a two-lane blacktop through the desert with nothing to see for miles and miles but the occasional Burma Shave signs or the steadily larger and more outrageous postings for "The Thing!" a roadside-shack freak show they wouldn't let us see. Janey and I loved the roller-coaster swoop of the road.

Daddy always seemed proud when he surreptitiously slipped a big bill to the doorman at the *Folies Bergere*, and he escorted us to a good table. One night we saw Eartha Kitt and afterwards went back to the room to get ready for bed. Mama had made her stash and she was ready for bed too, but Daddy went out to gamble a little more, and the next morning when we woke, there was no Daddy. Mama, worried and furious, sat us down for breakfast while she went to look for him. When she brought him back, his eyes were

ringed with red, and he was shame-faced. I gave him a sympathetic
glance. I hated seeing him look so beaten.

This time Mama drove, and Daddy sat with his hand grasping
a silver dollar, all he had left.

By THEN, AND FOR A LONG time, I had understood that alcohol
was the problem. I thought billboards advertising whiskey were
messages from the devil and wondered why God allowed them. But
my father's ups and downs on the alcohol merry-go-round tested
my faith. As the years passed, I became more and more angry. I
swallowed that anger, and sugar lows and a tight stomach played
havoc with my appetite. When my parents offered me sherry to get
me to eat more, I asked about the drinking, and they turned their
anger on me. Why did I keep bringing it up? Why did I have to
be so dramatic? These turns usually happened at the dinner table,
and the world tilted as my favorite person, Daddy, betrayed me. If
I corrected Janey or showed off, Daddy cut me down. "You think
you're so smart. You don't know anything," he'd begin, and once
begun, all bets were off. If I defended myself, his fury escalated until
I fled the table, tears spouting, ran to my room and slammed the
door. Once I threw my doll against the wall and broke her foot and
felt guilty about that. It wasn't his words so much as the deprecating
tone soaked in disdain that caused me to collapse. Mother had a
handy way with words, but they were nothing compared to the
scalding critique that rumbled out of Dad's mean mouth.

4. Duet

"Maybe I just haven't tried hard enough."
—"Four Eyes," *Little House on the Prairie*, B.W. SANDEFUR

CABRILLO JUNIOR HIGH SEEMED HUGE. An odd assortment of old and new buildings flung onto a big lot with a flock of Quonset huts set on bare ground in the middle as construction crews banged away. Toni and I were suddenly mixed in with kids from the other grammar schools and separated from each other. Mrs. Christiansen, my seventh-grade homeroom teacher, was tall and thin, adorned with a dramatic French twist and bright red lipstick. Dressed in a slim brown suit, she smelled strongly of perfume (to hide the smell of her cigarettes). The fact that so many of us had the same name—three Karens, three Jimmys—prompted her to designate us as Mr. and Miss.

As part of our training in democracy, we elected student officers. Karen Ewing was elected president, and I was elected program chairman. I wondered about Karen Ewing dressed in her sedate cream rayon blouse with the embroidered collar and her abundant wavy brown hair held by a barrette. All the kids automatically turned to her, and right from the start, I felt the need to compete with her. She had a quiet self-containment I envied, and one day I confessed my jealousy to Mama. She told me to look for what it was I liked about this other Karen, and I took her advice, never dreaming that by admiring her intelligence, I could transform my jealousy into deep admiration and love.

Every other Friday it was my job to provide some kind of diversion or entertainment. Often, I wasn't prepared with a little sketch or play or plan for the class, and I'd resort to a spelling bee. I thought it a good fallback since everyone could be included, at least at the beginning. And I was a good speller.

On the alternate Fridays, we held student meetings and practiced Robert's Rules of Order. We had a suggestion box where students put ideas for discussion, and one Friday, all the Jimmys were eager to read the suggestions. Short Jimmy opened the box, unfolded a scrap of paper, and read, "Miss Grassle should do better programs." He picked a second: "Miss Grassle does too many spelling bees. She should think of something else." I could feel the heat rise in my face as a stir rose in the room like a wind ruffling the tops of the kids' heads. Everyone looked at me, and the other Jimmys began to snort and cackle.

Short Jimmy pulled out the next suggestion and paused as the room vibrated. Looking miserable, he reached to hand the paper to the teacher, but she backed away with a gesture of—this is *your* bailiwick, and his face reddening, he began, "Miss Grassle doesn't do a good job with the programs." I felt a couple of hot tears fall to my wooden desk, and I glanced up at Mrs. Christiansen, who nodded. A moment later I was out the back door, running up the hall to the girls' room where I ducked into one of the stalls, fastened the door, and sobbed.

A few minutes later, Karen Ewing was suddenly there. Somehow, she talked me out of the stall, patted my shoulder, and told me not everyone felt that way. "Those boys were just being mean because they like you," she said. It took some time before I was calm enough so we could return to our seats, and they branded me "Crybaby." But at the end of the school day, Karen Ewing joined me to walk toward the exit, and as we walked together, we discovered a natural rapport. We offered each other tender confessions and philosophical puzzles, and after that, we left school together often and sat on the curb and talked until we had to walk in our separate directions.

When I spent the night at my new friend's house, everything was a wonder. The Ewings' house was a breathtaking Spanish home on the hill, with a courtyard instead of a front yard and a sunken living room where Mrs. Ewing played Peggy Lee albums. At dinnertime, Karen and I hung around the kitchen, and Mrs. Ewing came in wearing a floral sheath, revealing a darkly tanned décolletage. She had tucked a vivid orange hibiscus behind her ear, bright against her peroxide blond hair. To me she looked like a movie star, and when Mr. Ewing put his arm around her waist and gave her a kiss on the cheek, I couldn't believe what I was seeing. I was amazed that parents behaved like this. Lived like this. It wasn't only their beauty and grace, it was the ease with which they seemed to do everything. When we sat down for dinner at my house, there was a heavy exhale, as if my parents both were saying, "Made it through another day!"

But in the Ewing house, Mrs. Ewing asked, with ease, "Now, how shall we know which Karen is being spoken to?"

"You could call our Karen Karen One and her Karen Two," her little brother suggested, but Mrs. Ewing pointed out that then at my house, I would be Karen One and Karen Ewing would be Karen Two.

Neither of us had a middle name, which to me only meant we had that much more in common. "We sometimes call our Karen Karen-Dee," Mrs. Ewing said. "It's a kind of nickname. How would that be, Karen-Dee?"

And so it was.

Two or three afternoons each week, I carried my dance case to school and walked to the studio for classes, and before long Karen Ewing got permission to visit my ballet class. She wanted lessons, too, and her mother was all for it. She practiced with such concentration and diligence that she moved rapidly from the beginners' group to my advanced class, and many weekends, we spent the night at her house, dancing rapturously for hours. We choreographed tragic love stories

> "... and it seemed that our two natures blent
> Into a sphere from youthful sympathy."[1]

We also created lighthearted duets for talent shows and sock hops, and because it was the '50s, and it didn't take much for a kid to be considered "different," Karen Ewing and I became borderline freaks.

MRS. EWING TOOK IT UPON HERSELF to find performances of great ballerinas to inspire us, and dressed up in our best dresses, full of anticipation, we traveled together to shows in Los Angeles. At the Greek Theatre, the stage glowed as Alicia Alonso portrayed Giselle, a peasant girl who loved dancing. She was as light as helium, joy incarnate, and Karen and I were riveted as the follow spot carved out each consummate gesture in the mad scene. While this was not the first time that I was captivated by the story of a girl enthralled by dance who dies of heartbreak, this time when the show ended, I clapped until my palms hurt.

Mrs. Ewing led us backstage where dancers bustled about, and ladies carried sparkly tutus down concrete halls. Karen and I shyly made our way to Alicia Alonso's dressing room, which had a star on the door. Other well-dressed adult admirers were waiting too, but I had read all about Alicia Alonso, so when she appeared, sharp-featured with her black hair pulled tightly back, to sign our programs, I asked her how she had practiced in the hospital when they said her polio meant she would never walk again, let alone dance. She held one hand up, flat, making a stage, and her other hand became a dancer. Her fingers articulated a difficult combination ending with a *tour jeté*—just as if those fingers were her legs. She taught me that night the power of the mind, the meaning of determination mixed with desire, and I left inspired. I told Mama and Daddy all about it the next day. They were happy I had these opportunities and always gave me money to offer to treat everyone after the show.

That summer, when we were fourteen, Mrs. Ewing found a ballet school in Hollywood that would allow us to take classes for one week. Karen-Dee told me excitedly that some girls who had studied there had gone on to join the corps of real ballet companies. We could stay right across Hollywood Boulevard at the Roosevelt Hotel.

The studios were in a mazelike basement with sunlight slanting in through high windows. Huge mirrors hung above hardwood floors. The dressing room was dark, with little lockers. The regular students wore strange combinations of mismatched tights and homemade leg warmers, wool scarves or crocheted vests wrapped around their torsos. To me, bourgeois to the core, they looked raggedy. I had saved up to buy myself a sky-blue leotard with matching tights and soft kid, blue ballet slippers.

We began by working with a teacher so she could place us. Both Karen-Dee and I knew our French terms and easily picked up combinations. When I barely placed above her, I felt irritated, and irritated with myself for being irritated, recognizing I was so competitive I was almost willing to sacrifice our time together just so I could have more status. I kept quiet, we joined the same class, and the challenges began. While I had emoted my way through routines, Karen-Dee had paid attention to correct form, learning to shape the arm, the hand, the fingers into the flowing curve true to the art of ballet. I'd never paid much attention to that until that summer, and the teachers were forever correcting my technique. And when one teacher called out, "Blue! Feet together!" "Blue! In time!" I felt like the butt of a joke.

Even so, my respect for both students and teachers grew hourly, and each day, after the long, hard work, we rewarded ourselves at C. C. Brown's Ice Cream Parlor with its high ceilings, shiny white lacquer walls, and floors with black-and-white squares. We slouched in red leatherette booths and gorged on luscious sundaes. One morning, Karen-Dee and her mother told me I had cried out in the night—my muscles were screaming. I had never been so sore, but by the end of the week I knew this: either I had to start studying in Hollywood, or I had to give up any idea of being serious about ballet. Mama offered to drive me down to LA once a week for classes.

But I wanted to make a change, be more like other girls—go to football games, go out with boys. I discussed this excitedly with Toni and other friends when we went to the beach. I wanted to "belong." And despite her generous offer to drive me, I knew the cost of those lessons and all the driving would be a hardship. And so, at fourteen, I stopped dancing. Karen-Dee continued with Barbara.

When I gave up dancing, I see now, I separated myself from myself, distanced myself from that deep connection I had found in ballet. I would pursue plays and speaking contests and that was satisfying, but all the way back then I began to hide something tender inside.

IN HIGH SCHOOL, THOSE OF US who were college bound were put into English XL classes. Karen-Dee and I landed in separate classes and saw less of each other. I wasn't working hard, resisted memorizing anything, whether Latin or chemistry. I rationalized that memorizing wasn't actual learning. Toni and I were back in class together again. I copied her pierced ears and we both began to experiment with boys. Trying to be cool, I dated some of the "bad boys" from the senior class, and so did Toni. We made out in cars and came to class on Monday mornings with silk scarves now tied coquettishly around our virgin necks, as if to announce, "I've got a hickey!" In the '50s, a girl's reputation was paramount: There were good girls and bad girls and nothing in between. To be a good girl, you didn't actually have to be good, you just had to not get caught, which meant not get pregnant. I was decidedly a good girl experimenting and not wanting it to get around. I smiled in the halls no matter what was going on inside.

By then, Dad's real estate business was doing well, and he was able to build an office in front of our house, so I got the old office for my own room. I picked pink paint and wallpaper featuring French poodles in coy poses, and my mother helped me fix it up. By my junior year, football players were hanging out at our house after games, recounting every play and devouring Mom's pies. Toni bought a tiny Fiat, and some mornings she arrived at school, cigarette smoke wafting out of the windows, and girls bloomed out of the two tiny doors, colorful as circus clowns. Toni had become friends with the cool girls, sexy and sophisticated. They were like hot sauce to my cold porridge of student activities.

I began to be fed up with the Baptists. Pastor Parks was moved away when I was fourteen, and his replacement lacked imagination. For a while, I took notes on his sermons with the intention of challenging him, but I knew he would only tell me I had to have faith. And I had grown weary of the sanctimonious girls in the youth group, with their exclusionary beliefs that locked out many of my best friends, like Jerry, my close friend who was Jewish. He and I decided we were going to be prez and veep by the time we were seniors. Also, Toni and Karen-Dee were agnostic and the smartest, kindest people I knew, so how on earth could they be damned? For a while I tried another Christian denomination and youth organization, but they didn't satisfy my inner debate, and so one night when I was fifteen, I left Baptists in a huff and discontinued actively practicing Christianity.

One night near the end of the summer before our senior year, when I knew that Karen-Dee soon would be caught up as editor of our prize-winning student newspaper and I would be occupied as vice president of the student body, I invited her to spend the day at our house. We went swimming in the ocean, and back at the house we tried out colored rinses on our hair, enjoying our old intimacy and the sharp anticipation of the coming year. She was going to go to Stanford, where her mother had gone, and I had decided I had to go to Stanford, too.

I hoped that my extracurricular activities were going to buoy my less than stellar scholarly performance. Both Toni and Jerry were going to do a year at Ventura College to conserve money before enrolling at Berkeley. The University of California was incredibly economical for a college education and I could get admitted easily, but I was disinterested in Berkeley, thought of it as an "engineering school," much to my parents' disappointment.

SENIOR YEAR, MRS. MUNSELL, THE Dean of Girls, asked me to spearhead a new girls' service organization. Times have changed so much since then that it is hard to describe a woman like Mary Munsell. Her kind no longer exists. Perfectly coiffed and modestly dressed in a matching suit with those clunky mid-high heels, she spoke in a measured, modulated voice. There was a correct way to behave, and she was the personification of that. So much of my self-consciousness around mature women had to do with sex and how restrictive the standards were for young women. When Mrs. Munsell asked me to look at a paperback book about sex and give her my opinion, I read it avidly, knowing little of what it contained. (Mother would discuss anything, anything but sex.) But when she asked what I thought of the book, I reported it was good and yes, she certainly could recommend it to other girls, but I didn't dare broach any of my own confusion. I felt sure if she knew what Mike and I were up to when we parked on Saturday nights, she would lose all regard for me.

I see now that she could have been a much greater resource for me. She opened the door, but I couldn't walk through. The lack of honest communication between females was one of the ways we all were trapped. Secrets and shame deterred us from sisterhood. In reaching out to me to establish a club, an honorary service organization for girls, Mrs. Munsell, I see as I look back, was attempting to put us on an equal footing with the boys.

In junior high, I had advocated for a girl to be on the telescope team in science class. But this was my first chance to create something equal for girls that would last. The boys had the Knights, a kind of honorary service club, a precursor to men's clubs like my dad's Lions Club. They also had athletics with letter sweaters and prized jackets. But this was before Title IX became law, and we girls had none of those things.

My mother's life was being enhanced by the Business and Professional Women's Club, and I saw our new organization as a structure to advance girls' hopes and ambitions. The first person we included was Sara Sue, who I met when she and her family moved to Ventura from Missouri. Her dad and mine had a lot in common, and Sara and I both loved our school service work (she was President of the Girls' Association) and together had rewritten the student association constitution. We also double-dated with our boyfriends from Oxnard. As high-achieving, independent girls, we knew we had a better chance at a social life away from Ventura. We came up with the name: the Ladyes. All these years later, I wince at our quaint spelling and the image of passive ladies bestowing silk scarves on their favorites. Within a decade, I'd be challenging anyone calling me a "lady," lest it minimize my independence, strength, or freedom. But this was 1959, and I was taking one step toward equality.

At our first meeting of twelve, we held elections. Karen-Dee beat me for president, and I could see Mrs. Munsell hide her distress. For the remainder of the meeting, I kept up my mask, smiling as I handed the gavel to Karen-Dee. When the bell rang, I turned pale and shaky and pleading a sick stomach, I fled to the nurse's office. She called my mother, who picked me up, and in the car, I broke down. All my work to get the club set up, and they still chose Karen-Dee to lead them. Karen-Dee had known this was mine, and still she swept in and took it. I felt the rejection by my peers like a deep wound, and I couldn't stop weeping.

Finally, back at home, my mother said, "Wash your face now—that's enough," and put me to bed. I fell into a deep sleep. She woke me for dinner, but I couldn't eat. Karen-Dee called and apologized, admitting she "just wanted to see if she could beat me." Of course, I accepted her honest confession and said I understood. Singed by knowing my peers hadn't chosen me to lead, I determined to finish what I had begun. Besides, I needed the credit. The distrust I felt for the majority of girls, and my attempts to be liked, I realize now created an inauthenticity in me that they sensed. In truth I feared most of them. I chose only a very few to trust. And in separating myself so effectively from so many girls, and even from Mrs. Munsell, I lost touch with much of what I was actually feeling.

My dad's colleague at the Lions Club had a son who was pursuing a PhD in theatre at Tulane University in New Orleans, and Dad suggested I apply to the adjunct women's college, Sophie Newcomb. When I investigated and discovered that the university's theatre program was nationally renowned, I decided to apply. Sophie Newcomb was expensive, nearly as much as Stanford, but I was accepted, and when Stanford turned me down, and I turned up my nose at Cal, my folks let me know they would make it work.

The day I got the rejection letter, I called Karen-Dee and drove out to the beach house on the Rincon her family had rented for the summer. Karen-Dee was set for Stanford. She had excelled in every pursuit she tried. She was kind, empathetic, and sorry that we wouldn't be on the same campus, and as we walked on the foggy beach, she wished me well at Sophie Newcomb, and we talked about how good it would be for me to get away. By then I was fighting bitterly with my father, feeling constrained by our small town, and though I loved Mike, I ached to free myself from old expectations.

Part Two

Passion

"If I feel as if the top of my head
were taken off, I know that is poetry."
—Emily Dickinson

5. Undertow

"I hooked my feet under the seat, curled up my toes, and I really hung on."
—Ebenezer Sprague, *Little House on the Prairie*,
BLANCHE HANALIS

TIME ON THE SOUTHERN PACIFIC'S "Sunset Limited" coach car stretched to airy thinness, pure potential. Mama and I sat up for the forty-hour ride to New Orleans, economizing, reading, eating at tables set with white cotton tablecloths in the dining car, where kind Black waiters poured from bottomless silver coffee pots. Passed through Nevada, Arizona, New Mexico, Texas, Texas, Texas. At night, Texas moon, wide desert, clickety-clack. I was waiting for my future to begin.

Houston was a halt station where I had time to make a quick jump onto land—a blast of heat. A furnace? The engine? No, simply summer in Texas. Longing for a drink of water and an earth-bound toilet, I hurried out of the scorching sun into the air-conditioned station and stared aghast at the sign: "Colored only." The snack bar? The same. The drinking fountain? Shocked and angry, as I walked to the other end of the station towards the ladies' room, I stared gimlet-eyed at the white people, their drawls now bleached of charm.

I hoped I wasn't going to regret choosing a college in the South. I had pored over the course catalogue, and Mama and I had sewn clothes to mix and match with what I had carefully chosen and bought at discount from my retail job. We had packed everything, including my phonograph and favorite records, and my boyfriend's photo, into my big steamer trunk.

We arrived that very evening in sultry New Orleans. When the taxi pulled up between the hotel's elegant white columns, I realized Mama had not skimped. Inside, a gracious welcome. Real antiques. We telephoned my future roommate, a local girl. She and her mother invited us to come to their home the next day before going out for lunch. We soaked in the luxury of a real bathtub, dressed up, and found ourselves in the French Quarter. We ate French food in the Courtyard of the Two Sisters and wandered in the humid night, drinking rum drinks in hurricane glasses. I was amazed. In California, you couldn't even be served at seventeen, let alone flaunt your drink on the street. Walking in the street in a festival atmosphere with Al Hirt playing in a packed club on one side and a strip joint where a woman twirled tassels from her nipples, I was grateful Mama shielded me from nothing. I was about to learn what a truly different world this was from the only one I'd known.

My new roommate lived in Metairie, a new district of expensive, Colonial-style homes and sweeping lawns. When Nancy opened the door, I thought she looked like a cameo, her fine white skin framed by brunette waves. She led us in to meet her mother. Mrs. L. was vintage New Orleans, with roots in the "Gahden District," she let us know, not in this "upstart neighborhood." It was Mr. L. who wanted a *new* home; he was from Texas. He was "in oil." In Ventura, the people "in oil" were in the oil *fields*, employed on the rigs outside of town where the stink made us gasp whenever we drove by.

I noticed, as we left for the restaurant, a Black servant ironing in the garage. It was ninety-nine degrees, 90 percent humidity— unbearable—but Mrs. L. said as we passed, "You have to lock them out—they'd steal everything." Mother and I exchanged a look. We went to "the club" in the "Gahden District," where Mrs. L. told us about old "Noo Ohlyns." I wanted to hear everything, impressed by the big old homes and capacious lawns and everything growing green, but Mama later pointed out to me that the staid restaurant had dirt on the window sills.

Our dorm was filled with girls from the South and Texas and Northerners who hadn't been accepted into the Ivies. In Ventura, no one mentioned the Ivies. Nancy was obsessed with sorority rush, which I didn't do; she wanted me to go to the Baptist youth group; she didn't think I should be dating Jewish boys. And so, I stopped hanging around with Nancy and hooked up with girls like me, girls who wanted to explore the city. The streetcar named Desire no longer ran, but we took a bus into the quarter, had our tea leaves read, went to a hotel for oysters Rockefeller, drank coffee with chicory. As we were boarding the bus back to school, I strode toward the back, but one of the girls grabbed me and dragged me to a seat near the front. "Back home—" I started to tell her how things were, and how it was fun to sit in back, but she cut me off. "We don't sit back there."

The Negroes, as in those days we said in Ventura, or the "nigras" as people in New Orleans said, sat in the back of the bus. I ached with a sense of injustice at the sight of so many downtrodden-looking people. I'd never before smelled poverty. In the dorm basement, maids did the laundry, while dryers hummed to the click of cockroaches. And all of it filled me with shame. I thought we were better at home, though it was true Dad had used the "n" word until Janey and I insisted he stop. We had few Black families in Ventura, but when my sister planned to go to the junior high prom with a Black boy, the school put a stop to it. He and she decided to simply meet there, and they danced together anyway. My parents had to accept it. But in New Orleans, the segregation and the clinging to the past were thrust in my face and upset me terribly.

However, I also felt the liberation of being a student in a women's college. Our classes were small, our teachers excellent. Without boys around, I felt free not to set my hair and free to argue a point without fear of looking "too smart" the way I had in Ventura. The university, Tulane, had decided first-semester freshmen could not do theatre. I joined the school newspaper instead, and by homecoming, I had written three-fourths of the front page. When my heavy load, made especially hard by ancient Greek, began to get away from me, I quit the paper. I began to wake in the dark to study with the din of steam pipes banging as if there were a ghost in the basement. The Texans—more free-wheeling and fun than the other Southern girls—taught me to smoke and let me use their tubs for hot baths, "for my nerves." I identified with Blanche DuBois.

I went home for Christmas vacation but didn't study, so I had to cram for finals. When I was panicking, my Texas pals offered me Dexedrine; a lot of the girls used them as diet pills. And for seventy-two hours I studied with breaks only to eat or take an exam. I smoked to calm my shaking hands. Sitting at a desk in my friend's room, because if I went near my bed, I was going to fall asleep, my whole body was weak and trembling, and I thought, *This is withdrawal.* I had to sleep. When the girls tried to wake me, I had no recollection of anything. I took fewer pills to finish up finals, but one night, feeling homesick, I made a call home and burst into tears. My mother swung into action: She had my transcripts sent to Berkeley, and when my acceptance came, she procured a place in the dorm before I could have second thoughts.

The Sunset Limited left late from New Orleans, so my pal and I double dated in the Quarter. The boys were taking me to the train when I realized I didn't have my ticket. I placed a panicked call to the dorm, the boys raced back to pick up the ticket, and sped back to me and my girlfriend. I just made it onto the train where I sank gratefully into a seat. The train was full of young servicemen heading to be stationed in California. On that 2000-mile journey home, they taught me to play Hearts, and I ate a lot and let the train rock me to sleep, recovering from my experiment with drugs and swearing I'd never repeat that.

I'd lasted just one semester at Sophie Newcomb, and on that long train ride, I felt total relief, with nothing asked of me, between places, between people. I barely reflected on the experience, which is no surprise because I had exhausted myself. Just before we reached Union Station in Los Angeles, I washed up in the roomy Ladies' Lounge and put on my old black speaking-contest dress, my new beret, and high heels. When I descended the steps, Mama burst into tears and said, "She's all grown up!"

IN JANUARY, MAMA AND I HEADED to Berkeley. I loved it from the first moment. The air was clear and fresh after rain the night before, and I was enchanted by everything about the city. Had my mother known what was coming next, she might have wished me back in New Orleans, for then I was seventeen, a virgin, a naïf who thought Berkeley was a temporary solution on my way to Stanford. But the '60s were dawning, and Berkeley was an epicenter of change. I lucked out with an artistic, smart roommate, Barbara Glickman, who, unlike the other girls I saw from Beverly Hills, had held on to her nose, and was gorgeous and sexy.

We lived just a few blocks from campus in an eight-floor women's dormitory, part of a complex of four—two for men, two for women—built around a central dining room. At the south entrance to campus, when I saw card tables staffed by students supporting and informing us about everything from the Young Republicans to young socialists wanting to "Free Cuba," my curiosity was instantly piqued, and although the campus was enormous, and registration overwhelming, the anonymity offered a kind of privacy I liked.

One night on the way to dinner, I saw flyers announcing a meeting about the House Un-American Activities Committee (HUAC) to be held in our dorm lounge, and curious, I decided to go. The Danish modern orange couches and chairs were all taken, so I found a place on the floor to sit. Two or three grad students spoke, likening HUAC to the Senate committee made infamous by Senator Joseph McCarthy and his anti-Communist campaign of the 1950s. I remembered seeing actors I admired paraded before TV cameras, flash bulbs popping, though I hadn't followed the story closely enough to understand the damage wreaked on people's lives as a result. I knew the Senator's overreach had brought him down, and I understood that some people joined the Communist Party out of idealism, not because they wished to overthrow the US government. My own dad had been a youthful socialist, so I sympathized with people who may have explored Communism.

But sitting on the floor in that room I learned that HUAC had subpoenaed more than one hundred public school teachers, that people's reputations and livelihoods had been on the line without even a trial. My sense of the injustice of HUAC flared up in my chest, and I signed the petition advocating its abolition. The *San Francisco Chronicle* had condemned the hearings, and I knew a peaceful protest was planned, but I had a paper due, so I didn't board the bus to attend the demonstration.

But later, when I saw that peaceful demonstrators were attacked by police with fire hoses, sending students tumbling down the cold, hard marble steps of City Hall, and when I saw the arrests and heard authorities calling them "Communist sympathizers," "pinkos," "outside agitators," I knew that in fact they were just like me, only slightly older and smarter. It was then that the icy sheath of my family's Republican beliefs began to show hairline cracks.

AT DINNER WITH THE FAMILY, MY father told me I should be a teacher. "Then you can always earn a living," he said, but I had looked over the courses for the teacher track and knew that was not what I wanted. I liked English, philosophy, psychology, the arts, but I couldn't answer my father's questions about what I would be. I didn't know.

He was clear and direct that when I graduated, I would have to be self-supporting, and with that in mind, even as I studied the subjects I liked at Berkeley, I enrolled at the modeling school in Oakland. I used my summer earnings working retail for tuition, and every Wednesday night I took the bus to Oakland where, to my surprise, the manager talked me into entering the Miss Oakland contest.

The contest was a huge distraction from my work at Cal, and secretly, I thought if I could win an acting scholarship, my folks would let me go. For the contest, I performed a monologue from *A Streetcar Named Desire* that earned adulation. I didn't win the contest, but the dream I didn't let myself dream was further encouraged by strangers at the contest who told my mother how talented they thought I was. This had also happened in high school at speaking contests, but my parents feared the idea of acting, especially Mom. I suppressed the desire.

After the contest, my Greek professor asked if it was me in that photo from the Miss Oakland contest, and when I told him it was, he looked disgusted and shook his head. "Youth and beauty. And so it was when they killed Socrates."

His words stung. *I killed Socrates?!* I felt judged and discounted. I was on the verge of breaking out from my background into a new realm. I had fallen behind in my studies with the contest, too many dates, and a break-up from Mike. Anxious and overwhelmed, I went to the Student Health Center to get something to help me sleep. The first signs of trouble hit when I missed the bus to attend my cousin's wedding in Gilroy and, that same week, failed my Greek final. I realized I couldn't take drugs.

FOR OUR SOPHOMORE YEAR, TONI AND I scrambled after quitting rush for sororities to find living quarters. We landed in a boarding house with a pretentious French name—the Chalet de Longpre. Mrs. de Longpre was not French, but she did promise balanced meals and Sunday brunch in the "Chateau" next door—a brunch that ultimately turned out to be cornflakes. The houses were plain-looking and big with linoleum halls and floors, bare-bones, with worn couches in the downstairs living room we called "the lounge." They were nothing like the sorority houses, but Toni and I liked the odd collection of young women we now lived with—transfer students, last-minute deciders, sorority dropouts. That year we made friendships that would last a lifetime, though of course at the time we couldn't have known that. As I look back, I'm grateful for the turn we took away from the less unpredictable living style to the more adventurous women we bonded with there. Toni and I became ever closer; really, we could finish each other's sentences.

Just before the fall term began, some boys invited the two of us to a beer bust in Tilden Park in the Berkeley Hills. We both got so drunk that when they dropped us back at the boarding house, Toni threw up in the trash can, and I tripped on the change of pattern in the linoleum and fell flat on the floor, laughing hard, until I saw how sick my friend was. Never having tried my best at school, I determined that fall to apply myself. Every afternoon when I had no class, I went to the library to study.

Two of the new friends we made at the boarding house, Karen McLellan and Jeanne Lengsfelder, were complete contrasts. Karen grew up in San Francisco and Sausalito and treated the Bay Area with a casual diffidence that struck me as sophisticated. Jeanne was from Great Neck, New York, and had parents who had emigrated from Europe to escape Hitler. Karen's mother was a divorced career woman, a buyer for Roos-Atkins, a women's retail shop that sold typical "co-ed" clothes of the day: tailored skirts and madras blouses with button-down collars, accented by a metal circle pin. The allure of that East Coast preppy fashion didn't impress me, but all the sorority girls wore those outfits, and Karen did too. She had first headed to the University of Missouri to study journalism, but like me, she couldn't stand the South, and we had both bounced into Berkeley with no real plan. She was a beauty in the mold of Faye Dunaway (though Dunaway had yet to appear in the movies), and a quick wit. One day, she showed up at the boarding house in her own red convertible, so I thought she was rich and was still more convinced when I met her glamorous mother.

Jeanne's chemist father created perfumes and was a gifted painter. Unlike Karen, Toni, and me, Jeanne was inexperienced with boys but as irresistible as a puppy. Unlike anyone I had ever known, she spoke familiarly of Bach and used the word "fugue" as if it were an old friend. She wore thick black bangs that she pushed out of her dark eyes when she engaged with her thick New York accent in enthusiastic debate. I liked to argue a point, loved logic, but Karen and Toni were more amused by all this. I felt protective towards Jeanne—as if she were my super-smart little sister. Meanwhile, my own sister was thriving in my absence, played Aunt Eller in *Oklahoma* to great adulation in the school musical and was disinterested in any topics I brought home.

AT SCHOOL, IN THE DOWNSTAIRS LOUNGE, we gathered, excited to watch the first-ever televised presidential debate on a small black-and-white TV with rabbit ears. We were all familiar with Richard Nixon from his years as vice president and because he was one of ours—a Californian. But John Fitzgerald Kennedy was a new face, and we were very curious. And Nixon was shockingly bad, his arguments full of holes, and utterly non-telegenic. As sweat coursed down his face, and Kennedy remained so poised, handsome, young, and smart, we were enthralled. He spoke to our hopes and ambitions for a great life. When we heard about buses going to a Kennedy rally in San Francisco at the Cow Palace, we four signed up to go, and there Kennedy's vision of a moonshot and the Peace Corps won us over. He was our kind of leader. When I heard him say, "Ask not what your country can do for you, ask what you can do for your country," I felt a chill run up my spine, and my heart began to beat faster. I felt as if he was speaking directly to our generation, convinced that we all could make a difference.

Still, I felt compelled to listen to the other side, so Toni and I took the city bus on Saturday to a small park in Oakland where Nixon appeared and spouted homilies about his mother's cherry pie. I saw a man who didn't respect the citizenry, who believed his best method was to manipulate. I wished I was old enough to vote, but at the time the voting age was twenty-one, and it would be another eleven years before the law was changed to give the vote to anyone eighteen and over.

But politics wasn't my primary focus, studying was. I wanted to find out if I could do well at academics if I applied myself. My favorite class was Modern English Literature with Professor Parkinson where we could choose to write creatively in addition to writing literary criticism. Every lecture opened a new door to me: Literature contained philosophy *and* psychology *and* was beautiful into the bargain. I declared myself an English major. When I read Freud's *Civilization and Its Discontents*, I began to better understand the depressive moods that sometimes descended. I drove Toni crazy as I strode around our room declaiming Prufrock: "And would it have been worth it after all . . ."[1]

Over the years my relationship with Toni only deepened. We shared secrets and aspirations. We also both had fathers we adored but were drinkers who could be terribly cruel. And we both had mothers we thought of as critical and controlling. I can still see Toni in that room we shared—dressed in pajamas, rubbing her eyebrow as she concentrated on Chaucer's *Canterbury Tales*. We were serious about our studies, took NoDoz caffeine pills to stay awake to work longer. And before we went out on dates, with our penchant for alcohol, we both drank lots of milk to protect ourselves from getting too drunk. We also helped each other sneak into the Chalet after hours, tipsy and climbing the fire escape so we wouldn't get "campused" for the weekend. Toni also encouraged me in my project to lose my virginity.

One afternoon I received a letter from my father that threw me into a panic. His Lions Club had shown a short documentary created by HUAC called *Operation Abolition* that claimed student protesters at Berkeley were Communists or Commie dupes, and that they were violent.

He wrote, "If that's the kind of people you have up there, you can just come home."

I rushed into the bathroom, burst into angry tears, and tore his letter to pieces, but I feared he would force me to leave Berkeley. And I loved my school. So began my disillusionment with my father. When I visited home, I tried to explain to him how wrong he was about those protesters, and he backed off from his threat to force me to come home, but that began the many years of our excruciating political arguments. Whenever he put down the poor or derided my idealism or scoffed at liberal solutions like a guaranteed income—ideas that excited me—I was hurt to the core. Mom stood by, tried to deflect, and dreaded the knock-down-drag-out arguments that ruined many a family dinner she had prepared with care.

At the end of the fall term, a madman who ran out of the Berkeley Hills and onto campus with a sawed-off shotgun, shot and critically injured Professor Parkinson. The young poet who had been with him in his office was killed, and after that, I had to drag myself through finals. The struggles I had been having to find meaning in an absurd world grew heavier, and that was before the revelations I would soon learn at home.

Over the holidays, Mom and I went to Santa Barbara to do some Christmas shopping. We were sitting in a small restaurant on the Paseo del Sol, the old colonial Spanish courtyard lined by charming little shops and our favorite place for lunch, when she asked me if I remembered when Daddy had been in the hospital in Camarillo. I remembered. "We took a picnic out there. You told us he was sick, in the hospital. He was subdued," I said. I didn't mention to her how awful that visit had been, how nauseous I had felt, how confusing it was when he came home and no more was ever said about it. But I remembered the fight. It was somebody's birthday. Uncle Harry had come over for dinner, and later, when I was sleeping, I woke to the sound of pots and pans slamming against the wall and crashing to the floor. I heard Mama's voice full of angry tears and padded down the hall where I saw Daddy duck, then pick up a pan and put it on the table. She was screaming, "White trash? Trash? White trash! You let him sit here and call my mother that in our own home, Gene!" Another pan flew by. He stooped again, and as he rose, he saw me staring, turned and fled out the front door. I remembered the Venetian blinds rattling against the glass. I remembered being frozen.

Now, as we sat in the California sunshine, in the pretty Spanish courtyard, she had something to tell me.

"Your father left the house that night. He went out to the farm road in the east end." I could envision that road, the tall eucalyptus trees shielding the crops from the wind.

She went on: "He put a hose in the exhaust pipe, fed it through the window of the car, rolled up the glass as far as he could, and turned on the motor."

As I tried to contain my astonishment and fear, she went on to tell me he'd been found there unconscious and placed under seventy-two-hour watch in Camarillo. It was the law because it was believed that anyone who would kill himself might also kill someone else.

I asked for more information. She told me he refused to talk to the psychiatrists. He refused to speak. He said the medicine made him stupid so he wouldn't take it, and they kept him one more week with no progress, so they sent him home.

She went on to tell me how she had coped: Uncle Harry had refused to advance her any money, blaming her for Dad's condition. She couldn't cash Dad's paycheck; the bank account was in his name only. Her friend Mabel Miller had been her port in the storm, watching us while she went to the hospital, loaning her money for groceries.

In that courtyard in Santa Barbara, the sun was still shining, and the waitress brought more coffee. We lit up our cigarettes, and I put my hand on hers. She twisted her rings.

"Sometimes I find one."

"What, Mom?"

"A suicide note. In a drawer or in his pockets. They're not dated. I never know if they are new or old."

And when I asked what she did with them, she said she threw them away. She thought I should know. Janey didn't know yet, though this all started before she was even born. When my mother was pregnant with Janey, she told me, he'd gotten involved with another woman and felt so guilty that he made his first attempt.

In that moment I longed only to return to school. I felt I had to be brave and be there for Mama if she needed me and told her to let me know if there was anything I could do. We paid the check, visited the ladies' room, put on fresh lipstick, and drove home.

6. Surfacing

"There's no way to find out unless you try."
— "The Lord Is My Shepherd," Part 1, *Little House
on the Prairie*, MICHAEL LANDON

DURING SOPHOMORE SPRING TERM I thought losing my virginity and the writer's block I'd developed in my fiction seminar were my greatest challenges, but life had other ideas.

Over Thanksgiving break, I rear-ended my uncle's Cadillac, and a man named Larry, tall, dark, and handsome with glittery blue eyes, came to take my statement about the accident. He disarmed me with his glib salesman's jokes and his reference to "the illusive Miss Grassle" in his report. A grad student in business, paying his way through Cal by working for an insurance company, he began to come see me. We started to date.

Larry's father was an officer at the naval base in Alameda, so we could drink scotch for fifty cents a shot, and whenever we did, I loved the "lift off" I felt in my brain. When we zipped up in his red sports car to wine country or down to Carmel and Big Sur, I felt like this was real romance, and I was happy and excited. I didn't believe in virginity as a virtue, but I could not go "all the way." Even drunk, I couldn't let myself go, though Larry, with remarkable patience, did his best to convince me to make love. After months of making out in the car, doing everything but penetration at his apartment and in a motel in Carmel, he devised a plan. He knew I wanted to, and a friend told him to surprise me in the shower. One Sunday morning, he came into the shower with me. We were soaking wet when we finally landed in his bed and had intercourse. Finally, I had crossed that barrier. Although I was relieved, afterwards I felt a strange sense of disorientation. It was the second time I went to the Student Health Center to ask for psychological help, but I couldn't talk openly with the woman I saw, and when she suggested a male therapist, I didn't want to make her feel bad, so I said, no, I was fine, and I left. I buried my confusion. Instead, Larry and I had more sex, and began to spend every weekend together. That February, on my birthday, he had given me his fraternity pin, surreptitiously on a stuffed tiger, so I couldn't say yes or no. Both sets of parents were pleased and they believed we were moving towards engagement.

All sophomore year, I'd resisted the lure of posters announcing auditions for the Theatre Department because I was bent on getting the best grades I could. But when an old friend urged me to read aloud the final scene of *Look Back in Anger,* I couldn't resist. The character, estranged from her husband, had suffered a painful miscarriage. She describes her loss and they reunite in a powerful way. I felt compelled the next day to go to the audition where Stacy Keach—our campus star (whose name, while he was still in his twenties, would appear above the show's title on Broadway)—reached out to me and I was cast in the female lead. Because Stacy was blocked from the show by a university policy barring him from appearing in too many plays in one term, Vince Cobb, the son of the greatly esteemed Lee J. Cobb (the first Willy Loman in *Death of a Salesman*), was cast.

When Larry realized how keen my interest in theatre was becoming, he invited me to see *King Lear* at the Actor's Workshop in San Francisco. That production was a revelation: I couldn't take my eyes off the onstage kingdom, rough-hewn and primitive, its king tribal and willful. The costumes were simple, more medieval than Renaissance; Lear's fury burst upon Cordelia like the storm, and his sudden rejection reverberated, reminding me of my dad's lightning attacks. The young Michael O'Sullivan, only twenty-seven, carried me with him onto the thundering moor where he tore off his garments and was reduced to madness. Lear's need for forgiveness and unity with his honest daughter came too late, and as the lights rose in the theatre, I felt a powerful catharsis. I wanted and needed to belong to this kind of theatre.

Inspired, the next day I returned to rehearsals for *Look Back in Anger*. I was a quick study, instantly at home on the stage, and so by day I endured sociology lectures in Wheeler Auditorium that would be transformed at night into our stage for the performances. Berkeley's Theatre Department soared in the '60s, and a new PhD program attracted a fresh crop of talented actors and directors.

Even as *Look Back in Anger* opened, I continued to dream of *Lear*. And when Vince asked if he could photograph me, and I agreed, he and I began to share a secret affection for each other. Our intimate scenes together onstage deepened our bond.

The play was winding down, and Larry would soon be receiving his MBA. He drove over to the dorm to bring me the good news: He'd been offered a good job with Lockheed in Los Angeles. We went out for hamburgers and ate in the car, and he told me he wanted me to marry him and move with him to LA. I could finish school at UCLA, he said. Sitting in that car, I felt trapped and understood this was it: Move forward with him or end it.

I tried my best not to hurt him, but by then I had realized that if I didn't give myself a chance in the theatre, I would always regret it. He felt I could try in LA. When I made an excuse about LA not being where the theatre was, I realized I didn't love him enough. Not enough to go with him. I didn't say but I did see that we had less in common now than when we had first met. He was angry with me and said things to hurt me, so I closed off to him and our breakup was harsh. But for me, the idea of being on my deathbed and not having attempted to act seemed like the worst kind of failure. And Vince was ready to listen. He understood.

MAMA HELPED ME ARRANGE TO TAKE a summer course at the Pasadena Playhouse, an idea Daddy had suggested for some time. I arrived in Pasadena with a suitcase full of Shakespeare and Shaw and Stanislavski from the Ventura Library and spent the summer of 1961 lying on my bed smoking and reading through the night. I felt like a forest nymph overtaken by a lusty god, so possessed was I by the longing to act, to live in the theatre, to belong to the great traditions I was reading about and listening to on recordings. Toni and I were taking Physics at Ventura College night school, but I needed to miss the last two weeks in order to finish the Pasadena course. On Fridays, Mom came to get me, and I studied Toni's Physics notes in the car while Mom drove. She dropped me at the college so I could pass the weekly test and fulfill the Berkeley Physics requirement.

In Pasadena, another young woman and I recognized each other's determination and went together to the small theatre to practice our auditions for the next day. As Colette, an exotic brunette, began to perform her comic piece, a tall, gangly guy strolled into the theatre and stood back watching respectfully. When Colette finished, he walked down the aisle—his voice abashed and enthusiastic at the same time: "That looked really good. Can I show you mine?" he asked. Enter Fred Gordon: Twenty, exuberant, with a big heart in a huge frame he had yet to own.

Fred was lively in his monologue and wanted to know what we thought. I tentatively made a suggestion, and he leapt to try it. We instantly became colleagues, co-conspirators in art, and after rehearsing for hours, we walked outside into the warm evening and lingered, talking for a long time under the old magnolias. Fred was from the East Coast, had a metropolitan verve that was new to me. He was smart and quirky, quick to get a joke, and when he asked me a question, his keen focus suggested my answer might contain a life-enhancing secret.

Our dorm was an old brown Craftsman where I lived in a garret that trapped the thick summer heat. I looked down my nose at the girls downstairs having fun singing Rodgers and Hammerstein around the piano. As the six-week course progressed, Colette, Fred, and I became a threesome who stoked each other's passion for serious theatre. One night while listening over and over to Colette's recording of the third movement of Brahms's Third Symphony, I made up my mind to leave Berkeley, move to San Francisco, and somehow, some way, find work in the theatre.

That very night I placed a collect call from the pay phone on the small landing of the dorm to my parents to let them know immediately of my plans. I was going to be an actress. I was going to quit school. I would find a modeling job to support myself.

My mother was not having it. I could be an actress and finish college, she said, but this was not a conversation she was going to have over the phone, particularly not as I'd had to raise my voice to be heard over the girls downstairs singing "Oh, what a beautiful morning!"

Vince came to pick me up for a movie date, and I announced my decision to him. He seemed ambivalent, doubtful, but I didn't care. I was anything but.

The class in Pasadena ended, and I returned to Ventura, and once Mama realized I was not to be deflected from my plan, she took to her bed, drenched in tears and disappointment. "Anything but politics or the theatre!" she wailed theatrically. Mama was not a weepy woman, but my dad's remark brought home what had been obvious for years. He sat smoking at the kitchen table. "Well," he said, looking straight at me, "I've been trying to talk you out of this for ten years. Now, I'm through talking."

This was news to me.

Not long after that I had to have a tonsillectomy, and Mama never left me alone in the hospital. When I had unexpected bleeding in the dark, she was there to see that it was stopped. I think it was sometime during that hospital stay that she finally accepted my plans. During the enforced silence of my recuperation, I saw the journey I had traveled in my memory: the dancing, the plays I'd created for school and church, the role-playing skits I'd concocted with neighborhood kids and cousins. Throughout those years, not wanting to disappoint my folks, I had ignored what I now understood had always been my heart's desire.

My father had seen it. I had not.

And at the end of that summer, Daddy helped load my stuff into Mama's car, and off she and I drove to San Francisco where she helped me find a little studio apartment and fill it with basics. She even bought a bottle of scotch for the company she imagined I would have. And then she left me to find my way.

7. Art and Death

"Who's afraid? I ain't afraid a nuthin.'"
— "The Spring Dance," *Little House on the Prairie*,
BLANCHE HANALIS

I HAD ALREADY CONTACTED THE modeling agency and circled in red in the yellow pages the names of all the city's theatres, though there was only one I wanted. I ate breakfast, flipped the Murphy bed up into the closet, and began to pace as I stared at the heavy black phone, fearing that when I asked, I would hear no. The phone was black, mute, heavy. *Go on. Dial.* In a flash, I knew what to do: I got down the bottle of scotch, poured, drank, took a deep breath, dialed. A sonorous voice: "The Actor's Workshop."

It turned out they were just beginning a new apprentice program, classes were beginning soon, and the people in the program would be available to the theatre twenty-four hours a day.

"You would belong to us," the voice on the phone said.

For a moment I didn't know what to say. The modeling agency had offered me a two-day stint that would pay a month's rent, but this man was offering to set up an audition, and if I was admitted, the program would begin the next week.

I stalled for time. I would have to ask my parents for help, and Dad had been clear that I was to be self-supporting. But I said yes, and afterwards, when I called to ask my parents for one more year of support, they agreed to back me with one hundred dollars a month.

The Workshop was located in the Marines' Memorial Theatre downtown, a short walk from my apartment, and when I first entered, I did so like an acolyte nun. Alan Mandell of the sonorous voice on the phone met with me and my fellow students in the office. We were a serious bunch, from San Francisco State, UC Davis, Carnegie Tech, and one young woman who'd been in the summer show at Disneyland. Most of the others already had theatre BAs, but a few were, like me, undergrads still. Someone handed another young woman and me a bucket and cleaning supplies and dispatched us down Mason Street to the smaller Encore Theatre to prepare it for its fall reopening. We unlocked the big doors and let ourselves into the black lobby. Planning to attack the restrooms first, we nearly gagged at the stench and quickly developed a strategy: run in, splash Clorox all around, rush out again, and wait. Outside we smoked cigarettes and got acquainted. She was a graduate of SF State and had studied with our co-artistic directors, Jules Irving and Herbert Blau, the actual director of *Lear,* the show that had led me here. A cigarette later, I set about doing my first job in the theatre: cleaning the toilets. I was in heaven.

Each morning that fall I took classes with members of the company, and in the afternoon, we built sets, hunted for props, sewed costumes, or held book in rehearsals. At night we worked backstage as crew. Lunch was eating sandwiches while reading plays aloud on the empty stage. We were sponges soaking up the salty sea of our passion, surrounded by artists of equal passion and greater skills, like Beatrice Manley, the ferocious Regan in *Lear,* who was our acting teacher. Regal and gracious, Beatrice was married to Herb Blau. José was the tech director, a former dancer, wildly flamboyant in his short wool cape; he taught movement. Ronnie Davis, dark and intense, had a company, the RG Davis Mime Troupe, that performed socially satirical commedia plays free in Bay Area parks; he had studied in Paris with Étienne Decroux at L'École Mime, and now he was teaching us.

Even as I handed the actors huge paper cups of coffee that I carried from the corner coffee shop downstairs, and as I helped them change out of their sweaty tunics, I felt shy, but I studied them closely, tuned my ears to the loudspeaker in the dressing room as dialogue from *Sergeant Musgrave's Dance*, *The Three Sisters*, and *Lear*, rotating in repertory, night after night, floated into the room. After each show, we changed the set for the next night's performance, struck the costumes, and locked the props safely in the big black prop box. It was rumored that Michael O'Sullivan had, in a rage when rehearsing *Lear*, pulled the backstage phone out of the wall. To me it looked ever after like a holy relic. In the hall was a water closet with a single toilet we could not flush during the show because plumbing threaded across the ceiling above the audience. Things were bare bones, and I came to understand that in this business, money was spent where it could be *seen*.

Too young to join the others at the Curtain Call for a drink after the show, I often just walked the city streets, admiring the Asian antiques in Gump's windows, trying to ignore the pretty clothes in I. Magnin's, finding in Chinatown, for one dollar, a warm white bun stuffed with pork. My old prom dresses hung limp in the big closet behind the Murphy bed—the trappings of a former life—and I began to wear only jeans and a sweatshirt, and barely had time to launder them. My hair grew longer. I stopped setting it. When the mascara ran out, I did not replace it. My language grew looser, my priorities more certain.

The Workshop members felt a degree of dedication that the novelist Herbert Gold compared to a Communist cell: We lived in basement apartments, had barely any income, wore proletariat jeans and pea jackets. Many of the adults had day jobs and families, but their hearts resided almost wholly in the Workshop. The year before I came, Henry Hewes wrote in the *Saturday Review* a piece that resonated for me then and resonates still: "Most impressive in the company is Robert Symonds. . . . Mr. Symonds, who has chosen to develop within the Workshop company instead of aspiring to

Broadway recognition, is not a luminous personality who turns the role into a projection of himself, but just a fine actor capable of employing his superb skill and coordination to create any character an author or director has devised. . . . In general, this appears to be true of the other actors."[1]

The Ford Foundation gave the Workshop a grant that provided two hundred dollars weekly salary to ten actors. It seemed a princely sum to us kids who worked for nothing, but for grown men with families (Bob Symonds had three children) and the professional actors who came up from Hollywood for the season, the meager pay was a sacrifice they willingly made for the chance to play a variety of roles in great plays. This was the company, after all, that first brought a Pinter play to the United States, the first *Godot* to the West, and had also taken such works to San Quentin.

Every few months, Herb held a company meeting where he presented a paper full of literary references and high-minded theory about what the theatre was all about—ours and it—*the* Theatre. He laid out a shining path in which the theatre would challenge, nourish, and alter its community.[2] After only a couple of months, I understood I had dived into a world that would require me to learn much more. I definitely had to go back to school.

I did not forget my old friendships with Toni and Karen-Dee. Toni and I visited back and forth across the Bay Bridge, but my hours made it hard. Karen-Dee was having her junior year abroad in France. One evening, I was having a beer in my apartment when my mother called, and I knew instantly that something was wrong. The *Star Free Press* had announced that Karen-Dee and three other students had been killed in France. They'd crashed their car on a tree-lined road, exactly the way Camus had died. She was just about to turn twenty-one, and now her brilliance, her sweet spirit, her beautiful wavy hair, all were gone. I'd just had a letter from her full of concern that I had dropped out of college. How was it possible that she had died?

Feeling strangely alien, I pushed the sorrow and shock deep inside and returned to doing the work that was expected. And I didn't think to cancel or just not go to the Halloween party Vince and I had planned to hold at his apartment in Berkeley. As soon as we finished our chores backstage, we went to my place to put on our nose putty, white clown faces, black surprised eyebrows, and big red grins. I pulled on the old, blue leotard and tights, looked in the mirror, and saw that I looked the opposite of what I was feeling, but when his friends arrived, already high, to pick us up for the ride over the Bay Bridge, I went along. As they gossiped about people in Beverly Hills, I sat silently, lost, terribly sad. At the apartment, we quickly poured drinks, and, from the kitchen door, I watched dancing couples assume grotesque shapes in the dim light. In the neon-lit kitchen, feeling coldly superior, I thought how superficial they seemed. I was the real one, experiencing real tragedy; my grief at losing Karen gave me depth, and made me separate from the others.

Finally, near dawn, the guests had left, and I collapsed on the floor and began to sob. Vince didn't understand. He accused me of crying for myself, of being selfish, and this set off more uncontrollable tears. I screamed that he didn't understand, but a quick hard slap snapped my head around. The shock stopped my tears.

I knew he had seen such scenes in the movies: Slap a hysterical woman to bring her around. I did stop crying. I grabbed my work bag and shot out the door, my heart wild. I ran into the pale gray light of the deserted neighborhood. I ran with crazy clown makeup streaking down my face to Karen and Jeanne's apartment six blocks away. I woke them up. They brought me in, made coffee, listened, let me shower, and put me to bed. When Vince showed up, they didn't let him in. Soon after that, Vince and I broke up, and he left the Workshop. I couldn't know it then, but this would be the beginning of a pattern I would repeat time and again: drinking, fighting, and a spiraling into despair.

Back at the Workshop, my grief over Karen's death settled in me as depression. Walking down to the mime studio past Market Street, I wondered why it was Karen-Dee who died and thought it should have been me. I recited T. S. Eliot's "We are the hollow men, we are the stuffed men," and poured alcohol into the black hole that was me. Karen's death proved to me the absurdity of everything. Stanislavski said, "Shake the dirt off your feet when you enter the theatre," and I did, but every night on my way out, I picked it up again. I became that girl who makes calls in the middle of the night that she can't remember the next day. Toni took my calls and listened to my panicky, anguished voice until I calmed down. Looking back, I understand that although I had teetered on and off the edges of depression since I was very young, this was my first serious bout with depression.

In the midst of this, one day I was at the office desk when beautiful, soulful Rob Gove walked in. A Kenyon College wrestler, he had recently washed up on North Beach not knowing why. All he knew was he couldn't follow his big brother into the family business so he broke off an engagement and fled the Midwest for San Francisco. Within weeks we were lovers. He moved in with me without being invited. We lived on oatmeal, macaroni and cheese, and sex.

What I deeply wanted was to be held. Rob was depressed, too, and even joked about checking into the hospital across the street for a lobotomy. He and José became friends, and José often came by in his faded-blue VW van to pick up Rob to go to the scene shop or to do some other heavy lifting the Workshop needed.

Tim, the company's full-time production manager, ran the scene shop, a wooden warehouse with a tin roof down in the low-rent district below Mission. He lived next door with his wife and small daughter and showed us the theatre ropes in his kind, meticulous way—how to record the moves in a rehearsal, how to paint sets, properly store props. He often drove a bunch of us in the back of his rickety, all-purpose van down to the shop, and while we worked, he kept the classical music station playing on the small, paint-spattered radio.

One day I was in the scene shop helping to paint a canvas backdrop when the delicate pizzicato of *Sylvia*—Karen-Dee's solo—clubbed me. I dropped my paint brush on the bench and ran toward the costume storage where I hid between thick rows of old clothes to muffle my sobs. Rob found me and asked, gently, what was wrong, and when I told him, he said, "You don't have to hide."

I realize now I was surprised. I'd grown up believing grief was something I had to bear alone. Mama had counseled me throughout my childhood whenever I was sad or disappointed to "go to your room and have a good cry." She was a believer in the cleansing power of tears but holding me wasn't in her repertoire. Rob handed me his handkerchief; I blew my nose, stopped in the restroom to splash water on my face, and the two of us returned to the shop where our set designer, Bob La Vigne, offered me a cup of coffee.

It's a moment I remember vividly, because I felt accepted. I learned my sadness was okay. In that world, I discovered there was freedom for feelings, and for being someone who had not figured it all out.

Bob, serious and shy, was an accomplished painter, one of the Beats and a friend of Allen Ginsberg and Lawrence Ferlinghetti. He could design and execute both classical and abstract sets, and his representation of the autumn birches for *The Three Sisters* broke my heart. Many Mondays (our day off in the theatre) he took Rob and me on the Geary bus to the Palace of the Legion of Honor where the Rodins in the courtyard were real, and he wowed us by teaching us how to look at a picture with painter's eyes. He was mad for Rob and very kind to me.

Young, blond, and blue-eyed, clad in ragged navy sweatshirts, Rob and I were like orphans who shared our bleakness in private. Sometimes I scared myself: Skipping the spermicidal cream; bringing an actor home drunk from a party, ashamed when Rob got home, blanched at the sight of me with someone else, and left. Certainly, I knew that such acts were self-destructive, but I also was longing for romance while Rob was not. When I asked him to hug me, or to be more affectionate or expressive, he waved me off. I grew volatile: turning on the gas or running into the street in the middle of the night. I knew I needed help. I applied to two psychiatric clinics, but one rejected me and at the other a psychiatric social worker told me my suicidal thoughts were "boy-girl problems." I didn't go back.

And there was, too often, the drinking. *The Sunday Chronicle* ran the classic AA twenty-question quiz, and when I took it and was categorized as alcoholic, I declared it ridiculous—"Everybody I know drinks like I do."

A late arrival to our cohort of apprentices was a woman unlike anybody else I knew. JoAnne Akalaitis was frank, and unafraid to confront. She had dropped out of her PhD program in philosophy at Stanford to join the Workshop. Born to Lithuanian parents in Chicago, she was a first-generation American with a fierce intelligence. She had attended the University of Chicago. She was also striking, with high cheekbones and enormous blue eyes, so thin the doctor prescribed her beer and donuts. Though older than I, and far more educated, she befriended me and became my model of a strong female artist. We worked on scenes together when we could find the spare time. When one day I confided my dissatisfaction with Rob, she invited me to move in with her and her boyfriend and their other roommate, a writer, and their dog, Gus. I accepted gladly.

Rob and I remained lovers, but I moved into JoAnne's apartment. Each of the four of us kicked in five dollars a week. JoAnne, a wonderful chef, cooked for us all on the shoestring budget of an artist. I learned stuffed cabbage and shrimp curry from her, and her mac and cheese was the best I've ever tasted. Her one rule was that there would be no cooking until the dishes were done, but I never minded doing dishes, so all the roommates appreciated me. Often, she invited her brainy theatre friends from Stanford, and she whipped up big curry dinners with cheap California wine. Those were joyful community-building occasions, with lots of lively arguing.

We roommates went to the *nouvelle vague* French films and avidly discussed them afterwards. Though the young actors had snubbed us apprentices when we first arrived, by that spring of 1962 we were all going to shows they were in, shows in empty spaces around town. Lee Breuer directed a spectacular production of *The Maids*, searing and wildly imaginative with the ingenue from the Workshop and Lee's wife, Ruth Maleczech, also the mischievous Columbina in the mime troupe. I can still see in my mind's eye the gown made of parachute silk that flowed down from the rafters, a vision from the imagination Lee brought to his work for decades.

Work was my medicine. Co-artistic director Jules was set to direct a new production of *Henry IV, Part 1* with Bob Symonds as Falstaff. I was given a dual role: assistant stage manager and Lady Mortimer, both jobs a step up. I was excited about the chance to play a small role in a major production. In one exquisite love scene, Lady Mortimer, newly wed, weeps, sings, and says goodbye to her husband in Welsh, a lyrical contrast to the war scenes that follow. The actual stage manager, Jim, was a Teamster working out of town during much of the early rehearsals, so I had a lot of responsibility, my first opportunity to observe the entire rehearsal process from the first reading to opening night.

There is always a frisson in the air as everyone gathers for a first reading: cast, designers, crew, and staff, if possible. This is when the director presents his "take" on the show: why this play, why now, what it can teach us, and what it can contribute to the community. Jules Irving was our director and introduced the designers, who presented their visions, too. For *Henry IV, Part 1*, the set designer brought in a small-scale model of a massive steel structure with multiple playing areas and demonstrated how it would work, followed by the composer, the lighting designer, and the costume designer who brought drawings of each character in all his or her changes as well as swatches of the fabrics. My robe would be olive green with gold Renaissance patterns silk screened on it. In the rehearsal hall, it looked flat to me, but under the lights, it looked like rich brocade. Theatre magic.

This is also when the actors read the play aloud for the first time, and we hear it from beginning to end, together, as a company, bonding us and giving each of us a sense of our place in the whole.

This was my first experience of beginning a show in a company of professionals. And that excitement has never changed.

Each day after that first reading, we met in the church hall and conjured the play, from Jules meticulously discussing the beats with actors to beginning to block the moves to reflect the motivations of each character. Tim had trained me how to record all this in pencil, including the cues for sound effects and lighting to be added in tech rehearsals, and at the theatre, I worked with a recording backstage to learn the Welsh with my own idiosyncratic phonetics. I met with the musical director to learn my song.

In theatre, the excitement builds during the rehearsal period toward the day we will move from the rehearsal space into the theatre. I like to visit the theatre the evening before, seeing the set go up, anticipating the next day, giving in to the excitement. For *Henry IV, Part 1*, the day we moved into the theatre, the monster black structure was being welded and screwed into the floor, and Jules couldn't contain his emotions. As soon as the set was secure, he ran across the high wide bridge that spanned the width of the stage and climbed up and down the stairs like a small boy, yelling, "This is better than my erector sets!" Jim arrived and took over stage management for tech rehearsals, and I returned to my job as assistant.

Trying to do a perfect job, I did something stupid—something I can't remember but it must have been something like putting a precise cue before the dignity of the man. Jules called me into the office and told me how much good work I was doing but cautioned me to tone it down. As I look back now, I wish I had taken his words more to heart and learned diplomacy that day. The truth was that I hardly understood what the issue was or how easily a man's pride could be hurt.

During the long, arduous tech rehearsals, Jim and Jules worked in well-oiled tandem, setting cues for lights and sound just so, while backstage the actors adjusted to costumes, preened, tried on different shoes. Dress rehearsals unfolded. And the show was ready.

On opening night, as I left the stage manager's high desk off stage right to change into my costume and makeup, I was frantic with worry that I wouldn't be able to cry or that my singing would squawk. But I heard that Herb, the ultimate artistic arbiter, told one of the other actresses I seemed like a young Marlene Dietrich, and that praise went a long way toward building my confidence.

And so, on it went—one night I'd play Lady Mortimer, the next I'd set the table for twelve for the dinner scene in *The Three Sisters*. Completely integrated in my new world, I was deeply absorbed and left the work at the theatre feeling happier than when I'd arrived. Still, the low, dark mood seemed to dominate my hours away from the theatre and could be exacerbated when I drank, and I was never sure when those times would be.

When the Workshop announced the new season would include *The Glass Menagerie*, I asked Jules if I could talk to him. I waited in the turquoise booth in the corner coffee shop downstairs wondering how I would begin with the huge ask I was about to make. I'd seen photos of the original production, and I knew I looked right—slender, blonde, slightly fragile. But more importantly, I *felt* right for the part. I felt Laura's self-conscious shame, and I *knew* I could play her. He arrived and we ordered coffee, and I asked about what he was working on, stalling, and he didn't have much time and wanted to know what I wanted. I had to say, "I want to play Laura" or "Could I audition for Laura?" I don't know what I said, but his answer was swift:

"No." He answered without a beat. "First of all," he said, "you're too pretty for the part. A girl who looks like you does not have Laura's problems." (If he only knew.) He told me Bobbi would play Laura; she was deeply talented, one of our group, once his student at SF State.

I couldn't think what to say. I sat there holding my breath and silently telling myself not to cry.

"You know, Karen," Jules leaned towards me, "there's only one thing an actor ever wants to hear. Anything else is beside the point."

I looked at him and asked, "What's that?"

"You've got the part," he said.

"Ah!"

I nodded. He understood. After all, Jules was also an actor, and he knew how I felt without my saying anything.

It was so simple. And ever since, I have heard him say it many, many times.

FOR THE FINAL OPENING OF THE SEASON, we had an expensive period show, *Becket,* directed by Robert Goldsby from the UC Theatre Department. Anouilh's play had been a hit on Broadway starring Laurence Olivier and Anthony Quinn as Becket and Henry II. The story tells of their friendship, Becket's rise to power as the archbishop, their clash, and Becket's eventual assassination by the king's knights in 1190. The quote, "Will no one rid me of this meddlesome priest?" echoed through the centuries. The roles were played by Tom Rosqui and Malachi Throne at the Workshop. Herb was so conscientious about not "selling out" that he suspected even this serious play might be too commercial because it had done so well in New York.

By the night of the first performance, we'd been at the theatre for days and almost all night filling the lobby with costume production. Now, hidden behind the heavy sliding doors, on the other side of the lobby, sewing machines whirred while the actors went on, not knowing for sure what pieces of their wardrobe would be ready. We raced to finish—fake furs and jewels, velvets and brocades, gold tasseled cords to close heavy cloaks—then we grabbed the finished piece, ran upstairs, chased madly across and down the back stairs to the dressing rooms, handed it to a dresser, who draped it on the actor as he marched up the ramp to the stage.

By then, I didn't think anything of touching the actors, feeling their perspiration—only wanting to help them, get the show right, and afterward put it all away safely. I knew these (mostly) men now and fastened them into clothes with no self-consciousness. In the fall, I had been afraid of Tom Rosqui because he was so terrifying as Sergeant Musgrave; by the *Becket* production I knew him to be a gentle soul. Malachi Throne, with his imposing pronunciation, so superb in the Chekhov that season, I understood to be profoundly dedicated, even offering us free classes on his day off. They knew us, too, and wanted us to succeed. Wolfe Barzell bought me new sneakers to thank me for helping him with his lines. There was a way we'd all been naked together in the effort. Not in body, but in soul.

After the audience had gone home—they liked it!—we swept up the remnants fallen to the floor, loosened the threads from the machines. I felt a stunned satisfaction—exhaustion, too. JoAnne asked me about the apprenticeship, what I thought about it now that it was almost over. "Oh, yes. I've learned so much this year, exposed to all the stuff that goes into a play . . . the teamwork. Never get all that in an acting class . . . But that's it." Like the clasp on a suitcase, something clicked shut inside.

"What do you mean, 'That's it'?" she asked.

"That's the last time I work for no money." I felt I had paid those dues in full.

I was learning that in Europe theatre was recognized as a value to the community and as such was subsidized along with the other arts. Only here in the States, of all the first world countries, did actors and other theatre artists provide the subsidies through self-sacrifice and accepting a level of insecurity that a tradesman would scoff at. I was full of hope for the resident theatre movement in this country, where repertory companies were gaining a foothold in the '60s and hiring a company for a full season. I believed that that was how it would be and looked forward to a career in a company where we would play wildly different roles as the season went along. I believed it would be possible to have a life with some continuity and security in the theatre. That was our hope.[3]

I was determined never to work for no money, but I would one more time. And soon.

JoAnne told me about the Stanford Contemporary Drama Workshop, and she and I auditioned together for their summer shows. I felt it was worth it, for the chance to appear as the lead in the Tennessee Williams play *Suddenly Last Summer,* taking the Greyhound back and forth to my apartment in San Francisco, often sleeping on friends' couches in Palo Alto to save bus fare and time. Indeed, it paid off because the following summer Stanford offered me a full scholarship with board and room, and I won the lead in a production of Brecht directed by a genius director from the Berliner Ensemble, Carl Weber.

JoAnne was the star of the mainstage production at Stanford the summer after our apprenticeship. She earned a small stipend to play in Brecht's *A Man's a Man* in an inventive and incisive production directed by the New York director Alan Schneider, famous for bringing the first *Godot* to the States and for directing *Who's Afraid of Virginia Woolf?* on Broadway. I couldn't possibly have dreamed that not too many years later, I too would work for him, but this time on Broadway.

My loyal parents drove up to see the Tennessee Williams play, and after the show, as Dad and I walked toward the car, he drew me close and whispered, "That was impressive."

My heart soared. I knew he wouldn't say that unless he really believed I was on the right path. The fact that he was less afraid gave me courage.

8. Waking Up in Berkeley

"If enough people think of a thing and work hard enough
at it, I guess it's pretty bound to happen, wind and weather
permitting."
—*By the Shores of Silver Lake*, LAURA INGALLS WILDER

BEFORE FALL SEMESTER BEGAN, I RENTED a room in Berkeley
and visited the Theatre Department to sniff around for upcoming
shows. Travis Bogard, the Department chair, called me into his
office, where he and Bob Goldsby, the *Becket* director and a fine
acting teacher, were studying blueprints spread across Dr. Bogard's
desk. They were excited to share the plans for a playhouse-to-be,
replete with technical innovations and flexibility. Dr. Bogard
seemed curious about where I had been and asked if I would like
to join the department and take a double major.

At first, I was doubtful. I explained I had to graduate in two
years, and there were so many prerequisites, I knew I would never
make it, but Dr. Bogard, after questioning me about the apprenticeship, waived the lower division requirements, and I joined a
department swirling with activity. Three men from Brooklyn
College had transferred in and brought their muscular energy to
the school, and the new PhD program was stuffed with smart,

handsome men who also were good actors. In addition to the four main-stage productions, soon Friday afternoons saw the studio theatre packed with audiences eager to see adventurous, avant-garde one-acts directed by students like Stacy and performed by compelling actors like Michael Lerner[1], who had transferred from Brooklyn College.

By that time, 1963, Toni, Karen McLellan, and Jeanne were already in the final year of their English majors. Toni planned to earn her master's degree and teach English, Jeanne was thinking postgrad in psychology, and Karen wasn't sure. Often after an evening studying in my room, I walked to their apartments, and we sat around talking about everything from *Paradise Lost* to the difference between a clitoral and vaginal orgasm.

One day I saw Fred coming out of Cody's Bookstore on Telegraph Avenue. He had just transferred to Berkeley, and we were thrilled to see each other and reconnect. I learned that while he still had an interest in theatre, he was writing a novel, and that was his first priority. We began our lively discussions again—acting and plays—and enrolled in the same Milton class. He wanted to hear all about the Workshop, and he began to attend their productions regularly, ushering for free tickets. What I loved about this time was I was so sure of why I was there and what I wanted. That helped me to put my classwork into perspective. And soon, I was acting in shows. There was loneliness in my little room, but that didn't last for long, and I only drank on weekends and that fall had fewer incidents of hysteria. Rob and I took the bus back and forth to see each other and hiked in Tilden. My mood was blue, but calmer.

ONE FOGGY OCTOBER MORNING, I TROTTED from my rented room toward campus when a glance at the *San Francisco Chronicle* headline in a dispenser stopped me: "BLOCKADE IS ON." I bent down to read through the filthy glass, gave in, and bought the paper. Intelligence photos had revealed missiles in Cuba and, reading the story, I learned that the Soviets had secretly created long-range missile sites with nuclear capability and were at that moment delivering more nuclear material to Cuba by ship. US ships were already encircling the island nation, just 60 miles off the American coast, and Kennedy had given the Soviets an ultimatum: Turn back or expect war. The news rumbled down the halls and out to Wheeler Oak, where activists were making speeches from a wall that circled the tree. We were war babies. We knew what it meant to live with Mutually Assured Destruction—the phrase that "justified" using nuclear weapons to prevent war. We knew MAD was its fitting acronym. The atomic bomb was implanted in our flesh—after all, for years we had been drilled to face attack and knew in our hearts that nothing would save us if there were a nuclear war. We all felt it. This might be the end.

The United Nations had begun to try to intervene, but as the *Chronicle* reported, "Red Ships Stay on Collision Course." Students clustered together by the old Oak in strident argument, as if the arguments might make a difference. "We have missiles in Turkey, so why shouldn't they . . . ?"

I was furious with Kennedy. I couldn't imagine why he had taken such a wild chance, made such a threat. I kept seeing the poster of Khrushchev, fist in air, ready to blow us into nuclear dust. For days, I was terrified. I joined the debate and had trouble concentrating on my studies.

On Thursday of that week, four days since Kennedy's ultimatum, there was a fiery debate at the United Nations, with no agreement reached. In Los Angeles, six hundred miles south, hundreds of thousands of people stripped grocery shelves bare. On Friday, talk that we would invade Cuba began again, and knots of helpless students huddled at Wheeler Oak locked in debate. I saw Fred stagger over after listening to a replay of Kennedy's speech. He looked dazed, let me know he could barely speak, and left for home to wait.

As the day dimmed, I hung around the old tree until sunset and, shivering, I stopped at a pay phone to call home, wondering if this was the last time I would speak to my family. I was not alone in that fear. The defense secretary, Robert McNamara, later declared, "I thought it was the last Saturday I would ever see."

What did my parents and I say? I don't know. That we loved each other. They tried to tell me it would be all right. But none of us was sure that was true.

Finally, that Saturday, a UN truce was agreed to, and by Sunday Russia had offered to quit Cuba. Terms were set for negotiations. In the eyes of many, Kennedy became a bigger hero than he'd already been, but to me terror had come too close. Soon bright yellow signs for air raid shelters appeared all over campus. Some students stole them to decorate their apartments. We thought it was funny in our dark cynical way. We knew they were useless.

As OUR SEX LIVES GREW MORE interesting, my girlfriends and I moved into funkier, more independent places, and when I learned you could get the Pill at Planned Parenthood, I went there. The deep relief the Pill provided is almost impossible to describe—and we all knew we were living on a cusp. Unlike any generation before us, we had sexual freedom. That spring, I played Ann Whitefield, the personification of Shaw's modern woman, in a complete four-act version of *Man and Superman*. I practiced my lines with Karen McLellan, who cued me. Karen still wore her fine soft hair in a "style," still sported a circle pin on her lapel, but she was becoming bored with this persona and finally asked me how I managed to "look interesting." She wanted to look interesting too. I offered my simple solution: "Stop cutting your hair, and when your makeup runs out, don't replace it." To our mothers' horror, looking interesting essentially meant letting ourselves go.

It was in Karen's studio apartment where I tried pot for the first time. She had a huge print of Picasso's *The Old Guitarist* on the wall above her Murphy bed, and Jeanne was there, too. She had brought a record of Isaac Stern playing Prokofiev's *Violin Concerto in D minor.* We smoked a joint and sat and waited for something to happen, and almost without having noticed the change, I could *see* the music: those golden strings vibrating, bewitching me, and a blue haze softened the atmosphere. I felt the front of my brain tingle and let go as images flowed.

I loved having fresh eyes. Pot relieved me from thinking so much, from my brain that was constantly analyzing. Pot also was a different kind of relief; I no longer had hysterical episodes the way I did too often when I'd drunk too much. My friends and I began to use grass recreationally, on weekends, though I'd never think to use it during the week. That, I reasoned, might mean I had "a problem."

For my senior year, I lucked into a cottage behind a big, old, brown-shingled Craftsman in West Berkeley. One day while visiting Bob La Vigne, I told him about the place, and he gave me a lithograph of an exquisite woodcut he had done for "A Strange New Cottage in Berkeley," a poem by his friend Allen Ginsberg. It had the same sweet, shabby feeling that mine did. The cottage was ramshackle, but from the first time I put the key in the glass-paned door, I felt its spell.

Two rooms were connected by French doors; the kitchen had old appliances, the bathroom a claw-foot tub with feet painted apricot, and there were windows across the entire south side so light flooded in. At Woolworth's I found a red cotton bedspread and yards of colorful burlap and made curtains. McLellan drove me to St. Vincent de Paul in Oakland, where we found a fabulous '30s sofa for thirteen dollars, its soft upholstery once white, had pink lining peeking through. Rob brought over slews of used, multi-colored candles from his gigs at hotel banquets, and we stuck them in Chianti bottles, where they dripped in bohemian fashion. In the yard, I brought the rose bushes back by "playing the sunlit water, each to each" à la Allen Ginsberg. I bathed in the claw-foot tub and lay on my bed in the fading light watching a little mouse family come out from inside the wall to look around. Even they seemed sweet, good company. I loved this new home, all mine.

But as the year progressed, I began to fall into miserable moods, stayed alone a lot, lost sleep and couldn't rouse myself for an early French class. I fell behind, which only weighed on me more. I also experienced for the first time a strange psychic phenomenon: Time would change arbitrarily on the clock or my mind would play a song and when I turned on the radio, it would be playing the precise phrase I'd just heard in my head. I wondered if I might be mad. I wanted to run away and fantasized running to Big Sur, but instead I stayed in school writing papers and acting in plays, both of which anchored me.

IT WAS ONE OF THOSE SPLENDID FEBRUARY days, when a preview of spring lifts everyone. Karen McLellan was sitting on a wall singing, "I've got to crow!" when Michael Rossman, a grad student in the Math Department and an activist I knew from the Wheeler Oak rallies, spotted her. Soon after that she disappeared. Jeanne and I frantically phoned each other, asking each other if we'd seen her. On Sunday evening Karen reappeared, looking utterly different, completely happy. She announced she was helplessly in love.

Karen and Michael spent much of their time at his apartment on the north side of campus in a graceful, brown-shingled building full of their like-minded friends. One night at a party there, I met Barry Jablon, a sweet, sexy, sassy, smart man who took nothing for granted except his right to be happy. A guitar-playing, English PhD candidate, he looked like Paul McCartney, cooked Chinese food, and played improv with me in his comfortable apartment. The Dante on his desk was written in Italian. And he could read it. And as the months passed, I let go of Rob, and Barry and I became a couple. But I didn't move in with him. I stayed in the cottage.

Both Barry and Michael were supporting their grad studies working as teacher's assistants. Both were self-taught musicians and played guitar-recorder duets. Both had grown up in socially conscious Jewish families, and both had agile minds and were well-read and considered everything up for a stimulating discussion. It's hard even to imagine now, but in those days, grad students wore shirts, ties, and jackets to teach, and Barry and Michael were no exceptions, though they began to let their hair grow a little longer. Karen and I often went together to hear our boyfriends play Telemann and Bach at a local coffee house, and the four of us got high and listened to the contraband tape of Bob Dylan's latest music, feeling we "got it." *You know something is happening but you don't know what it is / Do you, Mr. Jones?*

When Barry and Michael went to San Francisco to picket car companies on behalf of jobs for Black people, Karen and I stealthily drove by to check it out as we headed down to Big Sur for a "spiritual" weekend. She and I, I realize only now—back then we had no idea—were milk-fed *shiksas*—a word Barry taught me—tiptoeing around the edges of activism. The first time Karen and Michael broke up, she was so traumatized she landed in the hospital on campus. They were destined to be together, but not without a lot of storms. My dear and vulnerable friend came under the care of a gifted Jungian psychoanalyst. Through her work with him, we both discovered *The I Ching* and Jung's concept of synchronicity. This idea of interconnectedness in time and space, at the level of all events and participants, transported me. I clung to this hopeful notion as much as to the theory (only a theory then) of black holes, which, though the opposite of hopeful seemed the objective correlative for the spiritual abyss I felt when I was depressed. Karen and I threw the *I Ching* to check on our romances and futures. Would she and Michael reunite? (They did.) Would I get my Fulbright to study in London? What if I didn't?

Karen persuaded me to see the psychiatrist who had helped her at the student health center. He was simpatico, but he had just lost a patient to suicide and told me he couldn't handle my depression at the moment. He recommended I drop out of school, get a job, and enter intense analysis. I rejected this. I needed the structure of school and wanted to graduate. My dark moods were oddly comfortable, like old slippers, except when they were excruciating.

During a brief breakup with Barry, one day I was sitting morosely at my desk in the cottage when Karen slammed in and ordered me to "Move over!" She and Michael, she announced, had broken up again. She and I shared the turbulence of our moods and our romances and began to share the cottage, sometimes sleeping up on the North side with our men or landing back home in our cottage. One night a dry east wind kicked up, and we smoked some grass and decided to the strains of Schumann that the blossoms were going to blow off the cherry trees anyway, so it would be okay for us to go out on McKinley Avenue, which was lined with cherry trees, and get some. In a Dionysian frenzy, we robbed small branches and filled empty mayo jars, wine bottles, and a bucket with blooms. We lit candles. The wind ruffled the flames. Our cottage glowed as the wild March wind whipped around the yard. And we didn't think about our men.

My senior year at Berkeley coincided with the four hundredth anniversary of Shakespeare's birth. The department was doing four full productions of Shakespeare, and I was cast as Portia in *The Merchant of Venice*. I was home going over my lines in the cottage when the phone rang, and someone gave me the news.

"They shot Kennedy."

"What?"

"Kennedy, in Texas—somebody shot him."

"Is he all right?"

"They don't know yet."

"Oh God."

I turned on my radio. He was dead. The grief over Kennedy's death was personal, and it was national, and it was global. I didn't know what to do with this news. I was too young to go to a bar to watch TV. I wondered if the department would cancel the play that night. I thought they should. When I called the school, the secretary told me that a decision had not been made, but she thought they would cancel. Everyone was in shock.

I waited by the phone for a decision and at last the call came in: "The show must go on."

It didn't feel right, but we all summoned our courage and commitment, held our heads high, and took the stage. At the time, it seemed an inadequate response to the tragedy. We had a small audience, and as I played Portia's words—

"The quality of mercy is not strained.
It droppeth as the gentle rain from heaven
Upon the place beneath. It is twice blessed . . ."

I couldn't imagine where mercy was. Within two days, Lee Harvey Oswald was shot dead.

AT CHRISTMASTIME THAT YEAR, I brought Barry home for the holidays. Dad's drinking was worse, and I thought he might be having money worries. Also, there was the potent eggnog, permission to drink in celebration. My sister had married and was often at the house with her baby because her husband did long-distance hauling and spent much time on the road, leaving her home alone, a young, single parent. Janey let me know she was feeling more and more nervous about Dad's drinking.

For several days, Mom and Barry and I tiptoed around Dad's drunkenness. His cheer, his humor, his bright but conservative political ideas came across in slurred words and with sharp remarks that wounded, and I saw that his hands were shaking, and he had a ragged cough. When his gaze narrowed and he looked suspicious, his eyes watery and red, I sank into myself—feeling shame mixed with anger, a toxic cocktail.

Barry and I escaped by driving to the beach, the place that had been my safe spot since I first could drive. I would park near the pier, write in my journal, release pent-up feelings on paper. But this time I was frantic, and Barry was calm and supportive. He had been in therapy for some time and asked if I could talk to my dad about how I felt. The awful story about his suicide attempts and my fear that he would try again came pouring out.

"I have to be quiet," I told him.

Barry shook his head. "But how can you live with this blade above your head?"

I didn't know how to tell him, but what I realized then was that I'd always lived with it. As a kid when I challenged Dad's drinking, he made me pay, and after I found out about the suicide attempts, I was afraid to question him or reveal my own dark thoughts.

Still, the next afternoon when Dad came in from the office, I asked if I could speak to him. He was not feeling well and lay down on the twin bed in my childhood bedroom. I sat beside him and told him how much I loved him and that I couldn't stand to watch him slowly killing himself. I told him if he kept on drinking the way he was, I was going to go back to school. And somehow emboldened, I upped the ante: If he continued to drink, I wasn't going to come home anymore.

I was completely surprised when he told me he would do something about it. Then the conversation was over. The next day he announced to my mother that he had made an appointment with a psychiatrist in Ojai. My mother confided the news to me in that secret way families of alcoholics do—a whisper, sideways, when we were alone in the kitchen. She said he had previously seen this doctor who had given him a book by Krishnamurti. Hope sprung up inside me.

Dad put away his cigarettes, took out a pipe from one of the times he had tried to stop smoking, cleaned up, put on a suit and tie, and handed me cash. "Here's your money for January," he said. "One hundred dollars."

That was odd since he usually sent me a check, but I thanked him and looked into his eyes. Something had changed. They looked cold, and I felt something had slammed shut in him. Then he told us he was leaving for a late afternoon appointment.

When he wasn't home by dinnertime, we went ahead without him. We washed up. We waited. We wondered. I asked my mother for more information, and she shook her head. We watched television. It grew later. Suddenly, the telephone rang, and when I answered I heard a local man's voice asking for my mother.

On his way home, he had seen my father's car off the road up on Foothill, and he thought my father was asleep inside.

Mama's hands were shaking as she tried to light a cigarette. "Come on, Mom, let's go see," I said, and she and Barry and I drove her Dodge up to Foothill.

As we came up the hill, we saw his car nosed into the dark hill, lights on, blinkers blinking. Barry and I jumped out to check. He was passed out over the steering wheel, an empty pill bottle was on the floor. Barry and I reached in and felt for a pulse. He had one, and I ran back to the Dodge to tell Mama he seemed all right. We shoved him over so Barry could drive his car back down to the house, and I drove Mama home. The three of us dragged Dad, six-foot-two, two hundred pounds, into the house. Somehow, we got him into his bed. Then Mama and I undressed him and put on his pajamas. I could tell Mama was on automatic, taking one task at a time, relieved he was alive, but frightened still.

I felt a cold anger embrace me. *How good it must be to have women to chase after you, carry you, dress you, put you to bed.* How selfish he was to put us through this, I thought.

We phoned our family doctor, who knew Daddy well, but his associate was on call. He came out with his little black doctor's bag and checked Daddy out. He told us he would be fine and gave us more pills, in case of pain, and I privately scoffed. *We have plenty of pain here.* The doctor left quickly, saying nothing comforting to us, and that night Dad slept deeply—though not as deeply as he had planned.

Dad had long ago rejected AA, and either Mama didn't know about Al-Anon, or there were no Al-Anon meetings in Ventura. We didn't know where to turn, what to do next. Barry had an uncle in

Los Angeles who was a psychiatrist; he thought he might have a suggestion, so he telephoned, and we arranged to meet him the next day. In the morning, while Dad was still feeling weak, we packed him into the car and drove him down to meet Barry's uncle in the San Fernando Valley, dropping Barry off to visit with his cousins. The three of us met with the psychiatrist together. Then each of us met with him alone.

I asked the doctor if I should quit school and stay home to help, but he was adamant I had to return to school and to my own life. He recommended a private hospital but told us Dad would have to sign himself in, and when we drove over there, Dad resisted. We begged. We cajoled. We cried. We threatened, and we begged again, and after hours of this, he finally checked himself in. We drove home and called Janey, and never again did I try to set any limits with him. He was holding all the cards.

BACK AT SCHOOL, AS GRADUATION approached, I grew anxious. All spring, I waited anxiously for a letter from the Institute for International Education regarding the Fulbright application I'd made. Apart from a scholarship to the Colorado Shakespeare Festival for the summer, I had no further plans, and I worried about what would come next. In April, the rejection arrived, and I realized I would not be going to London. I knew I would love playing Shakespeare all summer, but then what would I do? Return to Berkeley? How did that figure in my goals? I was frankly afraid of New York City. Hollywood? And do what, wait on tables? Every choice seemed too hard.

I went back to Berkeley and moved in with Barry. Karen McLellan had taken over the cottage. Then, that fall, out of the blue, Jules offered me a part at the Workshop in *The Wall,* a play based on John Hersey's novel about a family in the Warsaw Ghetto uprising. Working with colleagues I admired was joyful; we made fools of ourselves learning Yiddish accents and studied the show's

serious subject matter. I wished my life could go on like this forever—cooking new recipes with Barry, drinking wine, listening
to unvarnished news on KPFA, making enough money to get by,
acting at the Workshop. I pruned the old rose vine outside the
kitchen, and it bloomed, but I reapplied for the Fulbright.

When I had a long dinner break, I liked to come home and eat
with Barry. One night, he was on fire. Jack Weinberg, his friend,
had been arrested in Sproul Plaza for passing out leaflets. The police
car drove right onto the plaza, and as they shoved Jack into the
backseat, students surrounded the car. "Then they sat down!" Barry
said excitedly. "They couldn't move. They couldn't take him away
without running over Cal students!" Before I could say much, he
had grabbed some food and was headed back to campus. I had to
get back to the theatre, but I told him I would look for him in the
Plaza afterwards.

Students had been protesting for Black people to be given
proper jobs and housing. Under pressure from business interests,
the administration peremptorily withdrew students' rights to set up
card tables and distribute information. Many students, including
Jack, had been active in the Civil Rights Movement in the South,
and they responded to this repression with quiet defiance. News of
Jack's arrest spread quickly across campus, and that night, or soon,
there were thousands of us sitting on the cold concrete around the
police car singing, "We shall, we shall not be moved . . ." I'd been
acting in plays while Jack and others had marched, but I wanted to
be counted this time.

Soon, Mario Savio took off his shoes and climbed respectfully
onto the roof of that police car and spoke, giving the protest clarity.
The Free Speech Movement (FSM) was born. Mario was a quiet
young man whose activism sprang from his deep Christian commitment—he had worked with the poor in Mexico, and he had been
part of the Civil Rights struggle in the South.

Attempts to negotiate with the administration were dishon-
ored or stonewalled, which only fueled the fire of the resistance.

A steering committee formed from diverse groups, each with the common goal to be allowed to advocate. Barry and Michael both were on the committee and it often met in our apartment where decisions from the wildly divergent members requiring consensus often made some of those meetings last all night. I was proud to be a witness to their leadership. It was thrilling to be close to these brilliant leaders.

As Family Day approached, the university was eager for the plaza to be cleaned up, so they called in the Oakland Police, the Alameda sheriff's office, and the highway patrol. Five hundred officers in riot gear roared onto campus on their motorcycles and took positions behind Sproul Hall. That was a sound I don't ever want to hear again. The demonstration swelled to three thousand students. The tension was tangible. I didn't want to leave for the theatre and leave Barry and my other friends behind. California Governor Pat Brown forced a meeting between university President Clark Kerr and the protesters, and somehow violence was avoided, but there was no resolution reached. The university blamed "outside agitators, Communist infiltrators." The press reported the administration's version of events.

Those of us who were there knew there were no Communist infiltrators, no outside agitators. We were frustrated by the ease with which President Kerr could get his message out and control public opinion. The evening news was infuriating. After many broken promises, the administration lost all credibility with the FSM, and the Academic Senate formed its own committee to work for resolution. Many faculty members, outraged at the arrival of the highway patrol on campus, began more and more to take the side of the FSM.

On December 2nd, after yet another rejection of the FSM demands, Mario gave a speech and declared: "There comes a time when the operation of the machine becomes so odious, makes you so sick at heart that you can't take part, you can't even passively take part, and you've got to put your bodies upon the gears and upon the wheels, upon the levers, upon all the apparatus, and you've got to indicate to the people running it that unless you're free, the machine will be prevented from working at all."

Joan Baez stood on the steps of Sproul Hall, singing, "We Shall Overcome," and a thousand Berkeley students followed Mario peacefully into the building. I longed to go, but I had to be at the theatre, and when Barry went home to grab some food and papers he had to grade, he returned to find he'd been locked out. At two a.m., the FSM leaders began to prepare our friends for arrest, giving instructions on how to "go limp." Jeanne told me later that's when she felt terrified and excited all at once. At three thirty a.m., the arrests began. Over the next twelve hours, fourteen hundred police arrested 814 students. At first light, Jeanne was thrust out a side door of Sproul Hall. Were they hoping to avoid the press in the front of the building? It didn't work. She was screaming as a cop twisted her fingers behind her.

That morning Barry rushed into our apartment with the *Chronicle*'s front-page photo of Jeanne screaming bloody murder. Pickets had appeared spontaneously by dawn. Between the strike, the arrests, and the fragmentation on campus, many students were confused. Karen McLellan and I formed a speakers' bureau to carry information to the residences. We enlisted volunteers from the picket lines that had formed, met to review FSM talking points, and in the evening set out to visit the tidy sororities, the regulation dorms, the ramshackle independent houses to spread the news. I believed if people had the information they needed, they would take our side. Back then I had no idea how far those in power would go to maintain the status quo, but I was learning. The university was in disarray. No one knew if their classes were being held and the campus was largely deserted. The administration had lost moral authority with the arrests. The following Monday, Kerr called a campus-wide meeting at the Greek Theatre. I joined the fifteen thousand who piled into the theatre. The steering committee members walked up and down the aisles urging people to be calm, but the air zinged with tension. Some students were angry.

The energy was palpable. It felt as if a riot could begin. I looked for where I could leave if necessary. Kerr's message was, "Get back to class," but after he spoke, Mario walked deliberately to the stage where two security officers grabbed him and dragged him across the stone floor, and as they did, a roar erupted: "Let him speak. Let him speak!" When the officers let him go, he announced a rally, and we followed him, flowing like a big river from the theatre down to Sproul Plaza, where demonstrations became more impassioned than ever.

The Academic Senate was to meet the next day, December 8, 1964. We gathered outside Wheeler Auditorium where loudspeakers were set up so we could hear. Barry and I, along with thousands of others, sat on the ground and waited. The faculty supported the FSM and demanded complete amnesty for all activity prior to that day, with *"no restrictions on content of speech or advocacy" in the future* (italics mine). The faculty had realized that "we were doing what they had taught us to do—thinking for ourselves, standing up for our beliefs."[2] Many of us marked the FSM as a life-altering experience. I know it was for me. Integrity can be applied in every walk of life, and certainly in portraying human beings.

THE SHOW CLOSED. THE FSM WAS resolved. I found myself bewildered; faced with the uncertainty of my life ahead, I froze. One night, Barry told me triumphantly he knew who I'd been involved with before we met. I felt humiliated because that man had been married, and while Barry fell asleep, I lay rigid beside him, feeling betrayed by the way he crowed over discovering it. When I knew he was fast asleep, I slipped out of the comforter, and walked stealthily downstairs to our little kitchen. I threw a towel at the crack under the kitchen door, pulled a chair to the oven. *Nothing matters. Just stop the pain.* I turned on the gas and inhaled deeply. I waited and inhaled again.

I don't remember Barry rushing in and turning off the gas. I don't remember him opening the kitchen door and letting in the fresh night air. I don't know if he carried me back to bed, but I know in the morning I woke sick with shame. Bad enough I would do this to myself, but he pointed out that I could have blown the place up if anyone nearby had lit a match.

I promised him I would get help, and I asked Karen McLellan's analyst who recommended Dr. John N. K. Langton. To pay for therapy, I took a job teaching at a nursery school, and again, to my everlasting relief, my parents pitched in to help. During breaks at work, I sat in Barry's old Ford smoking, reading Ken Kesey's *One Flew Over the Cuckoo's Nest,* and feeling as crazy as the characters Kesey had created. I began working with the doctor doing serious dream work, and so I began to learn how out of touch with my feelings I had become—had been for a long time. I also learned how little I trusted my talent.

The psychotherapist was dispassionate and forthright with me, but this was short-term therapy, and essential as it was, I knew it wasn't going to last. I did, however, decide not to pin all my hopes on the Fulbright. I auditioned for the new theatre company being founded at Stanford. They offered me a position. I flew to Chicago for the national Theatre Communications Group auditions, and Ed Sherin, a director from the Arena Stage in DC, tossed my little snapshot of myself by the kitchen door and asked, "What is this supposed to be?"

"My photo?" I asked, though I knew what he meant.

"Listen," he said, "in New York, girls like you are a dime a dozen. You need to get yourself to New York, get a decent headshot and stop fooling around."

And as I flew back to California, I prayed for the grant so I wouldn't have to go to New York.

The reprieve arrived: a Fulbright to study at the London Academy of Music and Dramatic Art for a year. Barry proposed, but he had toyed around with commitment during the years we were together and had waited too long. There was no way I was giving up this opportunity. Just then, Herb and Jules announced they were leaving San Francisco to run the Lincoln Center theatre, and I felt a door clanging shut. There would be no Workshop to return to after LAMDA. I wondered if I would ever return to the Bay Area. The only serious acting opportunities had been at the Workshop.

Just before I left Berkeley for Boulder, there was an enormous outdoor teach-in about the war in Vietnam. On a perfect May day, I sat with Barry, McLellan, and Michael on the grass and listened to Phil Ochs sing, "I Ain't Marchin' Anymore!" and heard Dick Gregory declare, "I'll die for my country, but I will not kill for my country." That sounded right to me. The illusion that our country fought wars only for essential, decent reasons had been smashed. It was the beginning of the anti-Vietnam war movement, and I carried it inside me. Now, as I think back on my Berkeley experience, I feel a deep gratitude for a public education that had offered so much and so affordably: I found my calling, developed my moral outlook, and knew from then on how to seek out what I needed to learn in the future.

That summer in Colorado was a respite of acting, and I shared a place with Fred who had auditioned and been accepted. When the afternoon mountain rains swept in over the Rockies, we ran laughing to the theatre to spread tarps to keep our grassy stage dry. Cast as Ophelia, Miranda, and Lady Percy, I was most excited to play Ophelia. Our Hamlet, Barry Kraft, had registered as a conscientious objector and was being threatened with prison.[3] His moral fiber enhanced his passionate Hamlet. With Ophelia, I could pour my darkness into the cup of her songs and poetry. Fred and I relaxed in the kitchen smoking dope and doing satirical improvs, cracking each other up until our stomachs ached. He invited me to come to New York early on my way to London so he could show me the city he loved.

One night, in the foothills, we had a joyful party where East Coast friends roasted a pig underground, and we all stood around drinking while the sun slipped away. Sometime after the feast, an unexpected spasm of longing possessed me; rashly, I made a pass at my married acting partner. He was quick to reject me. I dashed out, headlong for the creek, sobbing in a hell of despair. Fred got me home. The next day, I was alone at home when my friends came to check on me. Too chagrined to face them, I kept the shades down, hid in my room like a fugitive. The trouble was I never could tell when my mood would turn on me. Or I would turn. Spin out like a car into a skid.

At the end of the season, Barry came, and we said goodbye, promising to write. My folks came, too, to see the shows and bring me home. Dad and I argued bitterly over the Watts riots then raging. My dad had had hard times and couldn't understand why other people couldn't simply "pull themselves up by their bootstraps."

My parents drove us through the Rockies, to the Grand Canyon and Bryce Canyon, and I slept in the back seat, worn out but deeply secure, without having to think or to plan. Once we were in Ventura, Dad made sure the local paper covered my Fulbright, and I spent time playing with Janey's little boys and hanging out with her. That might have been the visit when I testified for Toni in her divorce, and we planned for her to come to England to join me for the year. She was finishing some course work, but I told her I'd find us a place, and she agreed to share the rent for the first weeks.

On Saturday mornings, she and I stood in silent vigil against the Vietnam war, surprising the Ventura community, and then Dad shipped my old trunk to the *Queen Elizabeth*, and I followed, stopping off in New York where Fred had invited me to stay with him before my departure.

The world pulsed with possibility.

Part Three
The Way

"Hi-diddle dee dee
An actor's life for me."
—"An Actor's Life for Me," from *Pinocchio,*
LEIGH HARLINE AND NED WASHINGTON

9. *Practice*

"It was your teaching."
—"He Loves Me, He Loves Me Not," Part 2, *Little House on the Prairie*, MICHAEL LANDON

FRED TOOK ME TO HIS LOWER EAST SIDE apartment where he treated me to freshly baked bialys, and I pretended not to be horrified by the cockroaches scuttling across the floors, and so began my whirlwind introduction to his New York City. He borrowed a car from his folks and had his little brother take me on the Circle Line sightseeing tour so that I could view the city in all its magnificence. He took time off work to squire me to the top of Manhattan to see the medieval gardens and the Romanesque buildings that are the Cloisters, and he dropped me off at The Museum of Modern Art where I walked through the halls dazzled by the paintings I'd only seen prints or photos of—the Van Goghs, the Rousseaus, the *Guernica*. He got me comps for musicals his company was producing. As I looked at the splashy posters lining Schubert Alley, I was spell-bound and thought if I had seen this place when I was young, I'd never have gone to college. He took me to visit his parents in their Summit, New Jersey, Georgian manse, and I saw that Fred was their prince and felt their strong parental hopes and the pressure it put on him. It was a love fest with the four of us. My Fulbright seemed to shine on him, and I hoped it would give his artistic ambitions validation.

Fred walked me to the pier where we climbed aboard the *Queen Elizabeth* for pre-launch drinks and appetizers served by crew men in sharp uniforms. There were one hundred of us Fulbrights among the passengers. I was reeling, overwhelmed, and oddly nostalgic as the leaving would be a clear break with the past. Old fantasies of dropping out in Big Sur presented themselves as we ate tiny sandwiches on deck. I wanted to get going and knew these retrograde thoughts would vanish once the ship got moving. The blast of the horn, the swift hugs and goodbyes, and I was on my way to my dream, my destiny. I was in my own movie now. My cabin was far below, and there I met my shipboard roommates. We were all in a state of rapture, but I couldn't stay long. As the huge ocean liner departed from the docks, and rocked its way through the harbor, I was overcome by seasickness, and knew to hurry to the open air and gaze at the horizon. Soon my joy returned.

At dinner, sometimes the shipmates were at the same table. The first night, Alice, from New York, encouraged me to try the smoked salmon they offered for an appetizer. I loved it! And had it all five nights of the trip. Even in third class, the dining was elegant, and I watched closely to see what fork people picked up first. Liz, from DC, was also going to LAMDA, and both Alice and Liz would turn out to be my roommates in London, though at that moment I had no idea of what lay ahead—of the school holidays, when we would travel together, see Barcelona, the Coliseum, every park and theatre. For that moment, we had barely begun our journey together.

At the bar after dinner, many of us looked over the opposite sex, and flirting began. The atmosphere was happy and friendly. My colleague from Cal's *The Merchant of Venice*, Michael Lerner, our brilliant Shylock, was going to LAMDA on a Fulbright, too, and once there we experienced the kind of thrilling lifestyle neither of us had known. We tasted unfamiliar foods, met fascinating people, and explored London as we pursued our goal of becoming the best we could be.

I HAD A COLD WHEN WE DISEMBARKED in England, but that didn't stop me from beginning my life as a voracious acting student. I persuaded my ship roomies to race with me to the Aldwych Theatre to see the Royal Shakespeare Company's *Marat/Sade* on its closing night. Peter Brook's production of Peter Weiss's play had rocked the theatre world—revolutionary in theme and style. Set in a madhouse, each actor had created a singular disturbed character, and their energies caromed off each other in choreographed chaos. When they marched together to the front of the stage in a confrontational mob and hurled their angry song,

"Marat, we're poor, and the poor stay poor.
Marat, don't make us wait anymore!"[1]

I scooted forward on my seat captivated by and honored to be in the presence of the young, accomplished Glenda Jackson and the gutsy company performing the theatrical event of the decade. I knew that this was just the beginning of seeing theatre as I longed for it. I felt more certain than ever that I had come to the right place.

Of course, first we had to find digs. Liz, with her deep chortle, asked if I would like to share a place. I explained I was looking for a place for Toni and myself, that she would be arriving in a few weeks, and Liz said if we looked for a place for four, she would find a fourth to take the extra space. She was slightly younger than me, but I agreed to see what we could find. We searched but found only a series of big Victorian rooms with high ceilings, no heat, stained walls, teeny kitchens, and four single beds. We finally sought help from a rental agency, which sent us to an address near Holland Park. When she and I arrived, the landlord was standing just inside the open front door of the basement apartment talking to a few

Australian women, but as soon as I saw the two real bedrooms with matching drapes and bedspreads, dark red carpeting on painted cement floors, a lovely furnished living room with natural light pouring in from high windows, I knew we had to get this place, and the Realtor's daughter in me erupted by interrupting the Australians and declaring, "We'll take it!"

We moved in and discovered the place also had a big storage room and central heat, and while Liz advertised for a roommate, our other shipmate, Alice, came down to London from Manchester on weekends. Alice, with her tiny hourglass figure, had already been a professional teacher of the deaf in Manhattan and was pursuing advanced training in England. With her curiosity and enthusiasm, she was the perfect companion for touring London, so when she transferred to a center in London and moved in with us, we all felt lucky. With her sign language and innate charm, she was the ideal person to travel with where you didn't know the language, as I would learn later.

Toni had completed her master's degree at UC Santa Barbara, and her decision to join me and read at the British Museum seemed a fine opportunity to transition from the end of a mistaken marriage. Toni surprised herself with the power of her own intellect, and I look back and feel grateful that our friendship provided a bridge for her out of a painful time into her pursuit of her doctorate. She was an anchor for me then and always with her penetrating insight, deep understanding, and compassion for my struggles.

Our flat was an easy walk past Kensington High Street to the corner of Earls' Court and Cromwell Road. There stood Tower House, a huge white Victorian, where we attended school. The London Academy of Music and Dramatic Art was one of the finest drama schools in England. Its principal, Michael MacOwan, had discovered Iris Warren, a revolutionary voice teacher, when her name kept recurring on the résumés of actors auditioning for him at the Royal Shakespeare Company. Together MacOwan and Warren remade the nineteenth-century Academy of Music into the modern London Academy of Music and Dramatic Art for actor training, and although Warren had died by the time I was studying at LAMDA, her students were our voice teachers.

Michael MacOwan was an unimposing figure, considering the fact that he was a visionary. He was a gentle teacher, with an elf-like delight in the opportunity to reveal Shakespeare to us eager students. I noticed sometimes that his hands shook slightly; they reminded me of my father's hands when he was hungover. But when he said modestly, "Call me Mac," I felt fond of him. He made himself utterly approachable.

Each morning we seventy aspiring actors, including twelve of us in the overseas class, headed for the little dressing room in the basement, where we all had lockers. There, as we changed into our leotards, we had a chance to get to know the students in the three-year course, mostly English kids who began training right out of high school. One American girl, a peppy little redhead, was Swoozie Kurtz[2], named for her father's airplane, and already well-assimilated into English life. After changing, all seventy of us—American and English alike—filed into the big ballroom studio for morning warm-up.

In voice class, we came aware of our breath. "Just tune into what is actually happening in your body," our teachers explained. We stood with our hands on our middles while, one after another, our teacher walked around the room, placing her hand on our diaphragms. "Let your muscles and organs move freely out and in as breath moves through your bodies."

When she placed her hand on my middle, she asked, "Did you study ballet?" And when I told her I had—for seven years—she let me know I would want to soften my hard muscles. I tried to relax, terrified that I would never become the best I could be with my iron-clad middle, worried that I was already behind.

"What should I do?" I asked, anxiously.

"Don't worry. It will come."

Although I had been a dancer, our movement class was a new challenge, because of *how* movement was conceived. Trish Arnold, young, bouncy, with curly hair and a working-class accent, was the head of the Movement Department. A former dancer, by then fully in command of a different way of moving, she showed us how to let go to gravity, how to lift a leg with just an impulse, then let its weight swing it back the other direction. Rather than engaging muscle and commanding movement, we were learning how to allow movement, how to let gravity work for us. As I began to work with her images and just a thought, the relaxed movements began to come and what a pleasure—a brain-body connection that felt effortless. That first term in class after class, I was learning the difference between *doing* and *releasing*. Focus was intentional, specific, but that didn't mean tense. When we stretched our arms up, then released first from the wrists, then the elbows, then the shoulders, before engaging the larger muscles, I began to get it. Letting go of the head, rolling down through the spine, then building back up, attending to each vertebra, I began to discover how to have a posture that was relaxed but supported. It was the opposite of "Stand straight, shoulders back!"

We began each voice class in silence, tuning into our breath, making a small *f* with the mouth to feel the breath release from our middles. Often, we lay flat on our backs, needing no effort, focusing entirely on releasing to *allow* the breath to happen. This was the basis for learning to trust the inner process rather than striving for results. Again and again, I was learning how to come back to my center, how to *allow acting* to happen. I knew this was what I wanted for living too, and I trusted that this path would help me develop into a more trusting and spontaneous person. I had read enough to know that effort and control were not the answers to life, but my path—acting training—was teaching me in practical, daily terms, how to let go.

We trained from nine in the morning until six in the evening five days a week. It was such a luxury to spend entire days immersed in my craft. After a full day, often Liz and I took the tube to meet up with Alice and Toni in Piccadilly, grabbed a half pint and fish and chips or shepherd's pie in a pub, then sped to the box office to claim our cheap tickets, entering the theatre anticipating something wonderful. And usually, it was. In the English tradition, ushers encouraged us to move down closer to the stage when the expensive seats were empty.

Our exposure to the finest artists working in London and the multitude of plays gave us more than the equivalent of a graduate degree in theatre. Just as an audience walks out of a musical humming the tunes because their larynx muscles have unconsciously responded during the performance, our nervous systems were being fine-tuned. I was hypnotized by the dark mystique of Pinter performed by the Royal Shakespeare Company: Vivien Merchant, poised as a wild cat on the hunt in *The Homecoming*; David Warner[3] immediate and strangely loose as Hamlet berating Janet Suzman[4], as Ophelia; Paul Scofield[5] in *The Government Inspector*—so human, needy, and funny in his desperation as a starving stranger mistaken for an official and pandered to by the fatuous community. On the radio in an interview, he told of asking himself how to convey the hunger while hiding it from the townspeople he had to fool, and he hit on the idea of playing the scene as if he had to pee. I loved discovering how he had found a way to physically manifest desperation to us, yet in a way that would not be understood by the other characters. It was hilarious.

On Friday afternoons Mac gathered us all together and expounded on the philosophy underlying the training, but during the week, he took charge of Introduction to Acting Shakespeare for the Overseas Course. We were twelve very serious students from all over the country, and Roshan Seth was from India.[6] I'll never forget the day Mac revealed the scene in *Romeo and Juliet* when the young lovers first meet. They raise their hands and place them together, palm to palm, as required for the formal dance, and engage in courtship dialogue.

First, we broke down the text so we could clearly understand what the characters were saying. Once we understood, the movements became obvious: We knew how close they had to stand to each other, how they would touch, when they would kiss. I had specialized in Shakespeare at Berkeley, and in Boulder the previous summer, our esteemed director, Jim Sandoe, had us scan *Hamlet* out loud, letting the beat dictate the emphasis: the first line, a perfect iamb—not "*Who's* there?" But "Who's *there?*" But Mac's approach was revelatory. He possessed a treasure chest of clues we could use in studying the verse that revealed character.

Mac introduced us to the idea of respecting the end of the line rather than rushing to complete a sentence. This slight pause led to revelations of thought and feeling. We learned to find in a vowel the unfolding of emotion. Romeo's respectful but determined advance on Juliet, and her quick, witty response led us to understand who they were. In this single compact scene, their natural rapport and physical attraction are established. We delighted in the way they gamely tossed images back and forth—a challenge, a tease, and two kisses—all in nineteen lines. I'd known Shakespeare was a genius, but this! This astonished me.

Mac assigned us a partner, and with that partner we learned the scene, and brought it into class a week or so later. The day it was my turn, I was terribly nervous and mentioned my stage-fright to a classmate.

"That's just ego," he said, and I was caught off guard. I'd thought of these nerves as part of it. And anyway, wasn't it natural to want to do well and receive praise? I wondered at the idea of approaching this work with detachment and a sense of curiosity about what would happen, rather than investing in "getting it right" or worrying how my fellow students, or more importantly my teacher, judged it. This was another way of coming into the moment, being present.

Just as there was rhythm to our studies, we established a rhythm in our flat. We took turns cleaning, cooking, shopping, each contributing as JoAnne had taught me in San Francisco. If we used the telephone, we put thruppence in a cup. Often on weekends, because the English were polite but distant and we seldom had dates, we went places together. The food shops closed at noon on Saturday, so groceries had to be bought in the morning. And just as

I was dazzled by theatre, I was often amazed at this new world I was inhabiting—at the whole chickens hanging from hooks in butcher windows, the fresh vegetables and fruit displayed in stands, loaves of bread in bins with no wrappers.

On Saturdays we often shopped for necessities at Harrods or Marks & Spencer. As fall turned to winter, I'd noticed that my skin, ordinarily healthy-looking, had gone gray, and my sun-bleached hair had turned brown, and at Harrods a saleswoman sold me on a rich Estée Lauder cream but when she told me the price—one pound!—I began to hand it back to her, but Toni and Alice insisted I buy it. And it helped both my skin and my morale.

On Sundays, a peace descended upon the city, everything quieter, chilly weather dampening the many gardens and parks. The *Sunday Observer* and the *London Times* were so engaging I could while away hours reading Malcolm Muggeridge, Kenneth Tynan, and the actual news of the world—so much closer now than in the States. Even Africa seemed close when I read news of Idi Amin. Coverage of the Vietnam war was more critical of US policies as well. We had fine museums to choose from—my favorite being the Tate because of Blake and the Turners, and I took my time gazing at each painting, the way Bob La Vigne had taught me to do. After an exhibit or a movie, we might go to dinner at an Indian restaurant where I tried foods I'd never heard of—saffron rice studded with almonds and raisins and spices that made me feel almost high. I loved how exotic the words tasted in our mouths as we ordered: biryani, tandoori, papadam. And lager and lime refreshed the hot tongue.

In our first sensory awareness class, Norman Ayrton, the vice principal, guided us to pay attention to every sense. "First, just close your eyes and notice the breath. Don't *do* anything to it, just notice it. Gradually, become aware of the sounds you hear. A bird. The traffic. Bodies shifting around you." I had read just enough about meditation and Rob had taken me to see the Zen master Suzuki Roshi[7] in San Francisco where he gave me a lesson before I left the States, so that now I was beginning to practice the power of awareness, and as I settled into the exercise, I knew I could trust the teaching here. This was acting as spiritual path. Acting as Practice of Life. The way to great art, I hoped. I was thrilled to be there receiving this teaching.

Our teacher for the afternoon rehearsal class that term was an esteemed British actor, tall and formerly gorgeous, and also the designer of the LAMDA Theatre, which was compact and versatile, a gem with all the flexibility the blueprints I'd seen on the department chair's desk back in Berkeley had promised. At first, we sat at the front of the audience and read Shakespeare aloud. As the weeks went on, we kept reading, and I became impatient, wondering when we were going to get up. When we would *act*. When I groused to some of my classmates, I learned that they were fine sitting there, many of them inspired simply to be *reading* Shakespeare. I had read Shakespeare at Berkeley. I had played Rosalind, Portia, and Ophelia. And I had just one year at LAMDA to learn all I could. *Let's get going!* I thought, forgetting all about trusting the teaching.

I was pleased when a second year acting student invited me out, but he seemed to think drinking pints of bitters in the nearby pub was a date. I tried to remain cheerful as my stomach growled for food. Postponing dinner was often hazardous for me, and when he and the other students finally dropped me back at my place, I was feeling bleak. He said something crude to me, and I whipped around and slapped his face. He slugged me. And that sobered me up, fast. So ended the only hint of romance, and I retreated back to the quiet weekends of girlfriends and culture, relieved to have such dynamic and interested friends.

On the last day of the term, Mac called some students into his office. I waited nervously in the anteroom as one of my friends from the English group came out, looking pale. I walked in full of trepidation and noticed that Mac looked tired, his hands shaky. I watched him open the bottom drawer of his desk and pull out a pint of scotch. He kindly offered me a drink, which I properly refused. And then he began to talk to me about my attitude. It was, he said, creating a negative atmosphere. My impatience was not creative. He realized I was young—well, not so young—but not so mature either. I needed to correct this in myself, he told me. Stifling tears, I recalled Stanislavski's words about "the creative atmosphere," about shaking the dirt off your feet when you entered the theatre, and I knew that my nun-like devotion mattered not at all because my impatience and negativity were what stood out.

On my way home, I stopped to buy a pint of brandy, and back at the flat, I refused dinner, and when I went to the bathroom, I found myself on the floor sobbing. I hated myself. I heard Toni knock. I heard her try to cajole me out, but it was too late. I was in the black hole.

At last, when others needed the bathroom, I opened the door and ran to my bed. I was not only unreachable, I was inconsolable, and it was only years later that I began to understand that this darkness descended when someone brought one of my flaws to my attention and I realized that I wasn't perfect. I hadn't lived up to my own ideals. I treated the pain I felt by drinking alcohol, and that only sent me into darker pools of self-pity and remorse.

The next morning, feeling like a weak and wounded kitten, I packed my little bag and, with Toni and Alice, went to Victoria Station to begin our vacation. Liz was going to Europe with her parents, and we planned to meet up later in Rome. As we ferried across the channel in thick, gray mist, I felt my sorrow, if not my shame, begin to lift, and by the time we checked into a dark, cheap Parisian hotel, I'd forgotten the sting. The next day we shopped in Paris, astonished at lingerie even we could afford, and then I quickly purchased a bottle of wine on the platform as we raced to catch the evening train to Florence.

On the train, as the night wore on, hungry and thirsty, we watched in envy as families pulled out picnic baskets with full meals and bottles of water. A cute young Italian with a moustache and his father who spoke no English were sharing our compartment. As evening wore on, the conductor came in and bing-banged flip-flopped the compartment from two seats for three facing each other to six flat, slightly padded bunks so we could sleep our way through the Alps. Toni, Alice, and I went to the WC to change into comfortable clothes for sleeping, and then, parched, we climbed onto our padded slats.

I was on the topmost bunk, below me the young Italian, his father under him. My girlfriends slept on the other side. Before long, as others slept, high on the Bordeaux, I leaned from my top bunk over the edge and let my hair hang like a blonde curtain to the bunk below. He slapped at my hair, and after a little while, he stood and leaned in for a kiss. I pulled him up to lie with me, and as the train sped its way into the mountains, this handsome Italian and I fooled around, indulging in what Erica Jong would soon make famous in her wild bestseller, *Fear of Flying,* as the "zipless fuck." His dark moustache intensified his kisses, his ears all cartilage with lobes I bit. He liked that and entered me, and the next morning when I told Toni and Alice about my nighttime dalliance, their jaws dropped. They couldn't believe I had done it, but I felt no shame at all, just wickedly free.

And then came Florence! The Renaissance, the Uffizi, Botticelli. Never had I been so overwhelmed by beauty. Then Campari and soda, veal marsala, cappuccino. Everything was a wonder: the bathtub with its hand shower in the *pensione* where the three of us shared one room and covered the damp sheets with wool blankets. On the bus to Siena, I noticed "the morn in russet mantle clad, walks o'er the dew of yon high eastward hill" and *knew* that Shakespeare had been here. Alice negotiated with the hotel manager in Siena who declared "Americanas!" and she retorted "Studenti!" and got us a better rate. On Christmas Eve, Toni and I each bought a length of black lace and then gave them to each other to wear to midnight Mass. In Rome, at a family restaurant, the friendly son helped us order, and he and a handsome Danish student became our pals who took us to ride fast on the autostrada and out for drinks and dancing in small clubs. We deflected, but appreciated, their passes. Toni met an American and took off with him for Spain, and when an Argentinian architecture student invited me to Milan, I went, and on the beach, under the winter sunlight, we drank Marsala and lunched on fresh bread and cheese. It was so European! But the Argentinian and I were not a match, so I soon hopped a train back to Rome to find Liz, and she and I went to the sea and sang, "We're travelin' along, singin' a song, side by side." When we left Rome and the lively young men we'd met there, I wept.

Back at LAMDA, stripped of what we thought we knew when we first arrived, our group entered a self-conscious phase, even feeling naked, aware of the tight tongue, jutting jaw, toes surreptitiously gripping the floor, mind grasping for something to hold onto. I had to remind myself again and again to release, let go. Facing myself each day was a challenge, and I thought that if I'd known what it was going to take to learn what I wanted to learn, I'd never have had the courage to come.

This harder phase was accented by a London letdown, with its gloomy gray stone buildings, its gardens dormant, and no fun. The dressing room at LAMDA was freezing; just sitting on the toilet seat could take your breath away. In the theatre before rehearsal, I stomped around to warm my feet, and many days I thought how unsatisfying the blue airmail letters I received from Barry were—no substitute for affection and a man's arms around me. Except for our dear landlords, we seldom were invited to anyone's home. I fell into a depression.

In Berkeley, my psychotherapist had given me the name of a Jungian on Harley Street who recommended a woman analyst. I was uneasy about working with a woman, fearful of judgment again, but I knew I should go; overcoming that reluctance would be part of my therapy. Then, finding a time seemed impossible. I went to Norman for help, and he was sympathetic. He told me if I were late for morning warm-up every other week, to just come in and join. I dipped into the travel money I had saved since graduation, and one morning in the pre-dawn cold, I rose quietly, made coffee and breakfast, and hurried to the tube to make my seven thirty appointment. I rang the bell at the black shiny door and walked up the carpeted stairway with its lacquered banister to a serene home office of an attractive Jungian analyst. Sitting in a chair across from her, I began to reveal my unconscious. There I held dream images up to the light. The smell of her coal fire was comforting, and after the first time, I was eager to return. Over time I brought her my dreams in a journal, free-associated on the images in those dreams, and began to work my way out of my heavy mood. I was longing to free myself from the kind of wild hysteria that often seized me after a night at the pub.

One particular morning in the office with this intelligent and compassionate analyst, I remembered my sister's birth. It came back to me, as if it were happening before my eyes, doctors wheeling Mama in her wheelchair down a cement ramp. She was holding my new baby sister. She looked so happy. When Daddy opened the car door, he was grinning, and as Mama handed off the bundle to a lady in white with a nice cap, he helped her into the car. The lady in white reached in and put the bundle back in Mama's arms, and I attempted to scoot in beside them, but that day I had to ride in the backseat. Just for that day, Daddy told me. I couldn't see out the front window. I didn't like that.

Mama and Daddy got settled with the baby they named Jane. Daddy asked Mama if she was ready. "Yes," she said, and he added, "My side's ready," and they laughed together. He chugged the car motor, and we pulled away. "All right, Karen?" one of them asked, and I said I was, but I was not. I was mad, feeling tight pressure so big it hurt. They could have their front seat. They could keep it. My heart was breaking. A film of tight tissue seemed to grow across my center. I could deal. I looked out the side window. Life was going to change now. I could handle it. I was two and a half, transforming grief into a resentful corset compressing my body and the beginning of a life of collected resentments that would pile up into a mountain of unexpressed anger until it exploded in drunken episodes.

Now, in her well-appointed office, I wept so hard, when we were done, I had trouble walking out on the street. I couldn't face the Underground. I flagged a taxi and in a dissociated haze, holding myself in, I returned to the flat. Everyone was gone for the day, and I had forgotten my key. I walked upstairs to the landlord and landlady's flat and knocked. My face was tear-streaked and red, and when they opened the door, I stammered that I wasn't feeling well, couldn't go to school, had forgotten my key, and thankfully they asked nothing. In the flat, I felt safe. I made myself a hot coffee, walked into the bedroom, dressed in flannel pajamas, crawled into my bed, pulled the covers up to my chin, and gave in to exhaustion. Dark. Quiet. Sleep. And I dreamed.

In my dream I was comforted by a black snake. He was erotic and friendly, a companion, and soon he was penetrating me, and I had an intense orgasm that woke me. And I felt at peace. Before that day I had read in Jung's work that dreams could precipitate a healing. That day I came to understand how true that was. My storm had passed. I was twenty-three years old, and I had finally begun to discover the way I was.

IN VOICE CLASS, WE ISOLATED THE articulators—tongue, lips, teeth. I discovered I had a tongue that was thick and strong with holding on, over-exercised. That lump in your throat when you don't want to cry—that was my tongue. I couldn't let it go all at once, of course. Some vocal habits have to do with regional accents or parental habits, and we all had to learn to drop them so we could be "tabula rasa," blank slates, so we didn't limit the roles we could play. We needed a clear channel for the voice to move through.

Little by little, we became more familiar with our center, the initial impulse of the breath, and gradually we learned to allow it to pick up vibrations in our larynx (without squeezing the heck out of it in our throats), then let it travel up and out of our mouths. I was fascinated by the many tricks of the psyche and body we used to hide our deepest selves, and day after day as we showed up for what looked like simple exercises, we began to be revealed—to ourselves and to each other. One morning in the loo, I realized I was pushing even when I peed. The training was untying knots, the beginning of a lifelong process. We learned, watching others' struggles, that there really was no way to hide. The more we saw the beauty of our fellows revealed, the more we could trust that it was okay to let go.

We had been loosening our necks with head rolls in Voice class. Norman asked for a volunteer to do the new monologue. David sat in the chair while Norman took control of his head rolling it above his shoulders. As David lost control, sometimes the words slipped away, but returned as a freedom overcame him, and the text flowed out to us, transparent, full, and moving. When Norman asked him "What did you feel?" he answered, "Nothing, really. I was doing nothing." But we had experienced his nothing as a great deal. And that was the lesson. It wasn't about us feeling, but about being the medium for the playwright, for the human experience. I was even beginning to understand *how.* As we released all that unnecessary physical tension, we developed genuine strength—spines that supported the breath, legs that were in balance, shoulders that relaxed, jaws that no longer blocked vibration or emotion. I could feel myself making way for character to inhabit me, and the glory when a character came forth in a completely original way was a thrill every time.

Ronald Fuller was our ascetic monk of period history. He gathered us in a semicircle around him. The space heater glowed red, our toes grew hot, and our backs were freezing in the darkening room as he described the actual life of the people—the meals, clothing, diseases. We felt as if Fuller had come to us from the Middle Ages or the streets of Shakespeare's London to tell us what it had been like. He couldn't publish, he told us, because what he had written became obsolete before he finished writing—his knowledge forever deepening.

When our new rehearsal unit focused on Restoration comedy, Norman demonstrated how movements called "style" came directly from the restrictions or flourishes of the fashions. We practiced walking with our heads held high above our erect torsos (imagining ourselves in corsets), our elbows lifted so as not to crush yet to reveal the lace cuffs on slim sleeves. We walked in curving lines, passing each other, nodding graciously, offering flirty glances, displaying snotty attitudes. Back and forth we swirled, as if around traffic cones, making a scalloped path through the empty theatre. Norman arranged trips to great houses and to museums to study the portraits of the people of these eras, to gaze upon their gazes, to learn to see the world through their eyes.

We were rehearsing two Richard Wilbur translations of Molière plays. I was cast as Marianne, the ingénue, in *Tartuffe* and the society gossip, Arsinoé, in *The Misanthrope*. The ingénue was developing into a blissfully idiotic creature, but becoming the haughty gossip was more challenging. One afternoon, while I was striving to put down my compatriots in a particularly delicious bit of rhymed couplets, Norman grabbed my ponytail and pulled me up from behind.

"Keep going," he commanded.

I let myself be pulled up taller than I'd ever been, imperious. He pulled and pulled, demanding, "Show your strength!" Electricity shot up my spine—suddenly the breath was full and available, my diaphragm pumped and released without my thinking about it, and the words poured forth. Breakthrough! When we finished the scene, he said, "See: You are that strong."

"I know," I said.

"Ah, but you don't believe. *Believe it!*"

There was something I knew about strength. And that was that it often wasn't welcome. How to own it?

We went to Piccadilly to buy German makeup sticks and small pots of color, so much better than my old greasepaint—because they were *European*. During tech rehearsals, Norman told me we were going to rent a wig. I was shocked at the expense, and in the

Haymarket, I was very excited, entering the inner sanctum of the wigmakers. Norman described the character, and the wigmaker pulled out a few dark wigs. One was a good fit, and I saw the nametag sewn inside: Claire Bloom. I had just seen her in *Ivanov*, and the realization that I would wear this handmade wig of the famous and accomplished actress felt to me like crossing a threshold into the world where I wanted to belong. The wig was delivered to the theatre just in time for our dress rehearsal, and Norman showed me how to put it on and secure it.

On opening night, all the LAMDA students, faculty, staff, our roommates, and true to their word, our landlords, Mr. and Mrs. South, came to the theatre. The first play went well. My dim Marianne didn't land as many laughs as we expected (expecting them was probably the problem). During intermission, we changed for *The Misanthrope*. My Arsinoé was a sensation. The students were turning to each other asking, "Who is that? Who *is* that?" It had all come together. While I had experienced feeling completely in character before, this time was exceptional because of the distance I had to travel from Ventura girl to sophisticated aristocratic Frenchwoman.

That spring, Trish introduced more interpretive movement, and the day she brought in a big box of white masks, and we each put one on, we gazed into the mirror and let our bodies be moved by what we saw. Not being in my own "face," my own persona, created unusual gestures, strange postures, and foreign feelings. It left me feeling giddy. Next, we each looked at each other and let what we saw move our bodies. We tried on other masks, and as Trish guided us to stretch, energy seemed to explode like streamers through the room. We all agreed, this was pure fun. All our diligence was paying off in moments of exhilaration. We threw ourselves into stage fights, we lay on the floor and laughed on cue. We improvised little scenarios that ended in blood-curdling screams. The attraction of the art of acting that I had originally fallen in love with became more rewarding than ever, with more and more moments of pure freedom.

All of us roommates were working hard, and when anyone from home came to visit, we all welcomed the diversion. Friends from Berkeley and New York often came, and whenever parents arrived, we were treated to dinners at good restaurants like Simpson's with exceptional waiters in formal attire who carried great roasts on silver trays, and the salt was in delicate silver-and-glass dishes with tiny spoons.

A Berkeley friend arrived for a visit and stunned me when he revealed that Barry had let an undergrad blonde move in with him. I sent him a chilly Western Union telegram, and Barry responded with a blue letter that ended us. I got drunk and ran up an exorbitant phone bill to call him to rail against him, and I would still be paying off that bill for months after I returned home.

The atmosphere around us was swinging, and I got my first miniskirt, wondered if I should paint my lower lashes like Twiggy, listened to *Rubber Soul* with its sitar, and thought we were all getting enlightened together.

The performances at the National Theatre inspired us. Our whole class went together to see the Olivier *Othello* with the young Billie Whitelaw as Desdemona. Maggie Smith had gone on to *'Tis Pity She's a Whore* playing with her husband, Robert Stephens, the two of them reeking sex. And Albert Finney who was passionate and nearly unintelligible in the title role in *Sergeant Musgrave's Dance*, as he and his northern working-class contemporaries refused to adapt to standard English as a matter of pride. We Americans, meanwhile, struggled to learn the standard English vowels that would see us through any classic play, intoning, "Hoo Ho, Hoh, Ha, Haw," from our diaphragms.

I still can't believe how fortunate we were. Any Saturday afternoon we might waltz into a matinee of Ralph Richardson in Shaw's *You Never Can Tell* or see Lynn Redgrave, our age or younger, playing the mute daughter in *Mother Courage*, and breaking our hearts.[8] For John Donne's birthday, in St. Paul's Cathedral, we were privileged to hear Paul Scofield read one of

Donne's sermons and some of the poems. Combining these two was like "gold to airy thinness beat." For a young acting student, London was the equivalent of King Solomon's mines, and I dug like a thief for every jewel I could.

While I was there, Mom and Dad took their first-ever trip abroad, and I noticed that their mellow period seemed to be continuing. After briefly visiting me in London, they went on a tour, and then returned from Switzerland to spend more time with me. They were enthusiastic about their adventures, eager and open for more, and I looked forward to taking them to Hampton Court, where both Henry VIII and Queen Elizabeth I had lived. On one of those brilliant spring days that inspired the song, "It's May, It's May," we took a bus from a stop near our flat through the small towns outside London, and at the castle, my mind steeped in Elizabethan England, I was able to regale them with stories. As we were leaving the castle and walking toward the Thames, I told them how the young Queen Elizabeth shouted down to Sir Walter Raleigh as he was being taken by guards to a boat to the Tower—"Keep your head!" We hopped aboard a small boat just then leaving for London and glided down river, and I felt a drowsy, warm closeness enfold us. That evening, I felt safe enough to broach the subject of my needing more psychotherapy. My analyst had been suggesting I see her at least once a week, but to do so I needed their help.

"You have it all—talent, education, looks—what's the problem?" Dad asked.

"Just be yourself," Mom said.

I wept. I told them I didn't trust people, and wondered aloud about Dad's drinking.

"When did you start drinking again?" I asked him, and he said "a little red wine" didn't seem to bother him, not when they were traveling. And Mom agreed.

Still, after more conversation, and my tears, they agreed to help me go to therapy once a week.

Crocuses and hyacinths pushed up in the pocket gardens I

passed on my way to school—an English poem come to life—and some days we took lunches out to the patch of grass at school where we sat and discussed the latest show or the new Masters and Johnson research on sex. Other days, though, I'd feel my dark mood descending, and I raced home to be alone. I longed for Barry, then wished never to leave London, and then felt prickly with the teachers as if it were their fault our training was coming to an end. I slipped the Joan Baez album out of its sleeve and while I ate my Caerphilly cheese sandwich, I played that Dylan song again and again.

It seemed to describe the way I felt, a crossroads, a repetitive thought of the man, the weather shifting inside and outside and that line "Daddy, you been on my mind." There *was* an angular light that was new. The tiny buds on the trees outside our windows were finally opening. I gave in to Dylan's melancholy tune and was chewing slowly when I heard a clip-clop coming along the street, looked up and over the sill and saw an actual Clydesdale and cart, too good to be true. I quickly ran outside and approached the driver in his rumpled brown jacket and cap, his cheeks pink as an English schoolgirl's. The cart held row upon row of fruits and vegetables prettily stacked and protected from bruising—bright apples, even bananas. I asked what he recommended, and he spoke for the pears, fresh from South Africa. I wasn't sure. I thought I didn't care for pears, and *weren't we supposed to boycott South Africa?* but I wanted to be willing to try something new, so I went inside to get my purse, and came out to buy a pear. He picked a ripe one for me, and as he handed it over, I thanked him, feeling merry at the very notion of a fruit seller with a horse and cart right there on my doorstep. I rinsed the pear, dried it carefully with the dishcloth, and placed it on the table before me while I finished my sandwich. Then I settled in for dessert. The thin skin allowed my teeth to bite easily into flesh that felt as cool as a kiss, and the sweet juice spurted into my mouth and down my chin. I headed for the sink and ate it there, not wanting to bother with napkins or niceties. For days afterward, I hustled to the flat, prepared my sandwich, tuned my ears to listen to Baez and wait for the clip-clop of the big old Clydesdale and friendly man who seemed pleased by my rapture with his pears. There was no question about it. I was fully in the moment with that pear.

Liz grew tired of our housekeeping drill and moved out, and Anna Maria from Perugia, "where they make the candy," moved in. Her mother sent her *parmigiana* wrapped tightly in tin foil, and she made gnocchi with cream sauce, grating in fresh nutmeg. She taught us how to speak Italian, and in return, we taught her birth control. Then Alice's course ended, and we waved good-bye, sure we would write as she returned to New York, and Toni's mother came over, and they took off on a European tour. When Anna Maria fell in love with an Englishman, she was gone in the evenings, and suddenly I was entirely on my own at the flat, because I had little in common with the two young Australian women who had taken Toni and Alice's places. Anyway, the time was coming near for me to pack up the old trunk to go home.

I hated to leave the museums, the theatres, casual meals in pubs, the comfy, civilized tube, the Englishmen with their black umbrellas and the upholstered seats where everyone read two or three newspapers, the double-decker buses, the attendant carrying her change in a fanny pack round her middle. I comforted myself with the newest Beatles album, *Revolver*: "Turn off your mind, relax, and float downstream, / It is not dying, it is not dying..." This had been the theme of the year, really, turning off your mind, trusting. I slid it into the trunk to be taken to the ship, but leaving wrung me out, and this time I would be traveling solo, not with a bunch of American Fulbright scholars and the people who had smoothed our way.

My Jungian analyst strongly recommended that I continue my work once I was settled in back in the States. The letters of inquiry and eight-by-ten photos I'd sent to resident theatres had helped me to line up auditions in New York and DC, as well as an offer in Memphis for a whole season—which I was reluctant to take, my

Southern experience having been so difficult. Fred wrote to say, "Come ahead, stay with me." He had sold his book. But before I could write back, the editor left the publishing house, and they dropped his novel. He had a good job with a producer, but he wasn't sure he wanted to do that; he was beyond frustrated.

School ended, and with three days of freedom before the *United States* was set to debark, I flew to Paris on a cheap flight. The cabbie seemed to intentionally misunderstand my French, and humiliated, I got out and took the metro to the Left Bank, where my trusty *Europe on Five Dollars a Day* led me to a charming small hotel. I followed the hotelier to the top floor, where a sweet garret with a four-poster double bed and a little window—it was warm enough to leave open in June—was all mine. In the morning, I was astounded and delighted to receive a huge cup of café au lait delivered to my room with the newspaper.

At the Louvre, Americans crowded around the *Mona Lisa*, shot photos, and rushed on, and I wondered if people took photos to prove they had been somewhere. I bought a chartreuse, polka-dot chiffon summer dress for my summer auditions, visited the Impressionists' Museum, and stood in Notre Dame feeling awe. For three nights, I arranged for three shows: a tiny basement where Ionesco was performed with immaculate flair; the *Comédie Française*, which gave new depth to elegance; and last and surprisingly best—I arrived at a large courtyard behind a church where chairs were set up on the grass, under spreading chestnut trees. I sat down while an accordion set a nostalgic mood, and darkness fell. Lights in the arched corridors came on, and, magically, the young players appeared on the hip-high walls of the colonnade to perform in this romantic antiwar play that took place around World War I. A light rain began to fall, tapping on the leaves, adding to the dreamy atmosphere since those trees kept us dry, and as I slowly walked back to my hotel, like the dancers on the colonnade, my heart swung back and forth: anticipation, reluctance, excitement, fear. Back to London. Back to the States. Back to begin a new life.

10. An Actor's Life for Me

"Friends will stand by me in trouble. They will."
—*Missouri Ruralist* column, LAURA INGALLS WILDER

AUTUMN IN MEMPHIS, WHERE MY FIRST Equity contract—a full season of good roles—was about to begin, was crisp. I waited near the stage door for the artistic director, who was backstage congratulating his actors on their opening night. I heard someone say my name, and startled, and flustered too that someone here knew me, I turned and came face to face with Leon Russom, honey-voiced and kind, with a compact body that radiated vitality. I didn't know who he was, but he recognized me from my photo, and as we chatted, I learned he had also returned recently from studying acting in London. Later I learned he had taken one look at my eight-by-ten photo and said, "I'm going to fall in love with her."

Rehearsals began and he walked me home, as we shared our London stories. A few days later, I invited him for dinner where he acted out the entire production of the Christopher Fry play he'd directed that summer. He was impressed that Christopher Fry had been one of my teachers at LAMDA. We felt like two peas in a pod, both of us aspiring to greatness in the theatre, and both of us longing to have it all— a stellar career and a family. We moved into our own apartment across from the costume shop, where we shared a single bed and turned over in concert our first professional season. I learned he was an orphanage survivor. What I loved about him was the way he somehow combined exquisite vulnerability with fierce determination.

Near the end of the season, we were planning to go to New York for the big auditions and then join another resident theatre, expecting we'd be able to get contracts with the same company. We had planned to marry at the end of the season, and my folks offered to come for the wedding combining a visit to Florida to see Dad's brother and his wife whom he hadn't seen in decades. I preferred for them to come while we were still working so they could see our shows as well as visiting. We did have a wonderful time: I cooked for them and we shared the blues joint downtown where old blues musicians played and we were adults together. Daddy drank too much but his deep pleasure in the music was endearing, and everyone got along.

Then Leon had doubts. Then I did. My London analyst had suggested more inner work, and this tugged at the back of my mind, but life and love were calling. Most of my friends had married, and I'd been a bridesmaid at least three times. We were mid-twenties, not too old and not too young. I felt insecure enough about heading to New York with "no direction home" without exposing my private life to artistic directors I didn't know. I didn't want to go to New York as a couple unless we were married. We could apply to theatres individually if we weren't committed.

Following sessions filled with anguish and declarations of love, we took the leap of faith and set a date just after the season closed. Leon arrived at the Memphis courthouse carrying masses of yellow tulips for my bridal bouquet, and our friends, a merry band of players in tie dye and long hair, all bearing tulips, streamed into the courthouse, scandalizing the clerks. They showed us to a back room full of filing cabinets where the dusty judge frowned and lectured us: "This is a serious step." Did he think we were too happy, I wondered? Afterwards, Leon and I went to Beale Street to a photographer's studio for tourists where we had our wedding portrait taken with an old-fashioned camera in front of a canvas backdrop. Those black-and-white photos doubled as our postcard wedding announcements.

We took off for New York City in May in a little red sports car that cost us most of our savings. I'd let Leon talk me into it over the practical Volvo I leaned towards. Alice invited us to stay with her in New York while we attended the auditions. She had a small bedroom at the back of her apartment. Disappointed when we did not receive offers that would employ us at the same theatre, we debated what to do: Should we take the offers at separate companies and take the train back and forth for days off, or should we stay together and try our luck in the Big Apple? We turned for advice to colleagues from the Workshop, now at Lincoln Center. Bob and Jan Symonds were very supportive. Fred, who was working for a Broadway producer and writing his new novel on a roll top desk in his new Greenwich Village apartment, definitely thought we should stay. I sought advice from JoAnne and her husband, Phil—she and I had stayed in touch after we left the Bay Area; she'd written from Paris that she had met this fantastic guy, a composer, and they had been married by a Greek captain, traveled overland to India, and returned to New York to pursue their careers. JoAnne Akalaitis[1] was still an actress, and Phil was Philip Glass,[2] who was not yet known as a composer.

An agent who had seen Leon's work offered to send him up for roles, and Alice let us know we could stay longer. We auditioned, got no parts, and unemployment office clerks treated us like scum. It took months for our first checks to arrive, and they were tiny, based on the living expenses in Tennessee where we had worked, not New York, where we were now. The weather grew hot and humid, and Alice needed to move the extra bed to a friend's country house, which I suspected was the excuse she needed to get us to move. JoAnne and Phil were living in a commercial space where they had plumbed, erected walls for bedroom and bath, and made a living space, and they arranged housesits for us in their artist friends' lofts while those friends were away on summer vacations. Mostly illegal, these lofts had nothing in common with those that would be photographed, years later, for *Architectural Digest*, and my middle-class sensibilities were worn raw by the sound of mice (or were they rats?) scuttering across the floor at night and the roach armies that fled when we turned on a light. Leon, though, took it all in stride.

Phil and his artist friends, Richard Serra and Chuck Close, moved furniture for money, and when they needed an extra man, they invited Leon to help. Jan Symonds was recovering from back surgery, and I cooked dinner for Bob and the kids, and Leon and I ate too. Driving our sports car and having no money made me feel idiotic, but I did get a kick out of racing the taxis down 9th Avenue. We'd find a place to park—no mean trick—and return to find someone had simply lifted it to an illegal spot and taken our place, and our car had been impounded. Suddenly our food money for the week was gone. Fred's folks graciously invited us to stay with them in Summit, New Jersey, for a couple of weeks, but I was growing weary of being beholden to everyone we knew.

One evening that summer in New York, JoAnne told me she was worried. They were out of money, and she was having friends for dinner the next night. I felt terrible that I had none to give her, but she waved away my concern. The Tibetan thangkas they had bought in India, complex paintings mounted on silk brocade depicting iconic Buddhist figures, hung on their bare brick walls. JoAnne told me these were their insurance; if they had to, they would sell them, but they firmly believed they wouldn't have to do that. I was admiring her faith when the phone rang, and a moving job showed up. The money from the job arrived, and the next night I helped her put dinner on the table for six. Phil had given her a book of ancient Chinese recipes for her birthday, and she made chrysanthemum soup.

Just as I had learned from my teachers in London, I was learning from my friends, and their generosity and resourcefulness were a saving grace. I certainly did not want my parents to know how hard things were in New York. I phoned them collect once a week with a glossed over report on our progress so they wouldn't worry.

The day in June when *Sgt. Pepper's Lonely Hearts Club Band* was released, Phil brought it home, JoAnne cooked, and six of us sat down to reverently listen to it. Some of us smoked grass. I could listen more keenly when the background noise of fear dissipated as it did when I smoked pot. We paid close attention to every word and every note, declared it genius, a breakthrough—and even Phil, who turned out to be a genius in his own right, agreed. After all, we too were getting by "with a little help from our friends."

A casting agent who had seen Leon perform in Memphis took a special interest in him and set up a number of appointments. I felt threatened that he'd move on without me, and jealous of her attention. In our second month in the city, Bill Treusch, a young go-getter at the talent agency that had been sending Leon out, agreed to send me on a couple of auditions, and surprisingly I landed both jobs. *Wow!* I thought, *this isn't so tough*. It was reassuring that, after all, I did know what I was doing. The agency dispatched Bill, a sweet guy probably working for nothing, to take me to lunch at the famed Sardi's, and I signed with them. Bill was devoted to both me and Leon, as he eventually would be to other actors (notably discovering Sissy Spacek), but that summer, we were on a roller coaster. One day we were bleak and broke, the next it seemed we would rocket to success. My first job was a part on *The Guiding Light*, a popular soap opera. It could become a recurring role, and it paid more money than I had ever seen. Nearly simultaneously, I got a part in a pre-Broadway tryout about George Bernard Shaw.

My confidence soared. The chief agent and I agreed—I ought to go with the Broadway play, so he gave my notice to CBS (after only a short couple of weeks). But when I read the script, my heart sank. It needed a lot of work, and so I learned a hard, practical lesson: always read a script before accepting a job. How to manage the work-a-day world of the actor was not something we'd been taught in classes.

The producers promised rewrites by the writer while we were out of town, a common practice at the time. In July, crossing my fingers, I went off on a four-week tour, moving from one city to the next each week. Stephen Boyd, the Hollywood star, turned out to be well cast as the young Shaw in *The Bashful Genius*. Some other wonderful New York actors were in the show, and in Denver we played Elitch Gardens, the oldest summer stock theatre in the country where huge photos of stars hung high on the backstage walls. I knew my dad would be proud to know that I was playing in the same theatre where Raymond Burr, the lead from his favorite TV show, *Perry Mason*, had performed. Before every performance, I walked through the amusement park and rode the carousel, blissful to be working. I stayed in a little rented room, sleeping on a sagging single bed to save up money for that apartment we needed in New York. Leon was there appearing in an Off-Off-Broadway play that paid nothing but gave him notoriety since it costarred Baby Jane Holzer, one of Warhol's "superstars." Their photos were in *Vogue*.

Toni and her new boyfriend, Larry Thornton, drove over the Rockies to Denver to see me in the show. They were both working on their doctorates in English at UC Santa Barbara. I was impressed with Larry's devotion to my friend, and happy to be with her again. Seeing her felt like coming home, and she asked how I had resolved my doubts about marrying Leon that I had shared with her in my letters. I could only say I had taken a leap of faith. I was still hopeful that the marriage would go well.

When our company arrived in Falmouth, Cape Cod, we learned that instead of completing our tour and continuing on to Broadway after this week's shows, we would be closing. Several of us actors were sharing a big house, and when Leon came up for a visit, we tried to treat our time there as a holiday. I fixed scallops and blueberries to delight my husband and learned for the first time to be grateful for Actors' Equity, our union. My colleagues told us stories of the days when actors were left stranded out of town when producers ran out of money. Now at least we had our salaries and our transportation home assured. It was another lesson, and I never forgot it. My loyalty to the union has never dimmed.

After the intense three weeks on the road, the disappointing rewrites, and the quiet of Cape Cod, Grand Central Station's cacophony was a shock. Leon and I headed for Bob and Jan's, where we roosted in their children's bunk beds while the kids were at camp. I had saved most of my salary and told everyone, "Tomorrow, I'm going to find us an apartment." They all looked at me as if I were delusional, but the very next morning, Bill Treusch called and asked if we'd like to look at a rent-controlled apartment downtown. Now, their faces looked at me with fresh astonishment. It was $47.22 a month, so we raced down to 1st Avenue and 15th Street and rang the buzzer of the tenant who had the key. Richard Neilson, a charming English actor with blond hair and twinkly eyes, invited us into his and his wife's delightful kitchen; she was away on tour in a musical. When he told us that the available apartment was like his, a long railroad flat with four rooms, we could not believe our good fortune. He took us over to the apartment in an identical building two doors down where in the hallway a dreadful smell assaulted us. As we climbed the three flights of narrow, dark stairs, Richard joked that the tenants suspected the super had buried his wife in the basement.

But the apartment surprised us—with no building blocking the south windows, the kitchen was bright and light, though unlike Richard's place, the floor was cheap linoleum, not refinished wood floors. The walls were painted powder blue rather than the tasteful and subdued colors of Richard's place, but he pointed out that we could knock the plaster from the kitchen fireplace and have exposed brick like theirs. We needed no convincing. We returned to Richard's, where we called the landlord and took the subway uptown to sign the lease. We paid some graft and did not grumble about it.

Having been wanderers since our wedding, after four months, at last Leon and I had a home, our first. Leon went to Memphis to pick up our stuff. There was a terrifying accident when the trailer turned the car over, but no one was hurt, and he flew home in time for an important audition the next day. Our car was totaled. We were both up for the understudies in a British import. I was a wreck from the worry over the accident, but he carried it off with aplomb and got the job. I recall Leon returned and rented a car to bring our stuff up before he started rehearsal. The weather was changing and to stay warm, I'd begun to wear his long pants. Now I had my own clothes. We settled into life in Manhattan. Leon stood by for Ian McShane on Broadway while I worried my chance wouldn't come. It was painful to go to a party with the working actors from the show and be the one who wasn't working. While casting directors always said, "Let me know when you're in something"—they meant in New York City—so I decided to give myself two years to get onstage in Manhattan, or I would move to Hollywood to try there. One year seemed too quick and more than two, too long. Many professional actors moved back and forth, and while Leon thought we weren't attractive enough to make it in Hollywood, it would be my last chance to make a living as an actor. We'd had coffee with a few actors who had been hanging on a long time without making a living. I didn't want to kid myself.

IN THE LATE '60S, THE MOST striking thing about the Theater District was how filthy it was. Forty-Second Street was lined with one sleazy movie house after another. Sometimes, with JoAnne and Phil leading the way, we braved the clientele who needed a cheap place to sit down—derelicts, porn addicts—to catch a classic like *Diabolique* for a dollar. But the city was dangerous in those years, and I learned to watch my back and keep a good pace when I walked—no matter the time of day. I wore Leon's big army coat and a knitted watch cap at night when I took our newly acquired puppy, Molly, out for a walk. Even Molly had a theatrical pedigree since she was born to the Sardi's poodle when a beagle got into the kennel against the owners' wishes, and the litter wound up at my agent's office, looking for homes.

Leon and I worked on the apartment and stretched our budget by counting pennies at Safeway, the 3 Guys from Brooklyn fruit stand, and Pete's Spice on 1st Avenue. While I stretched awkwardly to paint the ceiling in the kitchen, I ruminated over the soap opera I had left so cavalierly and added up the salary I'd lost—maybe $100,000 that year. Whenever I landed a few days on a soap, I counted the months we could get by on two or three days' salary.

Looking for a job was my job. In training, facing myself day after day had been hard, but living this life presented hurdles I'd barely imagined. JoAnne said, "Being an actor is like being given a jail sentence," and while part of me revved up to the competition, another part quailed at the challenges. When you're raised to be polite, just getting on and off the subway is a lesson to be learned. I would stand at the doors of Bloomingdale's flummoxed, trying to find an opening to get through and into the store. So, putting myself forward for a part was challenging. Self-assertion for women had not yet reached my ears, and I traversed the tricky terrain between experiencing the joy of performing against a need to be invisible and not a target for criticism. After six months of receiving rejection after rejection, what confidence I had built up was sorely depleted.

When an agent calls an actor and gives her an appointment, it is either for an interview or one of two kinds of audition. The first is the general audition where an actor presents two contrasting short monologues; the second is the reading, for which an actor prepares a scene from the show being cast. My least favorite of these was the interview. Given a scene to read or perform, I could act, but I dreaded the stiff interview setup where three or four men sat at a table staring as you entered a nondescript rented studio space and took a chair facing them. Knowing they had the power to lift me from the unemployment line only made my anxiety worse. When I told people how I hated it, they told me "Just be yourself," but that was no help at all. Deep down, I didn't think I was enough—for the part, for the man, for life itself. Often the men at the table said nothing about the character. If they gave me a hint about the part, I could sometimes become that person before their eyes, but without it, I felt blank. "Tell us a little about yourself" were the words I especially dreaded, knowing they would be judging me for the part, and at times I shut down—dully reciting my training and experience. *Where was wit, vivacity?* As I talked, I seemed to hear myself, monotonous, and imagined their eyelids beginning to droop. At last, someone dismissed me, and I fled the scene.

But give me a reading, even a cold reading, and I was in my element. For Broadway, waiting to audition, actors crowded into the tiny stage-door anteroom, leaning against concrete walls or crouching on the floor, bent over our "sides" in an atmosphere thick with need. We arrived polished to a gleam, jostled against each other to let someone out from backstage while from inside we heard another name called. We stole glances at our competition. I studied everything: outfits, hairstyles, accents, and most of all whether or not they looked self-assured.

When I heard my name and walked with practiced poise to the stage, there was often a solitary work light burning onstage and a dark theatre. The bright lights from the lighting booth, when turned on, blinded you to the seats. From the black hole in front of me, I'd hear, "When you're ready," and I'd breathe, draw my energy to my center, turn into the light, nod to my reading partner—usually the stage manager. And begin. Afterward, a bodiless voice spoke from the dark pit: "Thank you." And I was offstage, moving past bodies, opening a door and stepping onto the concrete somewhere in the West Forties. I usually left those auditions wondering what to do next, feeling stunned. I had put my gut and soul out there in what felt like a high wire act, and then came nothing but the filthy Theater District streets. That first summer, Leon and I would often beat a retreat to the Village where scaled-down buildings, a quiet bar, and a stiff drink salved the sting. I knew day drinking wasn't a good sign, but often the shock of a cold martini felt like the right medicine. By the time we were settled, I wouldn't have considered going to a bar, too expensive. I drank only occasionally at home, maybe a beer.

When a reading went well and those strangers in the dark theatre decided I was right for the part, a callback came with the instructions to wear the same clothes I'd worn for the audition—so that they recognize me, and more: Don't improve too much on what you did because they liked it, but keep it utterly fresh and new, as if you've never performed this before. This usually followed days of rehearsing the scene while shopping in a grocery store, taking a bath, cleaning the house, or whatever other day job I had managed to land to help get us through the month.

After the callback came the waiting, the days of watching the phone, checking for a message at the answering service. Days passed and the acute phase of that purgatory of need and desire diminished, followed by a dull thud of disappointment or the self-laceration: If only I had done it better, truer, funnier, been more present when the fact was, sometimes, that the only problem was the leading man was two inches shorter than me.

Working out of town at a resident theatre helped put me back in the groove, and the day I returned to the city, I got a reading to replace Diane Keaton in a Woody Allen hit on Broadway. I went to see the show on Saturday for the Monday audition and felt well-prepared. Because the character made an entrance through a door, I walked to stand behind the set door, but it was pitch black back there, and I couldn't see my script, couldn't find the cue, couldn't feel the doorknob. I entered late—and rattled. Too inexperienced to know better, I didn't laugh it off and ask to begin again. Instead, I soldiered on as if nothing had gone wrong. *Acting as if nothing had happened.* Acting. Bad acting. Then came the "Thank you"—permission to run.

For an audition for Danny Simon, Neil Simon's brother, who was directing a comedy in Florida, I removed my winter boots so

I could move as if barefoot, and afterwards, he told me how well I'd done. Just one problem: I didn't have enough experience. As I hooked up the long laces of my boots, I felt as if I were dying inside but could only nod and say, "Uh huh," though privately I wondered how I could get experience if he wouldn't take a chance on me, even in *Florida*.

I know now that experience was exactly what I was getting— the experience of living an actor's life: showing up, putting the work out there, learning to trust myself, learning not to let fear jam my gears. The toughest days were those with no auditions, evenings with no hope, and financial insecurity looming large. I knew how to scrimp and make the money last, and that fall, Leon's salary was regular. He bought me flowers and the latest Stones album, trying hard to bring some grace notes in our life of uncertainty. We did all the labor on the apartment ourselves, removing chunks of plaster from the kitchen wall, waiting until night to surreptitiously deposit them in city trash cans. But no matter how hard we both tried, and no matter how pretty the flowers were, I could feel the darkness settling in again.

Jan persuaded me to see her analyst, though I couldn't imagine what the point was since I had no money to pay her, but I did go meet Dr. Alma Paulson who told me at the end of our meeting, "We Jungians aren't very well organized, so we don't have a clinic where patients can be seen for a reasonable fee, but I like to see some people on a sliding scale. What do you think you could afford?"

I was embarrassed to tell her how poor I was, so I fell silent until she leaned in and asked if I could afford one dollar per session. I quickly assured her I could do five, and we agreed to begin the next week. When I left her building, I wept tears of gratitude.

Leon and I also learned through friends about Dr. Soltanoff, the chiropractor, a man rumored to have put Bob Dylan back together after his motorcycle accident, and a consult with him in his low-rent clinic down on Houston Street changed my life. I'd never had a name for my ravenous hungers and moods around eating, but

Dr. Soltanoff explained that I had hypoglycemia, and that there was treatment. He also treated me with chiropractic adjustments for the spinal pain I'd had since puberty, and when he showed me the x-ray of the beginnings of arthritis in my lower back, I told him I'd felt better before I saw that. Still, he offered good advice, and though I felt gloomy about giving up drinking my daily quart of milk and eating cheese sandwiches, I felt the difference within weeks.

Once a week, after I saw Dr. Paulson, I went to the small health food store near her office to buy supplies to treat both mind and body well. I suffered from horrible nightmares, and Dr. Paulson encouraged me to write down my dreams, and with her and Jung as my guides, the nightmares changed and evolved and became fascinating. I began to see meaning in my path beyond whether I got the job or not, whether I could pay the rent or not. I was on an inner journey, a journey like that of Psyche in the myth, one with labors to be performed in order to come into wholeness.

It was the late '60s, and the city seemed to brim with danger. In April 1968, when Martin Luther King Jr. was shot and killed in Memphis where we had just lived, we feared that riots would break out in New York, and though we couldn't blame anyone for feeling fury and despair—I did too—I began to feel as if fear were stalking all of us who lived in this city. When riots broke out across the river in Trenton, New Jersey, my depression deepened. There seemed no reprieve anywhere. The little park where I liked to take the dog and read the *Times* filled with drug addicts and alcoholics, and one night an actor friend called us late from an uptown hospital to tell us that, after the show, he'd been knifed. We told him to take a taxi to our place where we gave him herbal tea and put him to bed on our pathetic sofa bed, and afterwards slept fitfully ourselves—was anyone safe? In June, I picked up the *Times* and learned that Bobby Kennedy was dead. I wept and wondered what had happened to the world.

Then one day a wolf came to our door. The ordinary-looking man in a suit wanted to collect for unpaid bills. I stood by the metal-sheathed door, puzzled, ashamed, and promised to take care of this right away, as soon as my husband got home. Months earlier, Leon had insisted he take over our checkbook and paying our bills. Glad to be rid of the responsibility, I'd acceded, but now I paced the railroad rooms, not wanting to believe what I'd heard. I was careful; I knew how to select the can of tuna fish that gave the biggest bang for my thirty-five cents, how to laboriously prep cheap lamb shoulder to prepare a palatable moussaka, but when Leon got home, I discovered he had written no checks *and* we had no money in our bank account.

I railed at him while he begged for forgiveness. He hadn't meant to do this to us, and angry or not, facts were facts. We were broke.

Leon had just received an offer to replace the lead in an Off-Broadway hit about a farmer in love and having sex with his pig. It was a *metaphor*, and in those days such fare constituted a career opportunity. The job paid about fifty dollars a week, and we were in debt, and being in a show in the city was key to getting a career rolling. I insisted: He had to take it. I promised to get a "real job"—a day job—until we were out of the woods.

The next morning, I slipped into a slinky pop-art dress and walked outside into the beautiful spring day. I bought the paper and checked want ads as I rode the subway to Midtown. One looked possible: "Size 8 Figure Model, Paraphernalia, College degree req." and a phone number. I dropped a dime into the pay phone near Times Square and dialed, and a woman with a heavy Brooklyn accent gave me the address and told me to come right over. I walked the ten or fifteen blocks to the Garment District where men pushed long racks of clothing down the street. It was chaotic and colorful.

Paraphernalia was known for its bright cotton mini-skirted A-line dresses with full length zippers. A design for the '60s, fresh and sexy, they announced, "I look great without trying, *and* I can be naked in nothing flat!" On the upper floor of this industrial building, I met Joe Cohen, the affable, hard-working boss for this hip fashion line. I described my background and told him my husband

and I had decided we could afford just one actor in the family. He okayed me, and I was led to an anteroom where I took off my dress and was measured, in businesslike fashion, by a nice older man. I was embarrassed by my ragged cotton panties, but he didn't seem to notice, and it turned out I was a perfect fit for their size 8. I got the job, and Mr. Cohen instructed their current figure model, a bleached blonde who was leaving to get married, to describe the job to me. Once in a while, she explained, I would "show" the clothes on the little runway in the long empty showroom, but mostly I would be available to the pattern makers as they created patterns for the designs and made samples for the designers to see.

And so, relieved that we would once again squeak by, I joined the working stiffs on the packed, oily-smelling subways, happy to be earning a paycheck. On my first day, they needed to show a finished sample to the designer Betsey Johnson who was leaving Paraphernalia to start her own company. A tiny, intense blonde, she was in a bad mood and ignored my smile, meeting it with a frown, tugging on the dress, and treating me as if I were a dummy as she gave notes to the pattern maker. Thankfully, the pattern makers were kind and truly sorry for pricking me with pins—again. I was given a light robe to wear and perched myself on an extra sewing machine near the industrial window where they didn't mind if I read while I waited for them to need me. And so began days of changing in and out of bell-bottomed pants, slinky fabrics, tunic tops, and sparkly textiles. My wardrobe improved—catcalls on the street were proof. I had learned to act tough, so I "flipped the bird" to the hard hats when they whistled, and my heather brown skirt and sweater got lost in the back of the closet. My confidence rose.

Leon was getting a lot of exposure and working with talented, up-and-coming actors, and often in the late afternoon when I was coming home, I'd find him and our funny mutt in our little neighborhood park. We walked home together where I prepared our dinner that we ate quickly, before he had to leave for the theatre. I often spent weekends or evenings cleaning the house or paying bills.

Ms. Magazine had not yet appeared on the scene, but I was getting ready to welcome the advice it would offer women—this division of labor was far from fair. Often, I met Leon late in the Village after his show, and while we got high with other actors, attended late-night concerts of the newest rock 'n' roll sensations—like Elton John—I was dismayed that I had no answer when people asked, "What are you in?"

All that summer of 1968, I rushed to join the hordes on the trains, ran up the stairs to the newsstand at Thirty-Fifth and Eighth, ordered an egg-cream (no egg, no cream), swilled it as I rode the metal elevator up to the shop. I ate lunch at Chock full o'Nuts or Jewish delis and prowled the District, where gobs of sequins, feathers, and glass beads fed my theatrically starved eyes. I wondered how long I would have to do this. At summer's end, when Mr. Cohen encouraged me to move up in the company, I felt despair rather than gratitude. I had hoped to get back to my real work. He was a good boss but making a commitment to this company didn't feel right.

After dinner one night, Leon announced that he wanted to get his own place. I was floored. Hurt. Silenced. I wondered if my resentment at carrying the financial load had caused this. I thought I'd been accepting and even cheerful about it. Maybe, I thought, I had challenged his opinions too often. Like JoAnne, in an argument, I could be challenging. And I didn't know how to "take it easy." I was tired, too, from the struggle to make it work. I didn't fight to make him stay; I had plenty of resentments that I knew impacted the way I was with him.

Soon after this announcement, Bill called with an audition for *Look Back in Anger* at the Charles Theatre in Boston, and on my lunch hour, I rushed over in my minidress to meet the director, Jon Jory. In a monologue where the character has lost her child in childbirth, I poured my heart out. I had played this role in Berkeley, but my approach had altered completely since then. I recalled how I had sat in a dark janitor's closet for thirty minutes to "prepare" myself to do it, but this time I went on my lunch hour, knocked it off, had time to eat, and landed the job. When the offer came, I took it. If Leon wasn't going to be at my side, I didn't have to sacrifice my career. I gave Joe Cohen my notice, and with a plan to be in Boston for two months, Leon and I agreed he could keep the apartment and take care of Molly while I was away. This would give him time to find a place and, I hoped, to reconsider our marriage.

In Boston, I found a room in a mansion on Beacon Hill with a tiny elevator run by water power. I felt as if Katharine Hepburn in her dowager role in *Suddenly Last Summer* might step into my room at any moment. I settled in, walked through Boston Common to get to work, began to know my colleagues. When our paychecks bounced the first week, together we went to Equity to make the theatre pay us in cash. A handsome man who was also rooming in the house took me to see the autumn leaves, and one night he and Kevin Conway and I accidentally got drunk on apple juice that had turned.

And then Leon showed up. He had been cast as the lead in *The Bacchae*—here in Boston, the next show. He wanted me to join the chorus and stay with him. And because I loved him, I ignored the Janis Joplin tune playing in my brain, "take another little piece of my heart," and I agreed to join the Greek tragedy.

During that run, on Sunday nights Stockard Channing and I became pals when we drove in her Volkswagen bug from Boston into New York for our Monday off. I went in to see Dr. Paulson, then took the train back on Tuesday for that night's show. One Monday I went to our bank to deposit my paycheck and get some cash for my train trip back. Again, I discovered our account was empty. I had deposited all my savings from *Look Back in Anger*, and all of it was gone. I traveled back to Boston in a fury, for the first time thinking about divorce. I simply couldn't believe he could do this. The last time I'd convinced myself it was a mistake. My parents had lived within their means; Dad had taught me how to make a budget in college. From time to time when I was young, I had overdrawn my account, but since I'd been on my own, it had never happened, and I knew I couldn't live like this. The insecurity was bad enough without having the money disappear. Much later I came to understand Leon better; he'd grown up an orphan and had learned to roll with the punches. It mattered less to him than it did to me to meet his obligations exactly on time. I should have learned not to put my money into a joint bank account, but those were days long before I had heard anything about codependence and knew nothing of compulsive spending. Instead of understanding it was Leon's challenge, I took it quite personally. My money was gone.

When our show closed in Boston, we returned to the city together but soon after that we separated. I faced the unfinished projects in the grim apartment that still had no decent heat. The big brown heaters the landlord had provided, Leon had insisted we move to the basement of the building—too ugly, he said. But replacements had never been found, and the holes in the walls where the old ones had been hooked up spilled plaster onto the floor. Everywhere I looked I saw work to do alone—partly stripped woodwork, just another dream left hanging. I needed to pull myself together and face and finish it, even if it was not what we had hoped and dreamed it would be.

And yet, some months later, when I ran into Leon at an audition, we went for a cup of coffee, and our conversation stretched on and on. There was so much that we couldn't wait to share with each other, and we were both so glad at how quickly the other "got it." Unable to part, we took the subway downtown together. He had a great workshop project to direct for Joe Papp, a play by a British writer we both admired from our year in London, and he wanted me to play a fantastic part in it. This was irresistible. As before, we dug into rehearsal, inspired and connected colleagues, and soon we were spending days, and many nights, together.

11. Eating the Big Apple

"Maybe everything comes out all right, if you keep on trying. Anyway, you have to keep on trying; nothing will come out right if you don't."

—*These Happy Golden Years*, LAURA INGALLS WILDER

TIME WAS RUNNING OUT: TWO YEARS in New York—mid-May—was coming up fast. California loomed. In April, just in time, I was cast in a prestigious workshop production with two Tony Award–winning actors. It wouldn't pay much, but I was elated. At last I would be onstage in the city, and I could contact all those casting directors to invite them. Workshops are nurseries for plays, an inexpensive way to get the play on its feet; everyone works for practically nothing and hopes for a hit.

Early in rehearsals, Bill called, excited. He had gotten me an appointment to read for *The Gingham Dog*, a new Broadway show, whose lead, Blythe Danner, had suddenly dropped out. I told him I was free at five, and he cried, "Karen, this is Broadway!" and thankfully the director let me go early. Embarrassed because I had no money to take the subway to the West Side, I worked up my nerve to ask the esteemed actor Jimmy Broderick if he could help, and without hesitation, he handed me a dollar.

Alone in the dimly lit lobby of the Broadway house, I read over the scenes, reminded myself to breathe, and to focus: The character was Southern, which was good. I knew the milieu. The stage manager introduced me to Alan Schneider, the director who had, for years, been bringing literary hits to Broadway. I knew his work from Stanford, when JoAnne had played the lead in his inventive Brecht production.

He had me read. Then again, with a suggestion. Next, he had the stage manager call the producer. More people arrived. I read again. Mr. Schneider asked me to do a couple of improvs, which were fun and left me feeling freer and freer. I knew I was getting close now to a real Broadway job. And then I heard, "Thank you," and it was over.

On the street, my sale shoes pinched as I headed for the subway, excited and at sea. *Would I get the job?* I hoped. *What would happen next?*

That evening as Leon and a friend and I sat around waiting, Alan Schneider called. He couldn't be sure I would get the part, but he could guarantee I would get the understudy. *Groan.*

Bill explained they were figuring out if they needed someone with more experience—a *name*. Just a few weeks before, I'd had a similar call from Hilly Elkins, the producer of *Oh! Calcutta!* an all-nude show everyone was buzzing about. For that one, the exhausting auditions had lasted all weekend—acting, singing, dancing, and, finally, each of us alone with only producers, choreographer, and the director, Jacques Levy. We had to take off all our clothes and improvise naked. Leon was already "in" and had recommended me to Levy. The next day the producer telephoned me to tell me I'd had an "excellent audition!" but they weren't sure "which way they were going to go." *Maybe they wanted a more obvious sexy look.* He asked me to let him know if I got another offer. That had been good news, but not good enough. This time I hoped against hope that I would get the job. The excitement and anxiety kept both Leon and me up very late.

And then in the morning Bill called. "You're going to Broadway!" The opening was scheduled for mid-May, just before my self-imposed deadline.

Lanford Wilson's *The Gingham Dog* was about an interracial marriage that was breaking up, and the script portrayed a heartbreaking, vicious divide. The isolation of the Black wife, played by Cicely Tyson, from her community and now from her husband resonated even beyond race. At that time, so many women were beginning to leave behind traditional expectations.

The first day of rehearsal, I was to report to the Golden Theatre at one p.m., but early that morning, I was scheduled to model in a big hair show at the Hilton Hotel. I was doing it because my neighbor, Luce Neilson, had shared the secret of how I could get my hair colored for a dollar, regularly—by modeling for L'Oréal's annual show. They experimented on our heads: one tint on one side of my center part and a slightly different formula on the other. No one could tell. I became a blond blonde, ever so much more castable than my natural dishwater blond.

That morning in the basement of the Hilton, scads of young women were getting fixed up at long, stainless-steel tables. The hair stylist to whom I was assigned had a complicated do in mind, and she set to work, setting, drying, teasing, curling, arranging, sticking in hair pins, and driving me crazy. A group of models was called. Another. And still she fussed. The room emptied. Still she combed. Finally, a line of us ascended to the catwalks, stood, turned, waited as the moderator droned on and on about the styles. We glided to the next spot, stood, turned. She elaborated. On and on. I had to be on time to the theatre, and as this went on, my pulse quickened; I feared this would never end, and when it finally did, I fled the catwalk, dashing through the nearest exit, ran into the kitchen where toque-hatted workers turned to stare. "Where, where? The dressing room?" They pointed, I burst in, dismantled the horrible hairdo, grabbed my work bag with the precious script, rushed to a service elevator, and dashed out through the revolving door, onto the cacophony of the avenue. Though only blocks from the theatre, I grabbed a taxi, and when I arrived at the Golden, all was quiet. The stage manager and his assistant were setting up. Silently thinking that I must apologize to L'Oréal, I sat down in the hushed theatre, ate my sandwich, and read over my script.

Lanford, a well-respected young playwright, was a skinny guy with lank hair that hung over his brow, protecting his shy eyes, and he already had several Off-Broadway hits on his résumé. He sat way in the back of the theatre during our rehearsals, respecting the protocol of running his notes for actors through the director. He rewrote as we "found" the play. Our leading man was George Grizzard, a handsome, boyish Broadway star, I was proud to work with as he had been the Hamlet in the ground-breaking Guthrie Theatre when I was first starting out. Cicely's role was predicted to make her a big star. The couple had all of Act II to themselves. Roy London, my age, played the fun neighbor-friend. He and I were both making our Broadway debuts, and from the start we hit it off. My character, Barbara, George's younger sister, was the *sine qua non* of Southern racism of some girls I had known at Sophie Newcomb.

We worked with gusto. Our leading lady seemed eccentric—she wore sunglasses in rehearsal, and I couldn't find her eyes, couldn't make a connection to her. During breaks, she stayed on the pay phone backstage talking to her agent. She resisted the director—told him that he was asking for "results," verboten in our American tradition of Stanislavski and "the Method." He backed off, cajoled, gave suggestions, tried to block the play. I began to stew about what I perceived to be Tyson's selfishness, but I knew little about the kind of pressures she was experiencing. During week two, she began to live on baby food due to indigestion, and she arrived at the theatre exhausted, distraught. People whispered that her former lover, Miles Davis, had harassed her by driving by her place all night long, honking his horn. And by the second week, finding my fellow actor was impossible. Still, in her climactic scene, when she phones for help from the Harlem family she has left behind, I was moved by the gutsy poignancy of her work.

One afternoon, George confided to me, "Remember, we are building a family here. You and I are going to be working in the theatre for the rest of our lives, into old age." He confessed that in a previous show, he had received raves and had become impossible, and that his behavior only hurt the play's "family." "Remember: No matter what happens here, whether people change their work when the audience shows up, whether you can count on people or not, we need to be true to the craft we love." I was grateful to have met such a gem of a man, and Roy and I also bolstered each other when spirits flagged.

Our costume designer, Theoni Aldredge, brilliant and vital, took me shopping for my costume, a neat suit. I had never been to the lavish dressing rooms at Saks, where saleswomen brought in designer clothes, made suggestions, and offered glasses of water. They brought out a bright yellow suit that looked great for the character and fit me perfectly, but Theoni said, "No, if you wear that, no one will even *see* Cicely." In the end, she selected a soft-pink wool suit custom-made for me. And until my claws came out in my scene, I looked demure. Carefully tailored, with a silk lining that slipped on smoothly, it looked put together, and I wore that suit to auditions until its lining shredded.

Meanwhile, the producers masked tensions with sweet solicitations. They offered Tyson many hugs and "Hi baby's." After our first complete run-through, I scrammed out of the theatre, headed to a familiar bar, ordered a whiskey sour, and waited for Leon's show, *The Boys in the Band*, to finish.[1] Roy joined us and asked where I'd gone, and I realized I had been such a wreck I had bolted after only the first act. The rush of emotion in the scene overcame my good sense, and the next day I apologized to everyone. But they had other, bigger problems.

On Monday, the call came that Cicely had been fired. Rehearsals were suspended until producers could hire a replacement. We would be paid during the holdover. There were few *known* Black actresses who could play this demanding role at the time but finally after about two weeks, Diana Sands stepped in, and we convened for a new first reading on Sunday at a producer's apartment in the West Village. Diana had played Shaw's *St. Joan* at Lincoln Center. She was upbeat, confident, funny, and although she lacked Cicely's delicacy and beauty, she brought to the show the vigor and spirit we needed. Our producers remained optimistic, but financial pressures were bearing down on them, and I was skittish too. When one of the producers tried to give me a hug and called me baby, I shrank away, blurting, "Don't hug me! Last month you were hugging Cicely" (and we know what happened to her). Roy was shocked at how direct I was, and as I look back, I see how anxiety so often caused me to utter some blatant faux pas over the years.

Excited for the first preview, I arrived inside the stage door to find Haile Stoddard, our sole female producer, posting the two-week notice on the call board. She felt terrible. She had been an actress, and wanted actors to be treated more humanely, but now, she had to officially fire us before we had even opened, just in case. In her distress, she thrust fresh daffodils at me.

Roy filled me in on the inside story—he and Lanford were lovers, so he had all the news: Diana's deal had so strapped the company that, on top of the payout to Cicely (who, if she had been let go in week one, would have been paid nothing but that week's salary), the producers had no cushion to keep the show running until word of mouth caught hold. We *had* to have a *New York Times* review, and it had to be a rave. And that was a high bar.

The night of that first preview, we were called at half hour from our dressing rooms to the stage for some final notes. Alan Schneider lashed out at me, because my hair was still in rollers, and I hadn't yet put on my suit. My entrance was an hour away, so I snapped back, "You're trying to 'bitch' me, and I don't know why." He raised his voice: "You'll never work in the theatre again." I burst into tears and ran up the three flights of stairs to my little dressing room. Our stage manager came up soon after and explained that Alan always did this, always had to have a scapegoat. "You are low man on the totem pole, so it has to be you. You haven't done anything. You're so good in the show. Just do your work." I thanked him, mopped up, and went back to breathing and getting ready. The show was smashing, laughs rolled in, and the eloquence of the final scene seemed to penetrate. As previews progressed, my husband heard scuttlebutt around town that I was the "next Sandy Dennis"—at the time she was a big Broadway star who was appearing in major movies.

When audience members come together in a darkened theatre, they become one organism, a great beast, and our audience on opening night was a different crowd, a cool customer. Some laughs came in spite of themselves, but the atmosphere was chilly, and I thought, *So this is the big time in the Big Apple*. Afterwards we attended a modest party at a private apartment in the Village and as was usual in those days, everyone stayed up eating and drinking until the reviews came out in the early morning papers. When the press began to appear, there was no announcement. People began to drift home. I appealed to Roy for news. Clive Barnes, the *Times* premiere reviewer, hadn't liked it. Our goose was cooked.

Leon walked with me through the Village, across town and into our neighborhood. It was very dark.

In the morning, the phone rang. It was my folks who were gleeful.

"Congratulations, kiddo! We heard you were great."

"No, no, we didn't get the *Times*," I corrected them. "We'll probably close soon. Depending what the Sunday paper says."

"But Frank called us. He said you're a star in the review in Los Angeles."

All I could think was that if I were in Los Angeles, that might have mattered. Here in New York, it did not.

The *Sunday Times* review moralized about the broken-hearted wife having picked up a stranger at a bar but didn't address the issues the play grappled with or any of our performances. We packed up.

I bought my costume. After the usual hugs and promises to get together for a drink, all the energy, concentration, and camaraderie dropped away.

After *The Gingham Dog* closed, I sat on my dingy couch and reflected on my situation. While George was going to his country house for a break and others were going on vacation, I was simply facing another blistering, stinking summer in New York with no money to get out. I was sick of going to commercial auditions where I rarely landed the job. Prestigious agents called wanting to represent me, but I was back on the unemployment line. How could I get some stability? The closing had been a bucket of cold water in the face, and I decided I was ready to make some big changes.

I had heard about Kristin Linklater, who had brought the LAMDA voice work over from London and was training voice teachers. I wrote to ask about enrolling in her teacher training course. She told me I could begin in the fall.

On the weekend I went to a new discount place called the Pottery Barn—sawdust on the floor, dishes displayed on packing boxes—and picked out a Danish skillet and Finnish dishes painted with deep cobalt flowers to replace the used ones I'd found at a junk store. Soon, I knew, I'd be afraid to spend any money. On Monday, the day off in the theatre, I dressed in the Mexican blouse and corduroy pants I'd just sewed for myself, and I waited for Leon. Since the theatre was closed, I assumed he would spend that evening with me. I made a special dessert and chilled the split of champagne the producers had given me for opening night. I waited. And I waited. He didn't call. He didn't arrive. And that night something snapped shut inside of me. In the morning, I wrote to him asking for a divorce.

IN NEW YORK, DIVORCE WAS NEARLY impossible without an eyewitness to adultery. Instead, as was common, I contracted with an attorney for a Mexican divorce. The fee included air fare and the next morning, in El Paso, two other clients and I were met by a Mexican attorney and ferried across to Juarez in a bright red VW bus for a perfunctory proceeding in an old adobe courthouse. After souvenir shopping and lunch (the all-inclusive divorce), we were driven back to the airport and boarded our planes. After the two tiny airline drinks were gone, I retrieved my souvenir package, went to the restroom, opened the tequila, drank, and bawled my eyes out. I retrieved Molly from my neighbor and climbed the three flights to the empty apartment. In the morning, I called my doctor to ask if he would prescribe a heavy painkiller; he said no.

At Dr. Paulson's, I twisted in my chair as I poured out the truth: I wanted heroin. I couldn't handle the pain.

"Karen," she said, "you have a broken heart."

I wept.

"If you had a broken arm, you would get it set, take care of it, let it heal. You must do the same for your broken heart. You have to grieve. Take time, take care of yourself."

I argued that I couldn't, that I couldn't face the market or anything, any people, even the people in the park where I needed to walk my dog. And no, I couldn't afford to go somewhere to rest.

"There's a place," she said. "A friend of mine goes there when she's finishing a book. It's a convent where the sisters take care of people in need. It's in Connecticut, not far from a train station, and it costs just a few dollars a night, room and board."

"Oh, I don't think I could face talking to people," I told her.

"You don't have to talk at all."

"Really?"

"Could your neighbor watch your dog?"

The nun's long habit trailed behind her like the tail feathers of a gray dove as I followed her up the carpeted stairs. For several days, I stayed in a large, hushed home in a room with a window looking out on the trees. I read and wrote in my journal. I rested. When I did go out, I walked along the wet road with its crushed autumn leaves on the shores of the Long Island Sound. I let myself feel as sad as I was. After a few days, I could hear the few other guests talking at the dinner table, but no one insisted I talk. And when my five nights were up, I returned to the city and began again, but this time patiently, gently.

THE GINGHAM DOG DID GIVE ME some credibility since many in the theatre community had seen the show and wanted to work with me. So over the next two years, I picked up roles on soaps, which paid well, and in stock and resident companies, working with marvelous, talented people. My new agent told me I was a star in Florida, and when I landed the stand-by on Broadway for *Butterflies Are Free* with Rosemary Murphy, in a role Blythe Danner had created, I had the financial stability and free time to pursue riskier workshops like JoAnne's in Grotowski techniques and voice teacher training with Kristin.

My work with Dr. Paulson also deepened as I retrieved my pale shadow from the sea and ran like hell from terrifying animus figures chasing me through the underground of the city. As we worked together, symbols transformed. Books by the female Jungians taught me to listen to my inner needs. Combining Dr. Soltanoff's fasts with a quiet day during my menses, instead of lashing myself mentally to be productive, I tuned into my moon self, the quieter me, drew primitive mandalas and modeled clay figures for the character I was rehearsing to become.

But Dr. Paulson was also practical and told me if I didn't finish fixing up my apartment, I wouldn't be able to move on. Some mornings, after breakfast, I smoked dope and faced the wood stripping, and when I could no longer take the fumes and the scraping, I painted the baseboards brown and called it done. I found pretty fabric for the darkest room's window and painted the walls yellow to go with a yellow brocade chair I found on the street. I forced myself to buy a decent couch. Dr. Paulson also taught me I must always have "mad money" in my budget, no matter how small it was, even if it was just enough to purchase chocolate cherries they sold in the subway station for five bucks or dinner out with friends in one of the inexpensive macrobiotic restaurants popping up in the East Village.

Kristin let me use her studio for practice teaching, charging a dollar a lesson, and Sissy Spacek came because her agent wanted her to lose her accent. She was just a kid then, and she never came back, but she did just fine *with* her accent. When Kristin developed a Shakespeare master class, I attended and assisted her. When *Cymbeline* was announced at the Public, I was ready, no longer an unknown there, having done a workshop production with Leon directing that Joe Papp had admired. Stockard Channing and I were neck and neck for the lead, a role some called "the female Hamlet." I called her a day or so before we expected to hear, wanting to connect with my old friend before one of us was disappointed. Stockard was practical: "We're so different. If they want you, they don't want me. If they want me, they don't want you."

They wanted me. AJ Antoon, the hot young director, cast Tom Aldredge (Theoni's husband) as Cymbeline, the king and Imogen's father, Chris Walken as the romantic lead. Sam Waterston was the evil buffoon and Bill Devane was cast as the seducer/bad boy. All were stars in New York, and I was gratified to get to work with them. Now, surely, this show would result in the breakthrough I longed for. Simultaneously, the *Butterflies* company offered me the role on Broadway—a yearlong contract. Foregoing the security, I went with Shakespeare. *Cymbeline* was only two months' work, but I wanted to make my mark in a role that hadn't been created by someone else and that used my training. Chris, my leading man, was wildly spontaneous and creative in rehearsal. We all worked hard in the summer heat, and when it was too much, we headed downtown to rehearse at the Public.

One evening after rehearsal, four of us—Kristin, her date, and her old friend Tuie, a screenwriter, and I—brought a picnic to the Delacorte Theatre in Central Park and stood in line for tickets for *Much Ado*. Tuie's wife was away for the summer, and he flirted outrageously with me. He and Kristin had studied at LAMDA together, and he had some British mannerisms. When it began to rain, he opened his big English umbrella, and we opened the wine and waited to learn if they would cancel the show. He entertained us all with a tale of his screen test in Hollywood years before where he'd worn a contact lens to correct a wandering pupil. During the audition—a love scene with a beautiful young actress—his lens slipped under his eyelid. He carried on stalwartly, blinking like mad as his eye began to water, then weep, then flood. Trained for the theatre, he never thought to simply stop, collect the lens, and begin again. As he acted his heart out, his bad eye tracked farther off to the side, one eye expressing ardor while the other wept. Later, he found out to his horror that the studio had pronounced the test so perfectly terrible that they had preserved it to show their contract players what *not* to do in a screen test. I doubled over laughing at his telling, and his wandering eye landed on me.

Much Ado was canceled, so we began to walk across the park toward 5th Avenue to catch the downtown bus. Kristin and I—of one mind—stepped right out into the rain, stomping in the puddles, then shedding our sandals. I turned my head up and opened my mouth—rain! Lightning flashed while windows of hotels and mansions on 5th Avenue blinked on in small yellow squares. Drenched, she and I ran into the glade laughing. I tore off my shirt and let it fly behind me; Kristin did too. We stripped off all our clothes and ran. "Free! We're free!" she shouted in her vibrant voice teacher's alto. "The muggers are all indoors!" We were laughing, screaming, running, until finally, breathless, we stopped, embraced, and howled. Then we turned to see the men dutifully picking up our garments, not looking at us, which only set off more peals of laughter.

Downtown, at Tuie's flat, Kristin and I took hot showers and emerged in big white terry robes Tuie loaned us, our heads wrapped in towel turbans. We sat around and drank hot coffee with brandy, now ravenous for our picnic. We ate at the table on the enclosed sun porch listening to the rain.

Dr. Paulson had been trying to convince me of the value of restraining my sexual impulses, but I had struggled so to break through my chastity and didn't want it back, and Tuie continued to press his case.

After *Cymbeline* closed, *Butterflies* invited me back as stand-by, and I played about one week of every month with Gloria Swanson. My folks were planning a trip to the Greek Islands and would return through New York, and the *Butterflies* producers agreed to let me play a matinee while they were in town. I rejoiced that my parents were going to see me on Broadway—a dream come true. I picked them up at their hotel, and we took a cab up to the Plaza Hotel. Fred's novel was being released, and we found him standing by the edge of the park hawking copies out of a baby carriage. *Benjamin Grabbed His Glicken and Ran* was a radical piece of fiction, including a futuristic novel-within-the-novel in its own transmuted English. Harper & Row had granted Fred carte blanche on the cover where he stood barefoot, vulnerable and so young. He called out to strangers, "Look! My book! It just came out!"

My folks congratulated him, and Dad bought a copy, and after my matinee, Fred met us, and we all went to Sardi's to celebrate. It felt to both of us as if now nothing could stop us. My folks' pride and relief were palpable. I thought back to the five years previous, years during which I had worked as a maid, a model, a salesperson, and trained to be a voice teacher; acted on the road, in summer stock, in soap operas, resident companies, Off-Broadway, in workshops, on Broadway, and in commercials, in Boston (three times), Florida (twice), Atlanta, Cape Cod, Denver (twice), Philadelphia, Massachusetts's North Shore, Cincinnati, and New York. And what I thought was that surely now, at last, I would be acting primarily in the city. At last, I felt like I belonged in the theatre community in New York.

AT FIRST, I HELD TUIE OFF, but he knew how to romance a woman, and it was "Autumn in New York" and "You Do Something to Me" and "Just One of Those Things." He shepherded me around the city in taxis, to dinner at Lutece and swank breakfasts in the after-hours clubs. His sophisticated flat on West 10th Street was a secret haven for me. His partner, an agent who had discovered Ali MacGraw, and his wife were energetic and fun, and we double dated. I heard their Hollywood talk. They were in development on a script Tuie was writing.

Tuie and I wanted one last end-of-summer fling before his wife came back to town. Each of us told friends we were out of town and instead stayed in the city where we binged on movies and restaurants and long walks. As fall arrived, we confronted difficult conversations over pastry and cappuccino. His wife returned to town, and he, plagued with guilt, returned to his marriage. But only a few weeks later, he was back confessing his love for me. I dissolved in tears. One night when Toni was visiting and Tuie was over, his wife called from a pay phone on the corner. She terrified us when she said she had a gun.

He returned to her, but I knew if he called again, I wouldn't be able to say no. So, when Kristin offered me the chance to take over the Voice department at LAMDA to help them get it back on track, I agreed. She was on her way to Europe for her Guggenheim to write her book, but she said we could meet in London first; she would lead a workshop to train a few teachers to work with me. It was a chance for me to run away, and off I went to London.

Though lonely, I liked the LAMDA students and wanted to share the work I believed in with them and felt I was gaining mastery over the voice work, too. Amy Irving, Jules' daughter, was in the first year, and I was able to offer her support, so work was good, but London was much more expensive than when I had been a student, and my salary was meager.

And then, just before Christmas of 1973, Tuie filed for divorce and flew to London to join me. He began a new script as I completed my contract. By March, both Kristin and I had been persuaded by Tina Packer to join forces with her in Shakespeare and Company, her vision of a Shakespeare ensemble, combining American actors' guts and British technique. When she offered me a production of *The Winter's Tale*, playing Hermione and Perdita, I couldn't say no. The company appealed to our high ideals, and with the backing of the Ford Foundation, seemed sound. We joined the small band of players in Stratford plus fine teachers like B. H. Barry, the legendary stage combat director, John Barton, and John Broome from the Royal Shakespeare Company, who inspired me with his pagan choreography for *The Winter's Tale*. Trish came from LAMDA, and we had one lone administrator. Tuie's script was optioned, and we all moved to the country with high hopes. We began to train and rehearse three plays under circumstances that turned out to be incredibly difficult.

By summer, when the company returned to the States to work at the O'Neill Center, we were ragged from work and long, contentious, red wine–soaked company meetings. One night, as the struggle to come to consensus wore on, my loose tongue wounded Kristin and she never was able to forgive me. My own health seemed in jeopardy as I spiraled down. Desperate about what to do, on my one day off I drove clear across Connecticut to see Dr. Paulson, and soon after that, I resigned from the company.

But I had no Plan B—until the night the phone call came from California.

Winnie and girls on the road again

swing Daddy made
PHOTO BY HARRY GRASSLE

with Dad Grassle and trike
PHOTO BY HARRY GRASSLE

what a good girl! 1st grade

Mamam, my mother, and Edith

with Barry in Berkeley
PHOTO BY KAREN MCLELLAN

a blonde looking for work
PHOTO BY WALT BURTON

Mr. and Mrs. Larry and
Janey Messmore
PHOTO BY HOLLAND PHOTOGRAPHY

home for Christmas with
Mama's pointsettias

Leon and I playing olde-timey serious
on our wedding day, Blue Light
Studio, 1966, Memphis, TN

John Glover and I in *Muzeeka* by John Guare
at Cincinnati Playhouse in the Park, 1972
PHOTO BY WALT BURTON

The Gingham Dog, with George
Grizzard and Diana Sands, 1969
PHOTO BY KENN DUNCAN © BILLY ROSE
THEATRE DIVISION, THE NEW YORK PUBLIC
LIBRARY FOR THE PERFORMING ARTS

Cymbeline, with Sam Waterston, 1971
PHOTO BY FRIEDMAN-ABELES © THE NEW YORK
PUBLIC LIBRARY FOR THE PERFORMING ARTS

with Fred after *Butterflies are Free* matinee, the day his novel was published, Golden Theatre

Mama with Karen backstage on Broadway

Toni and Karen at Nepenthe in Big Sur

day one, *Little House on the Prairie* Pilot

opening week of season one,
The Christian Science Monitor,
September 20, 1974, caption: *Victory
smiles? 'Little House' (Karen Grassle);
'Rhoda' (Valerie Harper): winners*

Vic and the twins relaxing while I seem
to be air-conditioning my backside

PHOTO BY GENE TRINDL; BY PERMISSION
OF MPTVIMAGES.COM

Mike cracking me up

PHOTO BY GENE TRINDL; BY PERMISSION
OF MPTVIMAGES.COM

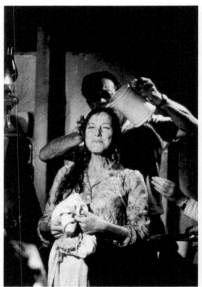

Larry wetting me down
for *A Matter of Faith*
PHOTO BY GENE TRINDL; BY PERMISSION
OF MPTVIMAGES.COM

relaxing between scenes
PHOTO BY GENE TRINDL; BY PERMISSION
OF MPTVIMAGES.COM

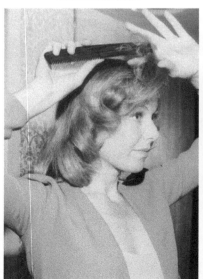

prepping for PR in Hartford

visiting Plum Creek on PR Tour
PHOTO © *WALNUT GROVE TRIBUNE*,
LAURA INGALLS WILDER MUSEUM

ERA march, Century City
PHOTO BY ALOMA

Toni's Larry at the
Hollywood house

Allen Radford and yours truly
on our wedding day
PHOTO BY GEORGE HALL

dancing with the Turnbaugh
Prairie girls
Photo by George Hall

Janey and her Sissy at the wedding
Photo by George Hall

reunion with Little House family
at Mt. Rushmore
Photo by Paul Valenti

Part Four

Breaking the Waves

"Go out and try your luck
You might be Donald Duck!
Hooray for Hollywood!"
—"Hooray for Hollywood," JOHNNY MERCER
AND RICHARD WHITING

12. Hooray for Hollywood

"How could you get a miracle?"
— "The Lord Is My Shepherd," Part 2, *Little House
on the Prairie*, MICHAEL LANDON

MY SHAKESPEAREAN WORK SUDDENLY concluded, Tuie
and I planned to pack up and leave Connecticut. We invited Fred
and his girlfriend for our last weekend and went down to the docks
to pick out lobsters. Contemplating returning to my grim New York
apartment, the chasm of unemployment, the dangerous walks with
my dog at night oppressed me. Molly would be glad to see me. That
was something. But Tuie refused to let my mood drag him down,
and he cheerfully picked fresh mint from our landlady's garden and
mixed up a batch of mint juleps.

In show business, living on the edge can be scary, but knowing
that a phone call can change your life is exhilarating, too. Expecting
to hear from Fred, maybe, I picked up the ringing phone and it was
Otis Young calling from California. And he had a job for me. I'd
met Otis one year earlier when I was walking home from Fred's
place on Christopher Street. It was one of those muggy nights when
so many people are out late trying to catch some air. In Sheridan
Square, I noticed two tall, good-looking Black men. As I passed by,
one of them called out, "Hey, he's Otis Young!"

I kept moving and said, "You are not."

The one identified as Otis Young beamed excitedly. "You know who I am?" I shook my head and kept walking, and in a good-humored way, they followed me. "Seriously," the other one said, "he is Otis Young. You know? From *The Outcasts*? On TV. Did you watch the show?"

I didn't mind the banter, but I didn't even own a TV, and I told them so.

"But you know my name?" Otis Young asked.

That made me laugh. I couldn't help but empathize with this out-of-work actor. By the time we reached Third Avenue, I'd stopped to give him my number, and when he called, he was mightily impressed to learn that I was about to go into rehearsal for the lead in Shakespeare in the Park's *Cymbeline*. We dated a few times, but by then Tuie's savoir faire and idiosyncratic style were sweeping me away, so Otis and I established a fun friendship.

And now, a year later, here he was, with a job for me. He was set to direct an independent movie he had written, and he wanted me for the female lead. The working title was *Leave That White Woman Alone!* And it would star Bob Dylan as a white cowboy, Sal Mineo as a Hispanic one, and Otis as a Black cowboy. I felt as if Otis had plucked me from doom. I was worn clear through from poverty and disappointment, and now there was this. Tuie had a new script almost ready, too, along with many LA contacts. He wanted to join me. Otis promised a ticket would be waiting for me at the airport, so suddenly I was on my way to Hollywood.

On the morning of our departure, Molly was growing sleepy from the tranquilizer I'd administered to her for the trip when Tuie buzzed me from the street to let me know he had a cab. I was stunned when we reached the street to find a sleek black limousine waiting for us. I knew we hadn't the money for this luxury, but for once, I didn't care. I was just grateful for the quiet, and the smooth easy ride.

But when I gave my name to the ticket agent, she found no record of a paid fare for me. Tuie's ticket was there—he had arranged it. But there I was with a drugged dog, bags packed, apartment sublet. I summoned my nerve and wrote a bad check for my ticket. I was sure Otis was good for it.

My folks met us at the airport in LA. I hadn't seen Dad in over a year and pulling him aside to confess I needed to cover a bad check wasn't the best way to reconnect, but I assured him that Otis's movie company would pay me back, and Dad was, as he so often had been, generous. Janey and her two little boys, my nephews, had come too, and on our drive to Ventura, I heard about how Mom and Dad's investment in the Ventura Hotel had done well ever since Mom took over as manager of this home for senior citizens. The place was thriving, caring for a lot of older people, and Mom and Dad were planning to put it up for sale and retire. Dad's real estate office had expanded too with Sara's dad and Janey having become salespeople.

For dinner we drove up to the old duplex on Main Street, and I began to feel thoroughly relaxed. My parents had never had an ounce of pretense, and I had the comfort of knowing that I was starting work any day. Tuie was optimistic about his new film project. For now, he and I would sleep on my parents' couch, but that would be temporary. Dad was cheerful about this new turn of events. For years he'd tried to convince me to move to California to find work.

The first weekend we borrowed Mom's car and drove down the coast to Otis's small rental house on a cliff overlooking the Pacific where he lived with his girlfriend and a menagerie of pets. We laughed a lot over the outrage the neighbors expressed when he planted watermelons instead of flowers. He told one ironic tale after another, each one on the theme of how in episodic TV he was forever being directed to act subservient to white characters. Now that he was going to make his own picture, things would be different.

But as the shoot date approached, no one reached out, and I hadn't yet received remuneration for the plane ticket. The picture was a Western, so I knew there would be costumes. I called the production office to ask when I would have a fitting, and Otis's girl-friend told me he was frantic. One of the financiers had pulled out.

"Well, what should I do?" I asked.

"Don't call us," she said curtly.

I had no contract, and now, it seemed, I had no job. I was in debt to my dad, sleeping on their sofa, an ignominious beginning to a Hollywood career. When one of their apartments behind the house became vacant, my parents—kind to a fault—let us stay there free and eat meals with them, and what I'd felt as the blues when I left Shakespeare and Company, shifted quickly to depression. For years I'd been able to support myself, and now I was broke and dependent again.

Mom, empathetic to my mood, and a spiritual seeker herself, gave me her book *Psycho-Cybernetics* to read. I began to practice the mental imaging exercises she thought would help lift my mood. Mom had discovered the Science of Mind when I was still a teen-ager, and the positive changes in her, I believe, saved her life. Now she introduced me to the exercises: recall a time when you did well, when you were at your best. When I closed my eyes, an image of myself playing Ophelia's mad scene or debuting on Broadway when I nailed the little Southern stewardess's narrow-mindedness came to mind; then, I allowed the triumph I had felt infuse first my mind and then my middle. This imaging helped to counteract the terrible self-criticism and anxious dreams I was having—of falling, drown-ing, slipping down a cliff—and I would feel all right for a few hours.

My practical side knew it was time for me to consider another career. For so long, I'd believed that if I followed my destiny, I would find my way, but now I felt lost. In college I had considered majoring in psychology, and ever since I had discovered Jung, I was convinced that meaning could be forged from psychic pain and confusion. I began to make inquiries about how long it would take for me to become a Jungian analyst and learned it would take years. But I could go to graduate school and become a psychologist in two or three years. The problem was how to pay for it. I had a few friends working in episodic TV in Hollywood, and they made more for one episode than I made in weeks of theatre work or in a year working with Shakespeare and Co. So I decided to try to get some TV work and go back to school.

Years earlier, when I was in Denver doing *Butterflies*, Maureen O'Sullivan told me her story. When she was a very young Irish beauty, Hollywood signed her to a studio contract, and after a couple of years, she had a vacation, bought gifts for her Irish relatives, and returned home in glory. But when she came back to Hollywood, the studio summarily dropped her contract. Young and stranded, she had to make a decision. She knew she had to bet on herself or no one would, so she gave the last of her money to a great photographer, and the photos he took of her landed her the job as Jane in the Tarzan movie. When that turned into a lucrative franchise, Maureen O'Sullivan became a star who was still working in her later years.

I decided I needed to bet on myself. A fellow actor knew a terrific photographer, and Mom loaned me money to pay her and for a new haircut at Vidal Sassoon (and gave me a little payment book and charged me 5 percent, which helped me keep my dignity). The night before the shoot, we drank wine and watched the Dick Cavett interview with Katharine Hepburn, and when she said, "You can't have it all," I sobbed, suspecting that was so. I pulled a razor blade from a razor and tried to cut myself, feeling despair. It had been years since I'd done that. I felt ashamed the next day. In spite of my swollen eyes, applying ice packs, and using my blouse to hide the scratches on my wrist, incredibly, the photos came out well.

I took the prints, including a topless photo—it was the '70s, and I wasn't the least bit embarrassed—to the Creative Management Agency. A number of young men made their way down the hall to look over those prints, and all these years later, it only makes me smile to think about the interest those photos aroused. But the agent and I settled on a photo, I had copies made, and CMA began to submit me for roles.

I planned to change my identity and changed my name to Gabrielle Tree. To me the name Gabrielle was made of curlicues while Karen was plainly chiseled. I chose my new "family" name combining theatre and glamour. Herbert Beerbohm Tree, a famous actor-manager in late-19th-/early-20th-century London made up his last name because, as he put it, it would be "too awkward for the audiences to shout 'Beerbohm, Beerbohm!'" Penelope Tree was a supermodel from British aristocracy on her father's side, with a mother who was an American socialite and political activist. Photographed by Cecil Beaton and Richard Avedon, Penelope Tree had lived with David Bailey, the hot *Vogue* photographer. So: Gabrielle Tree was born.

Many afternoons, I paced up and down as I tried to sit and read, waiting for a callback from the agency. Ventura was only an hour from Los Angeles, but the agency's phones were blocked from the area code. Thankfully, Tuie, with his great networking skills, discovered that his old friend, a studio executive, and his wife were going to London for a few weeks, and we could house-sit for them. So, we moved into a darling little Spanish house in Beverly Hills, and my father arranged for us to rent a powder-blue Ford that belonged to a woman who could no longer drive it. Lodging, check. Wheels, check. Now we had three weeks to hustle up some work. And we set to work, calling everyone we knew, trying everything we could.

Just before our housesit was scheduled to end, my tax refund check showed up and saved us. Tuie found a group of tired '30s bungalows with tiled roofs around a patchy lawn with worn canna lilies in Hollywood that were scheduled to be leveled in two months. We easily negotiated a very low rent—most people weren't looking for temporary, unfurnished places—and I felt as if we'd moved onto a set for a '40s noir film. Dad had just listed a small house in Oxnard for a young couple who were getting divorced and wanted to sell their furniture, so we bought their bed, refrigerator, sheets, and towels. Mom loaned us a dining table and chairs she had stored in the basement, and Janey's husband, Larry, loaned us his big pickup truck for the move. We were glad to be set until the end of 1972.

Now, to get some work.

THE AGENT CALLED ABOUT A PART and told me to "wear a dress and no makeup." Sure, I agreed, though there was no dress in my closet. In the '70s, it was common for actresses in Hollywood to wear tight jeans and little tops that revealed their midriffs, false eyelashes, and plenty of eyeliner. That look was "in," but the look, the agent said, was not helping Michael Landon cast Caroline Ingalls, Pioneer Mom.

I had to ask: "Michael Landon—which one of the *Bonanza* brothers was he?" Little Joe. *Okay*, I thought, *the cute young one, got it*. For years *Bonanza* was the top-rated show on television, an American institution on Sunday nights.

The agent went on: "Landon's becoming a good director. He just did an episode on *Love Story*." I had actually watched it on our little old TV with no cable hook-up. Its rabbit ears provided mostly black-and-white fuzz, but I could hear the marvelous Eileen Heckart.[1]

The interview was in a few days, so taking a deep breath, I went looking for a dress—most of my clothes were still in New York. At Design Research, known for modern designs like Marimekko fabrics and the classic bentwood rocker, I got lucky. The dress was made to order: soft, light brown wool with a fuzzy texture, a modest turtleneck, a flared skirt, and not too short. It fit softly over me, revealing enough to let them know what I looked like. And only forty dollars. I gulped and bought it. *It's an investment.*

I was encouraged when I arrived at Paramount Studios by a drive-on pass, much nicer than the usual routine: make a U-turn at the guard gate, hunt for a place in the large parking lot outside the studio, and hurry in the glaring sun down the hot asphalt streets bordered by cement "stages" with no windows, usually to a nondescript office building with poor signage. But that day, I got to park near an old office building at the northeast end of the lot where I saw "Desilu" on the pavement. I climbed the stairs to a dusty hallway and some offices once capacious and luxurious, now looking as if they'd been closed up since the '50s. The wall-to-wall carpet was faded to a noncolor, the furniture retrieved from the prop shop. A window onto the past. Since I'd arrived in Hollywood, I had been in a few casting offices—Universal, MGM, Fox—and none looked like this. Like our old Ford, it had seen better days. Like our bungalow, its heyday was past. It felt as if I had fallen through time into an old movie, just long enough to find my way to the future.

Halfway down the silent hall, I arrived at the office, my face naked, almost—I cheated with a little brown eye shadow. The secretary showed me to a waiting room. It was completely empty but for me. Puzzling. I was used to waiting rooms full of young women who looked a lot like me, quiet rooms where we eyed each other, competition zinging the air we tried to breathe. This time I waited alone, no script to study as this was only an interview. I'd rather read a scene any day, but at least that day I felt pretty good and figured my frozen disappearing act would probably not descend when the interview began.

After a short wait, Al Trescony, the NBC casting director, entered, introduced himself, and led me to a spacious office where I met Ed Friendly and Michael Landon, the producers. *Ah yes, that's the young guy from* Bonanza—*wow, handsome*. Mr. Friendly sat behind the big desk. Michael Landon sat off to the side in a chair. They were both tanned and smiling. A warm welcome, some chatting, and then the usual: "So tell us a little about yourself." I launched into my story in brief: a Broadway show that closed in five days, a Shakespeare company that had leeched all my savings, this past summer a movie lead that brought me to California only to fall through. My perspective on all this was darkly funny, and I was amused, myself, as I told the story. Mike's giggle was infectious. We all laughed at my recitation of the ridiculous lineup of hardships. I didn't mention that I was contemplating packing the whole thing in and heading back to school to study psychology.

Afterward, driving down Melrose, I thought, *Oh no! I told them I'm a loser!* Then, quickly, a moment of clarity: *I told the truth. If they don't want me, so be it.* When I got to the bungalow, Tuie handed me the phone. It was my agent. "Go back to Paramount and pick up the sides. They want you to read tomorrow." Then he confided, "Karen, I think we can get this one." My heart was thumping all the way back to the studio, my mind searching. *What do I know about acting on film? Nothing.* I had done some TV in New York but never prime time. I didn't watch except when visiting my folks at Christmas. All I knew was that I shouldn't be too loud; after all, I wouldn't have to reach the back row or the balcony. But I'd been trained to be aware of the space anyway—so I could do that. I broke down the two brief scenes into "actions" and back home, I practiced. A lot.

The next day when I arrived, I knew my lines by heart, but I held onto my pages. They asked me to sit on a big couch by the window. Mike got down on the floor beside me to read his part and looked right into my eyes. I needed all my concentration to keep from being distracted by how close he was. I hung onto the work, and we finished the first scene—a slightly comic one in which Caroline is puritanical about Charles mentioning the gender of the horses. He said, "Good." We read the second. Then he sprung up from the floor like a jack-in-the-box and exclaimed, "Send her to wardrobe!"

I was amazed, elated, confused—*I got the job? Just like that?*

Then Ed Friendly, with his toothy smile and silver hair, interrupted: "Uh, Mike . . . " he continued, "Karen, could you excuse us for a moment?" Mike looked over at Ed, surprised, but he and Mr. Trescony led me back across the hall, past the little reception area to Mike's big office where they asked me to wait. Apparently, there was a problem. Maybe Friendly hadn't liked me for the part? I was in an odd state, hanging fire, waiting. After ten minutes, they invited me to come back in. They were all very nice but made no mention of my getting the role, and as they said goodbye, Mike was still full of enthusiasm. There was no explanation, but his look told me I had the part. *I think I got it. I hope I got it . . .* all the way home.

I ran from the garages down to the bungalow, and Tuie came out all smiles as I lifted my arms in victory, exhilarated. He hugged me tight. "They want you to do a test!" he said, as if this were wonderful, but his words deflated me. I thought I *had* the part. I called my agent who explained that they had to get network approval, and NBC was asking, "Karen *who?*"

For Christmas holidays, Tuie and I were taking an important trip to Phoenix, Arizona, where I would meet his mother for the first time. She was a widow from a prestigious DC family and known for her imperious bearing, and this too would be a scary audition. She had settled in Phoenix when it was still small and wild when Tuie's father became the Episcopal bishop. Both sons had been sent to prep school back East. Now I, as "the other woman," had a steep hill to climb to gain her approval.

Thankfully, the *Little House* producers kindly set the test for December 26th, and on Christmas night I flew home alone to get ready. I felt that Tuie's mother had approved me, and back at home in our bungalow, I ordered pizza and tried to watch *The Waltons* special. The picture was so fuzzy, I felt like I was watching the road with double vision in a snowstorm, but I could hear the show, get the tone. I imagined *Little House on the Prairie* to be something like that.

I went to bed and tried to sleep but woke early and taxied over to Vidal Sassoon to get my hair cut. It never occurred to me they would provide an actual hairdresser. In the theatre, I had to research my hair style, dress it myself, and do my own makeup, but when I arrived at Paramount, I met for the first time Larry Germain, the hair stylist, and Allan "Whitey" Snyder, the makeup artist, who would become loyal allies. They were dyed-in-the-wool professionals, supportive without being too personal. Both had worked for years under the old studio system and had only recently agreed to do television. They had worked with some of the biggest stars ever, but it wouldn't be until later that I would hear those stories. That day they were simply reassuring, letting me know that when we got to NBC in Burbank for the test, they'd do my makeup and hair, and then stand by to fluff me up or powder me, as needed. I thought the lights and nerves would probably make me sweat. Indeed, I was sweating already.

Mike had gone ahead to prep for the test. When we arrived, he explained the plan to me. He had decided that dressing me up as a pioneer woman and trying to do a scene without an appropriate set would be ridiculous. Instead, we would do a simple interview to be broadcast on closed circuit to NBC executives in New York City. He and I sat on two tall stools, a table between us, on a generic living room set. Then a man named Teddy, who wore a camera lens on a cord around his neck, went to work. He turned out to be Ted Voigtlander, the Emmy-winning cinematographer, whom Mike had asked to come in that day to be sure I looked my best. The setup was taking quite a while, with the high studio lights hung from steel bars near the ceiling for shooting soaps on videotape. Teddy was used to the more complex and adaptable equipment used for features. I would learn that he had worked on *Lawrence of Arabia*. And although waiting was hard, Mike distracted me with funny anecdotes and jokes, and I laughed nervously. Waiting, waiting.

Finally, they were ready. We sat down on the set, and Mike asked me a simple question: Where did I get the idea for changing my name? I launched into a complicated explanation that included Carlos Castaneda, the notion of persona in Jungian psychology, a dizzy theory about identity, mystery, and power that was likely to convince my future employers that I had a screw loose. Maybe I did, but we didn't want to announce it.

"And cut it." We stopped. Mike asked if I would like to start again. I had gotten myself tied up in nervous knots and was grateful for the chance. We took a break, smoked a cigarette. I was powdered and fluffed, and we began again. That time, I kept it simple, much like our interview in the office, and in about ten minutes, it was over, and Larry and Whitey and I were back in the station wagon winding through Laurel Canyon toward Paramount, my head spinning. Before I could get back to the bungalow, NBC New York had called to approve me. Tuie returned from Phoenix, and we celebrated with champagne. I called dear friends in New York to tell them I was moving to Hollywood. I asked Fred if he would lose respect for me now. "Of course not," he said.

We drove up to my folks' place in Ventura for the weekend, all of us thrilled that the crisis was over. They were tickled that, at last, I would be nearby. I read the entire script that night and thought not only was Caroline not sexy, she was not at all shiny. In fact, she was a bit of a drag on her heroic husband, who was moving the Ingalls family out into the wilderness. She was a prig about her husband's reference to the horse's gender, not thrilled about the vast emptiness he called "home," and when the endearing Mr. Edwards showed up, she disapproved of him. It didn't seem exactly a star-making part nor a character who would generate lots of spellbinding roles in other projects.

As we lay on my folks' couch-bed in their living room, I followed these thoughts to their dead end: *It was a part. It paid. The show would run for some time—maybe as long as three years* (!), I figured. *But wasn't that exactly the problem? I'd be stuck in a TV series playing a negative woman who, at least in the writing, showed no sense of her own strength. Rather, she mildly chided her charming, violin-playing, adventurous, and handsome husband. But what else could I do? Gamble on getting another part?* Just one month earlier, I'd been ready to quit acting altogether, and now I had a job. *Wasn't it good enough for me?* I fretted through the night, and the fold-out bed kept reminding me that I was still in my parents' house, our bungalow would be torn down soon, my parents were getting ready to retire, and where would I be if I didn't do it?

Take the damned part and be grateful you're working, my self concluded. The show would help me get a name, gain some cachet, and experience.

After we shot the pilot, Ed Friendly took me to lunch and talked me out of my newly acquired stage name, and I'm forever grateful that he did. I *was* Karen Grassle, and I accepted that. And it meant so much to my father. It has to me, too.

Little House on the Prairie was set to begin shooting on January 5, 1974, my dad's birthday. A few days before, we threw my folks a retirement party at Janey's home. It was a glorious time for all of us. Mama and Daddy finally were going to have time for themselves, I was going off to shoot a pilot for a television series, Toni and her husband Larry were finishing their dissertations in Santa Barbara. Sara was there, too, along with her folks, both of our fathers being two Missouri boys carved out of the same mold: funny, loving, and sometimes manic. Tuie and Larry "streaked" the party, giving everybody a good shock. Running through an event naked was all the rage at the time. Daddy got good and drunk in a cheerful way. And so did I.

13. Having It All

"I want you to be my wife."
—"He Loves Me, He Loves Me Not," Part 1, *Little House on the Prairie*, MICHAEL LANDON

WHEN THE CALL FOR THE AUDITION first came, I knew nothing of Laura Ingalls Wilder's *Little House on the Prairie*. Although her books became children's classics as early as 1932 when they first appeared, for years they had been out of print or unavailable in my local library. The story of the Ingalls family as told by the middle daughter began in Wisconsin (the Big Woods) where her parents, Charles and Caroline, grew up, married, and started their family. They had three daughters, I learned as I began to read the books: Mary was nine, Laura, seven, and Carrie, three. Charles Ingalls was a restless spirit forever seeking new possibilities, so the family begin their trek to Indian Country—the prairie.

The pilot told the story of that journey to find a new life, the challenges of moving to an unknown part of the country to homestead, in what would later be called Kansas. In the end, when a government treaty with the Osage required the family to move on, they would lose their new home. The tall trees in the mountains of California not far from Yosemite would stand in for the Big Woods.

And since I'd never been to that part of the state, I looked forward to seeing places I'd only read about in stories like Mark Twain's "The Celebrated Jumping Frog of Calaveras County."

I packed the first two books, *Little House in the Big Woods* and *Little House on the Prairie*, to take with me up to the location, and flew with the cast to Sonora. Everyone was booked into a two-story motel but I had requested a bathtub, so they put me next door in the Gunn House. Much too nervous to sleep before our first day of filming, when my alarm sounded at four thirty a.m., I was already awake. Then the wake-up call came from the desk of the Gunn House a little before five, and I stumbled from my room outside to the parking lot next door where a brown station wagon awaited me. I crawled into the passenger seat, said a cheerful good morning to the driver, who seemed surprised by my cheer. He had the heat blasting, for which I was thankful.

It was still dark as we drove through the little mountain town of Sonora onto the highway and up the steep, curving mountain road toward the location. Close to Twain Harte, at nearly eight thousand feet above sea level, the car stopped. Dazed, I had no idea where to go. Someone pointed me toward a trailer, where I found Larry and Whitey who had arrived early and organized the makeup trailer: bright lights, makeup, and a big, hooded hair dryer run by a generator. This would be the first of a thousand mornings when Larry sprayed my head with water he had warmed and set my hair in little curlers, then put me under the dryer for twenty minutes. I was happy to learn the union required we be fed breakfast on these early calls, and that day the second assistant director brought my favorite meal—bacon and eggs—on a paper plate along with some coffee from the catering truck. I tucked into the food while my hair dried, then returned to Larry who would "dress" my hair. I could see the hair pieces on a shelf, both for the bun and for the long three-quarter fall—Ma's hair when worn down.

My hair was short, and when I first was cast, I'd been concerned about that. Mike didn't think it was a problem, but I explained to him that women didn't start cutting their hair until the 1920s, so he called out to Evelyn Maloof, the secretary, "Get Larry Germain on the phone." Hair was expensive and took time to create and to match, so it was decided: My hair would be rented, for now.

Larry artfully combed my short locks into pretend waves on the sides to look as though they belonged to the fake bun at the nape of my neck, and next I moved to sit in Whitey's big flexible barber-like chair. Whitey had a gentle touch with the makeup sponge, which, as the years wore on, I would learn to appreciate more and more, and when I was made up and ready, I walked outside.

In the freezing early morning light, the crew was unloading and setting up. Our assistant director, Miles, spotted me the moment I emerged from the trailer. A kind, energetic man with prematurely white hair, he directed me to a long trailer with many small steps and doors—our dressing rooms and the crew lavatories. Richalene, our costumer, was waiting for me as I climbed the wobbly metal steps into my narrow dressing room and private toilet in the "honey wagon." Later, when the weather warmed up, I understood where that name had come from, but that day everything was new, and strange. Richalene helped me into my costume as I wondered about the peculiar chemical smell coming from the small heater. But I didn't ask. There was too much to take in. Dressed in tights, long underwear, and petticoats, even turning around in the little toilet was a challenge. Once I laced up my black leather boots with their many grommets, I climbed out of the trailer, back down the wobbly steps, careful not to trip over the long skirt. I shivered in my inadequate jacket. The day was dawning and the scene struck me as an Ansel Adams photograph. Steep snow-padded mountains, thin crisp air, giant pines everywhere. I spotted a storybook cabin dwarfed by immense trees just up the snowy road. A yellow gleam shone from a window. This would be the home of Caroline's parents in Michigan, and on this, our first morning of shooting, we would play a scene of goodbye—the Ingalls family was leaving the little house in the Big Woods to begin their trek west.

Men in puffy dark coats were setting up black-and-silver equipment they carried from a huge truck. Those men were strong, and I was impressed with how they were able to work so dexterously; they seemed to possess secret skills, and they had the union cards to prove it. Other men in cowboy hats hitched horses up to a simple covered wagon; these, I learned, were the wranglers. Real wranglers dressed in real jeans. After all my years in the London and New York City theatre scene where the men were artists—men Vice President Spiro Agnew scornfully dubbed "effete intellectuals"—I suddenly felt as if I were a tourist who had somehow landed in a foreign land. When I spotted Mike high up on a crane looking through the camera, I was relieved that at least I knew someone here. The crane carried him down, then lifted him back up, and I could see that being in charge put him on top of the world.

I headed for the catering truck, where the caterers were beginning to prepare lunch for about a hundred people. There was a spigot for hot coffee on the outside of the truck, so I filled my cup and walked around unsure about what to do. I spotted Melissa Gilbert, the little girl with auburn braids who would play Laura, and when I said hello, she quickly piped up: "Do you have your tears ready?"

At first, I could only think, *Egad, oh no! Now I'll never be able to cry,* but I recovered enough to say, crisply, "Yes, they're in my pocket." Actors have a cardinal rule: Don't focus on results—where we're supposed to arrive emotionally in a scene—and *never* tell another actor what we expect them to do. I could see that working with kids was going to be really different.

Seeking to build rapport, I walked towards the adorable twin girls, only three years old. Children their age could work only a few hours, but with twins that extended the time to six. "Hi," I said, "I'm Karen, what's your name?"

"Sugar Lump," said the first one in a muddled sing-song voice.

"Oh," I said, barely understanding but carrying on. "And what's yours?" I asked the other darling girl.

"Foxy Robin," she said in a cutesy voice.

Well, I thought, this is Hollywood. What did I expect?

Melissa (Missy) Anderson, ten years old, modest and polite, was playing my oldest daughter, Mary. She and I had met earlier at a costume fitting at Paramount where stunned by her fairy-tale princess looks—long, flaxen hair and penetrating blue eyes—I whispered to her mother how pretty she was. I was surprised that her mom seemed surprised. That day the girls were all dressed in their nineteenth-century calico or plain cotton with modern jackets, while I was plain in my dark-brown raw-silk suit. The location filled me with awe, but standing around was making me jittery. *When would we get to work?*

When they called me for rehearsal, I headed for the cabin, stepping carefully on the gravelly road where mud puddles had formed from melting snow. The incongruity of all the equipment, and modern dressed people tromping around so purposefully in this high mystical forest, seemed—well, like a movie, and I was excited to begin. I called hello to Mr. Friendly and looked up at Mike, killer good looking, funny, and whip smart, as the crane carried him to the ground. As the girls and I arrived, he began to describe what we—the family—were to do. We would walk away from the older couple, the man and woman playing Caroline's parents. Then I was to climb up into the wagon seat—a neat trick in long skirts—and Mike would hand Carrie, still a baby, to me. He would settle our other little girls, blond Mary and spunky Laura with her buck teeth, under the canvas and join me on the buckboard.

We rehearsed. We tried it for the camera. I figured out that the wagon wheel was my purchase to easily mount to the seat. And finally, Pa swung up onto the driver's seat and called to the horses to go. A slap of the reins, and out we moved. But we hadn't moved far when Mike called softly, "And cut," and the wranglers halted the team.

Then we got out of the way. Lighting and camera crews made adjustments. They practiced again with our stand-ins. The crane with the mounted camera swooped slowly down and focused on the action on the wagon. I stood nearby and smoked as I watched, and I could feel adrenaline rushing through my veins. Onstage I had to create the entire atmosphere that supported my character's reactions—trees, sunlight, snow gradually melting to crash heavily from the branches onto the earth—but here it all was for me. The entire scene alive, present, powerful. And I was moved by it all, feeling the enormity of this moment for Caroline, who, in all likelihood, would never see her parents or her home again. She was leaving for the wilderness with three little girls and no idea who or what they would meet on the way or where that way would lead. By the time the costumer arrived with capes and coats, I was in a near trance. Larry adjusted my bonnet. Off came our jackets. The children, better prepared than I, had good ski jackets, but of course, they had their parents. My winter coat, a black wool princess maxi coat, would have been silly here, and besides, that was back in New York, another world. Here, I wore Caroline's wool cape.

Miles called for the cast, everyone was ready for our first take. Somehow Mike was able to both play his part as Pa and direct. We shot it. Mike checked with the camera man to find out if he was happy with it, conveyed to me that he liked the phony little smile I gave him as we pulled out. I was glad for the feedback. I'd wanted to reveal she was on board but not happy, making a sacrifice in order to be loyal and brave even as she left behind the comfort of the only home she had ever known.

Then the scene was broken into parts, and we began to shoot what is known as "coverage." The camera shot each character individually, each angle requiring a completely new setup. As the sun rose higher, lights had to be adjusted so each scene looked precisely the same, although they were shot over hours of takes. Last came the back of the wagon with Laura's little face in view for the narration. None of us had yet spoken a word of dialogue, and when Mike was directing, if the shot didn't reveal him closely, his handsome stand-in, Hal Burton, a skilled horseman and stunt man, sat beside me and called to the horses, "Ha!" and we pulled away.

When the assistant director, Miles, called, "Lunch," I was surprised the time had flown, but I was also ravenous. We walked over to the long tables that had been set up with folding chairs on a relatively flat area near the catering truck. When I got in the line by the truck, Miles came after me, "No, no, you go up front," he said as he led me to the head of the line. That embarrassed me. In Berkeley I'd learned respect for labor, believed in equality for all. The last thing I wanted was to seem snooty or more deserving than others. But I was learning protocol. The steaks and vegetables smelled fantastic and I carried my tray to the tables and found an empty spot where some of the men in cowboy hats were eating and talking, and I smiled and said a shy hello, and they clammed up.

I couldn't imagine what I'd done wrong. How could a woman stop a group of men engaged in conversation? I wondered if it was because I was a woman. Or an actress. Or playing a lead. I fell back on friendly and quiet and cut into my steak to fortify myself for the cold afternoon's work ahead, chewing away, feeling energized to be thirty-one and learning a new craft.

As the Ingalls family moved across the country, the *Little House* company moved down the mountain to shoot short scenes that would create a collage of their journey. Between shots, the girls and I warmed up at smudge pots. Though the land was more rolling and varied than Kansas, this part of California was relatively flat, with open land carved by big rivers providing panoramic visuals. Hal Burton drove the wagon over roadless acres, and seated on the buckboard, I bounced along beside him, my appreciation for my pioneer foremothers growing ever deeper with each new bruise. For the rest of that January, we settled in at a Great Western motel in Stockton, equipped with a family-style restaurant where we ate dinner. We rode out to the big ranch where we would "build" the cabin and to the county fairgrounds, where a huge Quonset hut became our studio for interiors.

Each day I began early when Larry arrived at my door with his spray bottle and curlers to set my hair. Despite Larry's gentleness, being sprayed wet and set in tight curlers before dawn felt like torture to the night owl I was. The big dryer was parked in my room for the rest of the shoot. Once I was dry, Larry artistically camouflaged my curlers with a chiffon net, and he and I would walk down to meet Whitey and the driver to head out to location, where it would take an hour to get Ma ready to shoot. Fortunately, none of us were morning chatter bugs, but we were the early birds since it took Mike and the girls just thirty minutes to be made up and dressed.

Mornings were beautiful. Our caterers dispensed fat, hot breakfast burritos wrapped in big white tortillas that will never taste better than they did out there just after sunup in the wintertime in the wilderness. At eight a.m., barring surprises, we rehearsed, then waited for the crew to reset lights before we rehearsed again, got our final make-up, hair, and costume touch-ups. Mike worked precisely and also managed to be the main entertainment, cutting up or chatting with everyone right up to calling, "Action." As the years went by, I became familiar with his repertoire of jokes and his Olympian memory for them. It was incredible to me, who could never remember a joke in the correct order.

ONE DAY DURING A DANGEROUS RIVER-crossing scene, I arrived on the bank of the river and found the crew hard at it— stretching ropes from one side to the other downstream of our wagon, just in case. *Just in case of what?* I wondered. *Oh, just in case the wagon goes downstream!* We climbed aboard. Pa and Ma feel truly worried and warn the girls to hold on tight to Carrie. Then Hal Burton took the wagon into the middle of the river, where it was secured with lines stretching to the shore on either side. Both he and the stunt woman were dressed as the Ingalls parents.

Mike and I sat safely on the buckboard, while Ma and Pa appeared to be near toppling over. Some of the crew wearing tall boots rocked the wagon as we played the fearful scene, acting our terror, but afterwards we stood safely on shore while Hal and Jeannie Epper[1] brought the wagon over the slippery rocks to the riverbank. I wanted to do the scene myself, but no one else would entertain the idea. When I thought of real danger, I thought of flaming car crashes or flying trapezes, but this was only a river.

Hal drove the horses hard, again and again, shouting and cracking the whip, to bump the wagon wheels over the rocks, and as I realized how dangerous it truly was, I held my breath until they made it to shore. Jeannie jumped off the wagon and asked me for a cigarette, and I saw as I lit it that her hands were shaking. I felt a rush of gratitude and amazement at the way Hal seemed to take it all in stride, though later I would learn he had broken his back three times.

THE FIRST DAY IN THE QUONSET HUT, we leapt ahead to a scene in the cabin Pa and Ma hadn't yet built. Each night I studied hard to be sure I knew what Caroline had already experienced, where she had just been in the moments before the scene began, where she would go when Mike called cut. I had never before shot anything of any length out of sequence. I reflected on interviews with famous actors and apocryphal stories I'd heard young actors tell about how the great ones did it. Marlon Brando, whom we all idolized, talked about creating an organic relationship with his props, which is what I had done in the theatre, using props as a way of expressing my character's inner life. That day, when I walked into the "cabin," I had been given a large basket of laundry. I studied that laundry, figuring out which pieces were Charles's, which the girls', what needed mending, and as I concentrated on the laundry, our rehearsal moved right along until suddenly there was a big blank silence—it was my turn to speak! Little Melissa Gilbert piped up with my line, and I looked up, hot with embarrassment, but Mike just laughed, letting me off the hook. When they gave me the cue again, I said the line, and we broke for another setup.

As he touched up my hair, Larry whispered, "So you've had your baptism by fire," and that day he became my ally, confiding hints to me about what other actresses had learned to do to take care of themselves in the controlled chaos of a movie set. Jennifer Jones wouldn't talk to anyone between rehearsal and shooting; Susan Anspach walked off to sit by herself. He let me know I didn't have to hang out with the crew, be jolly and social the way Mike was. Of course, the children were shepherded off to school at every opportunity, and I had no other actresses to talk to. Mike was busy directing, the actor playing Mr. Edwards hadn't yet arrived yet. But as Larry blended my short hair back toward the bun, he became my friend.

The basket of laundry was whisked away, and I never saw it again, and that turned out to be the way with our props, no chance to build a relationship with them, to imbue them with history or feeling. I discovered I would need to find a new way of working with props, and it would take all season one to do that. I found an out-of-the-way corner for my director's chair, and that became home base.

In the theatre, lines had never been an issue for me. By the time we had blocked the scene, the words seemed embedded in both my mind and body, but now I was needing to learn lines cold, all alone, in a motel room, repeating lines to myself after a twelve-hour day of shooting outside in the cold. Each night I sat in bed writing them out, checking and testing myself again and again until I conked out, page in hand.

We worked in the Quonset hut when it rained, and there we shot many night trekking scenes. Truckloads of dirt were brought in and spread about, and long grasses "grew" from it. Big heaters took the chill off the vast, uninsulated space. One afternoon, as we were shooting a family scene around a campfire by the wagon, I noticed a ladybug. They're good luck, so I showed it to the girls. Soon we saw one after another and they were everywhere, and we were all delighted. The heat had caused their eggs, hidden on the sage or grasses, to hatch and cover us with good fortune.

Then came the turkey. In a Christmas scene, the girls in their Sunday best are listening to Pa play the fiddle by a roaring fire as Ma plucks the turkey. Pa and Ma are putting on a brave front, since they have no presents for their girls. And suddenly a frozen Mr. Edwards, a large bearded man shrouded in ice, arrives. He had forded a freezing stream and made his way to the family, bringing along potatoes for dinner and shiny tin cups for the girls. Ma's antipathy toward him melts, and from that day on she accepts him as a friend. And indeed, Victor French had climbed down a snowbank and wearing nothing but pink long johns, strode into the mountain stream up in the Gold Country. I could hear his whoop across the snowy field as I headed for the trailer.

It was a bright, sunny day when we were to do the Christmas scene and, as I walked from the set to the makeup trailer and back, I noticed a turkey tied to a stake on the grass, but I didn't tarry to befriend the bird. I wasn't sentimental about its fate, but I also didn't want to bond with it before the scene. When it came time to shoot the scene, there was the turkey on the rough table where I needed to pluck it, and when I placed my hands on it, it was still warm. Suddenly, I was blubbering over that turkey, my eyes flooded with tears. The rehearsal was stopped. I was allowed to mop up, and Whitey repaired my face. The warmth had gotten to me, but Ron Chinique, our prop master, trying to help, told me he had left it to lie in the sun, thinking that would make my task easier. For a city girl like me, who only knew meat in refrigerated cellophane packages, the warmth of that creature undid me.

When we had wrapped up all the interiors, we left the Quonset hut and spent the rest of the shooting schedule at the ranch/home site. One dark morning, when we arrived, we discovered that the heavy rain in the night had mired the trucks deep in the ranch road mud. As we sat in our toasty car, Kent McCray, the unit production manager, and many of the crew were trying to dislodge the trucks. "You don't see a production manager out there like him. That Kent McCray is one of a kind," our driver said. I had met Kent in the hallway outside Mike's office soon after I was cast, and Kent exclaimed when he saw me, "Look at that face!" I couldn't imagine what he had seen in my face. I had no idea what "type" I was, but from his comment, I guessed it was good.

An enormous man in height and girth, Kent was in his early forties when we began *Little House*, and his whole crew reflected his fine work ethic. There was none of that "not my job" attitude I had noticed backstage on Broadway. Everyone pulled more than his own weight, and that energy flowed from Kent. He was second generation show biz; his father had been drawn into radio while working in insurance in Hartford and become a station manager. Kent liked the entertainment world and had an interview with a renowned professor of theatre at Yale who offered him his first job. Working for the professor, he learned all the elements that go into making theatrical magic, and while still young, he ran the Central City Opera House high in the Rockies, where he dealt with everything from housing to high-strung divas.

NBC moved Kent's father to Los Angeles just as television production was exploding there. The groundbreaking coaxial cable made national transmission from the West Coast possible for the first time. While visiting his folks, Kent attended a party where he met a vice president from NBC. The VP invited him to interview, but Kent demurred. His father, he said, wouldn't approve of nepotism, but the man simply said, "Come on, we'll deal with that if you get the job." When he told his folks he had, his dad hit the roof and left the room to call the vice president. He returned to the table mollified, saying, "It's only week to week, so we'll see what happens." What happened was that Kent's career with NBC lasted for more than forty years. He grew with the medium, absorbing lessons and incorporating skills as television itself developed.

After many years in television, Kent was tapped for *Bonanza*—the top show in the country, but Kent's first contact with Michael was challenging. On his first day, Mike called down to him from a high rock where he was rehearsing a scene, demanding a car to take him to an appointment that afternoon. The schedule showed Mike shooting all day, but Mike reminded him again. Kent didn't contradict him. Rather, he drove to a service station for a pay phone to call NBC to see if there was some mistake. No, Michael Landon was to shoot all day. Armed with the facts, Kent returned to location and told Mike he was scheduled all day. Mike laughed and told Kent he'd been "testing" him, and Kent had proved a star couldn't intimidate him. This may not have been the test Mike had in mind, but it paid off in a relationship that lasted for over twenty-five years, and I was just one more beneficiary of this great team. Kent, I knew, was the secret weapon behind the success of *Little House*.

That dark morning, Kent saw that muddy mess on the road as just a problem to be solved as soon as possible, but it was harder than they thought, and we were sent back to the motel to wait. Soon, we got the call to return to the ranch. Scheduling, equipment, budget—all this rested with Kent, and all of it worked beautifully. From the earliest days, I counted on him, depended on him, and knew if I had an issue with anything, I could take it to Kent.

On the ranch, we moved from hill to crevice to give the impression of different backgrounds. Wanting to be a good worker, I carried my chair, traipsing up small hills and down to the cabin site, though eventually I learned why carrying chairs was the prop guys' job. I needed my strength for my job. When we were shooting the collage of the cabin building, the Ingalls parents worked side by side like a team, and I thought of my folks. Next, Caroline dug a ditch. Mike called, "Action," and I dug, and dug, and dug some more. *What does he want*, I thought, *real sweat?* Finally, I looked up and saw the whole crew just standing there, and Mike burst out laughing. They had long since turned off the camera, and once I got the joke, I felt silly but joined in the laughter. Mike used such practical jokes to keep the atmosphere light, and it worked.

VICTOR FRENCH ARRIVED AT THE RANCH, bringing support to the Ingalls and fresh energy to the company. Vic's character, Mr. Edwards, was the lovable rascal, an untutored scamp whose loyalty and fun lighten the struggle of the Ingalls family. He and little Laura were a match as he taught her how to spit some distance, making Ma frown. She disapproves of him until his loyalty and affection for the girls wins her over in the Christmas scene. Once we were on the air, people fell in love with Mr. Edwards.

One day, Vic and I sat on a log getting to know each other while Mike was shooting scenes with the girls. He loved to talk. And I began to get to know this big, lumpy man, whose gnarled face fit his rough prairie costume, whose breast expanded with love—love of his art, love of his son, love of the diminutive actress he'd wooed and won. A fine actor, passionate, so dedicated to his craft, he'd expound on the art of acting until your ears buzzed.

When I learned he was engaged to Julie Cobb, I felt as if we were long lost cousins. Her brother, Vince, and I had fallen in love all those years ago during my first show in Berkeley. Back then Julie was still a young girl and lived with their mother, Vince with their father, the famous Lee J. Cobb. While Vince and I were going together, Mr. Cobb and Vince's stepmother did not invite me to stay with them, but his mom, the actress Helen Beverley, welcomed me with actual open arms. On nights I stayed over, Julie spent the night with a friend. I had slept in her bed.

Vic was happy to be making a break with the tough guys and criminals he'd been type-cast as previously. He aspired to direct and told me excitedly that he was pretty sure he was going to have his first crack at directing an episode on the final season of *Gunsmoke*. After we finished the pilot, he asked me to play a part. I counted this as a vote of confidence, and all of us in the cast had such fun working with him and together that we all bonded.

Vic turned out to be a drunk, too. Of course, neither of us knew this at the time. As years went by, we would both pay a price. But that day on the log, it was all blue sky and optimism.

THE SHOW WAS SET TO AIR in March, and pressure was mounting to finish on time. Two weeks in, the editor came up to work on a rough cut, while we continued to shoot. To speed things up, the dailies, flown down to Hollywood each night, were transferred to videotape so the editor and Mike could edit, on site. Sometimes the tule fog in the valley grounded the small planes.

One evening after work Vince Gutierrez, the editor, approached me and said, "You know you have to match your work." I had no idea what he meant. He explained that in medium shots and close-ups, I had to do the same thing I'd done in close-up, but I still didn't understand. Everyone talked about Dustin Hoffman's brilliance for doing something fresh and different for every take.

I took my question to Mike, who wasn't happy the editor had approached me. Things were going well, and he didn't want me to begin to feel self-conscious. But he explained it simply: If I opened a door with my right hand as I said a line, I needed to repeat that in all the covering shots, so they could cut different takes together. Many times, over the years, Mary Yerke, our diminutive script supervisor with the eagle eye, called out, "Braids back!" meaning Laura's braids had been behind her shoulders during the master. Mary wrote furiously in her script the details of our gestures and behavior, and her script was the postproduction bible.

Movie companies take months to shoot a two-hour movie, but we had four weeks to shoot our pilot, and Mike and the cinematographer were aiming for high-quality work. Many actors prefer shooting television to features because of the quicker pace, and for me shooting outdoors was invigorating. I had plenty to do to keep up with my character's development, continuity, and the new technical skills I was acquiring. I ate like a horse, and I lost five pounds.

At the end of the shoot, Tuie drove up to take me to Big Sur, my favorite place, for some rest and relaxation. We were on top of the world. He had found us a house to rent in Laurel Canyon and had moved our sparse belongings in. We had a home again. His divorce had been finalized at long last, and when he proposed, I accepted. It seemed as if suddenly everything was right with the world.

14. "We're Home"

"We'll all fare better if we work together."
— "The 100 Mile Walk," *Little House on the Prairie*,
WARD HAWKINS

MY FOLKS INVITED TONI AND LARRY to join us at their house to watch the pilot on March 30, 1973. They prepared steaks and baked potatoes and plenty of red wine. And we all settled in to watch. A Saturday morning screening of the pilot for cast and crew had been a week or so before, so I knew my work was pretty good, but I was anxious for their approval.

When the NBC announcer mispronounced Grassle, we all groaned and shrieked, but by the next commercial break, they had corrected it. I was breathless to hear what my parents and my dearest friends thought of the show and my work. (There was only one scene where I cringed at my acting.) They were positive, and we were all so happy. My folks did not give compliments. Dad might have said something like "Pretty good, kid," but I could see they were very proud. Toni approved and that meant a lot because of her intellectual standards, and this was, after all, television. But she and Larry were enthusiastic, and we all looked forward to having many fun times together.

That weekend Tuie and I found an inexpensive lamp in Ventura for our new place, and when I offered to write a check, the store owner said, "You have an honest face. I trust you," and I whispered to my fiancé, "Twenty million Americans can't be wrong." I felt lighthearted and free about becoming famous. For a while.

In my hometown, recognition was vindication for all those years of feeling unpopular, rejected by my peers, misunderstood. One Christmas, when I was visiting from New York, one of my dearest friends had said, "Oh are you still doing theatre? I thought that was a phase," and that had hurt so much. I couldn't help but celebrate having "shown them all." Weekly national appearances at eight p.m. on a top show with second billing to America's favorite guy: this kind of success, everyone understood. My father was especially jubilant that we had received the green light and we were set to produce twenty-four episodes, beginning in May. Tuie and I stripped wallpaper, painted, and feathered our new nest. We bought an old Volvo, and I drove the twenty minutes or so over to Paramount to see the set while it was under construction.

At the gate, when I told the guard my name, he checked the list quickly and waved me through. Driving onto the lot felt a little like being *in* a movie. Near the back corner, I found the enormous warehouse-like space, our stage—Stage 30. I parked beside it, another privilege of my new job. All was open and bustling that day.

Near the entrance, I found the Little House under construction. Mike introduced me to Trevor Williams, the art director, and proudly showed me around: the authentic size of the Little House—and it was *little*—the way the walls and ceiling could fly open to make space for camera, lights, and crew. On soaps I had shot in New York, the sets were more like the theatre, with three-sided walls, the camera positioned as if they were the audience. This set opened like a doll house and was reassembled with hinges so the camera could move in and around it, able to shoot as many angles as possible. The Little House would be a warm place, where the table held platters of scrambled eggs, family discussions took place over rabbit stew, and Pa's fiddling inspired the girls to dance in front of the cheerful fire.

One third of the double-sized stage was curbed off and filled in with dirt. Within that area stood the barn. As the scripts developed, the barn became the dark place on the prairie, the place where one night Mary would start a dangerous fire when she secretly wanted to study after bedtime, where Caroline, during a thunderstorm, would try to rescue a wayward cow and faint. Here, standing by the fence, Charles would tell Caroline that Mary was going blind.

Opposite our home set, past a wide concrete area, was a second huge space, where the interiors of Oleson's Mercantile, their home, and the church/school were built. A collection of miscellaneous flats was shoved against the back wall, ready to be assembled as needed. Eventually, the set designers built the Edwards family and later the Garvey home interiors. The design team, ably led by William Jefferies and Donald E. Webb, painted, wallpapered, curtained, and furnished interiors as required. Or, as if by magic, they created a tent hospital or art gallery that would be filmed, then dismantled. I loved this evanescent aspect of show business, so much like life and so exquisitely expressed by Shakespeare:

> " . . . melted into air, into thin air. . .
> And like this insubstantial pageant faded
> Leave not a rack behind."
> —*The Tempest*, act IV, scene 1

Once the show was up and running, craft service tables with gallons of coffee and boxes of sugary donuts were set up on the concrete island between the Little House sets and the town sets. Nearby was a rolling telephone stand with two phones for the entire company, phones that were automatically silenced when we were rehearsing or shooting a scene. And in the far rear of the main stage stood the makeup mirrors and tables, set back far enough so their bright lights did not interfere with the set lighting. There we sat in barber chairs, while Whitey and Larry put on our masks, packing up at the end of the day when we were going to shoot on location.

To the side and behind the makeup section two heavy doors led out to a row of small huts that looked as if they'd been thrown together thirty years before; these were our dressing rooms. Mine was conveniently located just past the big doors, across a wooden walkway. Inside was a twin bed with an old spread and bolster, a makeup table with poor lighting, and a chair as well as a hook to hang my clothes. Meant to be a private place, a place where an actor can study or prepare or nap as the hours drone on, ours had bugs and heating that either blasted or was off entirely, and although I was used to the bare bones of theatre accommodations—even on Broadway—I was surprised to discover these to be so poor in Hollywood. As time went by, I would read and hear about other TV actors' trailers with their favorite color bedspreads and kitchenettes where they could rest, study, even prepare food, but Mike's production style was austere. He didn't care about dressing rooms or trailers and the parties were noticeably economical, but at that moment, everything was exciting.

JUST BEFORE WE BEGAN SHOOTING season one, Mike invited Tuie and me to dinner at his home up above the Beverly Hills Hotel. We drove the curving road, passing one large estate after another, some hidden behind walls, others behind massive greenery, some boldly displayed for all to admire or envy. Jangling with excitement, I hunted for Mike's address. "There!" Tuie spotted the grand house of indeterminate Southern California style, and we followed the driveway around to the back and parked in the expansive brick courtyard. Above, to the left, we saw a terrace, pool, and large pool house for entertaining. Tuie had savoir faire with everyone, regardless of their money or status, and I took comfort in his ease. As we walked towards the impressive front door, I flashed on the maze that had been my life: Shakespearean heroines, sudden call of "You're on" on Broadway, rigorous Growtowski method on bare floors, planes and trains and Greyhounds, rented rooms, rising to the occasion, in love and bitter breakups, all leading here. We rang the bell.

A uniformed servant led us to a downstairs bar, decorated like a Western saloon. Mike, bristling with vitality, burst into the room followed by his wife, Lynn, a knockout in her casually expensive outfit, her luxuriant brown hair with sunny highlights flowing over her shoulders, her dazzling tan. She was perfectly made-up, and her ample breasts were hinted at but not displayed. She perfectly personified a type—sexy enough for a *Playboy* centerfold and already a mother of four. She greeted us warmly.

Mike was proud of his bar, designed around his *Bonanza* treasures taken from the set when the show wrapped, including a wagon wheel. He poured us each a drink, and the other guests began to arrive—Eydie Gormé and Steve Lawrence, Jay Bernstein, the publicist, thought to be the man behind Farrah Fawcett's sudden fame. After drinks, we all walked upstairs to the dining room. Mike and I were seated opposite each other at one end, with Jay between us while Lynn and Tuie sat with Steve and Eydie. The chairs were high-backed, upholstered in lipstick-red velvet; the china was gold-rimmed, and the surprising "silverware" was gold-plated. Everything seemed to trumpet expense.

Mike asked Jay about his vacation, and Jay gushed, "Just extraordinary. Very small party. Great guide. We were hunting grizzlies."

Grizzlies! Hunting grizzlies! At first my astonishment puffed out in air that would have turned to a guffaw, but Mike cast me a quick admonishing look: *Don't laugh at him!* I smothered my incredulity, stomped on my lightning-quick Freudian analysis of the short, goateed man with his silver-knobbed cane. *Important to our show. Get along.* He was hot in Hollywood: His name evoked an aura of mystery, because he knew how to make people suddenly and wildly famous. Mike had hired Jay to promote *Little House*, and this, it turned out, was the reason for the dinner: to let him get to know me, and maybe for Lynn to see I was no kind of threat—after all, I was so *nice*.

At the end of the evening, Lynn said, "You're going to see more of my husband now than I will." The fact struck me. Yes. The hours. That would be so. Except weekends.

IN THOSE DAYS, TELEVISION SEASONS RAN like the school year. Each series produced twenty-two to twenty-four episodes each season, and from Easter until the May sweeps, the networks, there were only three, ABC, CBS, and ours, NBC, showed reruns. For the May sweeps, every effort was made to pull in the audience for those all-important ratings that set the price for the commercials for the following season. The stakes were high; a good lead into the evening could secure a network a win for the entire night.

Once the season began, each week the time to produce an episode grew shorter. We needed seven working days to shoot one episode—nearly a week and a half, but episodes aired week after week with no pause, so we had no margin for error. Post-production—editing, looping, sound effects, color correction, scoring, and recording the original music, which David Rose wrote to suit the story—took time too. So once the season opened, the pace began to gallop. With a filmed show, like ours, the ratio was one hour of product (actually forty-eight minutes because of commercials) produced more than twenty times over ten months. We worked as if making a full length feature every fourteen days! Mike had explained all this to me before we began—when our start date was delayed because of problems finding a location the pressure increased. The week after Labor Day, the all-important air date, loomed.

They finally secured a ranch in Simi Valley and leased it from the Getty Oil Company. The Ingalls home site and the town sets had to be built, and we could begin. The irony of the location was not lost on me. Before my big break, I had traveled to England,

New York, and a multitude of towns in between only to wind up in Ventura County, less than an hour from Main Street. It had a kind of poetry to it, T. S. Eliot's:

We shall not cease from exploration
And the end of all our exploring
Will be to arrive where we started
And know the place for the first time.[1]

And yet, all of it seemed necessary. Oddly, I don't think I could have accepted it before then.

I LEFT LAUREL CANYON IN THE early morning darkness, drove the curving road east to connect to the Ventura Freeway North, then further east on De Soto Road to a small spur of freeway. As dawn broke, I passed by the Garden of the Gods, massive, rugged red rock outcroppings I recognized from dozens of Westerns, the spot where the bad guys set up an ambush for the good guys. New tracts of homes were being developed, growth that would explode during the years we worked in Simi, but that first day, building had just begun, and mostly I drove past modest, rural homes some with little windmills and gnomes in the front yard under a stand of eucalyptus trees. I felt tenderly towards Simi Valley with its dry desert hills softened by golden grasses. It looked much the same as it had the summer after my freshman year of college, when I took acting lessons with a European coach who lived in Santa Susana, a few miles from the Getty ranch. As I drove, I thought of how I had nearly dropped out of college back then.

As I turned onto the ranch road, I passed one small farmhouse, then big trucks hauling gravel rolled by, and at last I came to the unpaved parking lot. From there, I was ferried up a dirt road in one of the studio's brown Ford station wagons with some of the other early arrivals. Near our new home, I climbed into the brand-new makeup trailer, designed for the long haul by Larry and Whitey. They were standing there smiling, ready to go.

The ranch was ideal for us. There were no telephone poles or other modern detractions. It had miles of unspoiled, rolling terrain with grand oaks—completely unlike the actual prairie but serene in an old California way. The first site was for the Little House. "Plum Creek" had been installed and ran alongside the house. Sprinklers were turning the desert scrub green. The barn and barnyard, off to the side, were ready for their occupants. Just up the hill was the outhouse. When the story begins, the family is living in a sod house built into the side of the hill, while Pa builds the Little House. That day the atmosphere was full of optimism and enthusiasm, both for the Ingalls family, relieved to be settling in, and our company, anticipating years of steady employment.

When Charles exclaimed, "We're home!" and lifted Ma up to carry her across the threshold, both surprising and embarrassing her, everyone could tell Ma was pleased. And I was pleased, too. It was like a moving day that promised more permanence than I had known in years.

We began with episode two, "Country Girls," a sweet show, inspired by *On the Banks of Plum Creek*, with all of us still dressed in our clothes from the pilot. New to the town of Walnut Grove, Mary and Laura are insulted by Nellie Oleson (our town brat), who calls them "country girls" and ridicules their simple clothes. The way Mrs. Oleson (Katherine MacGregor) negotiates like Scrooge with Caroline over the price of her eggs, everyone knew this character was going to be a lot of fun. Ma spends more than she means to on pretty blue cotton print material when Mrs. Oleson suggests a drab homespun would be more "suitable." Once Caroline hears about the insult to her girls, she cuts it up for two little dresses. When I saw what the costumer had designed, I was tickled because they looked just like the first-day-of-school dresses my mama had made for Janey and me each year, with puffed sleeves, a ruffle at the hem, and a sash that tied in a bow in the back. Ma sews all night. Then Laura writes an essay and is chosen to read it aloud to the community. It's full of appreciation for her Ma. The synchronicity with my own life made me feel very connected to the story. Like Mary and Laura, Janey and I went off to school together in those homemade dresses in the morning and came home in the afternoon.

The dirt service road that went past the Little House both served the practical needs of the company and was the route for wagon and horses to reach "Walnut Grove." A narrow path high above served as the short cut for the girls to walk to school. Often Ma took little Carrie and her eggs to sell at Oleson's Mercantile. Shot from a distance, the small female figures in the tan hills that seemed to stretch without interruption to the sky gave the perspective of a land unsettled, a brave family breaking new ground. In these scenes, the girls and I were isolated from the crew, without microphones, and those moments allowed us to develop an intimacy. I told the girls stories from my own youth to entertain them and to weave the personal connections that resonated ineffably in our new "family." I hoped as Mary and Laura, they would feel close to Ma, and in fact over the years, the bond the girls and I forged through our work and our off-camera times became so strong, it has lasted all these years.

But back then, in the beginning, I wanted to infuse our private scenes with the intimacy I sometimes had felt with my own mother, those afternoons when we shared a quiet connection while she was making dinner. I remembered standing at the kitchen counter beside her, feeling the crisp snap as the end of a green bean gave way, pulling away the string, one side then the other. At that time of day, with Janey out playing and Daddy not yet home from the office, I had my mother all to myself, and the kitchen felt peaceful. I could confide in her as we looked at our tasks and not at each other. During those times with her, my chest would swell with an anticipation of what life might bring, would surely bring. She, with her large practical hands and her little crippled finger, made dinner for our family every day, day in and day out. "Feeling like it" didn't figure into it. Chicken broth breathed fragrance into the air, a promise of the dumplings that would soon bob like buoys in the rich liquid. In that atmosphere, I was open to her philosophical lessons, and by the time I was in sixth grade, she had taught me that when I "didn't like" someone or something about a person, it probably meant that it was something I didn't like about myself. Snap, string, toss. Snap, string, toss. When my frustration with not being popular was painful, she promised me that when I got to college, it would be different. She taught me patience.

She'd fry up bacon or salt pork, sauté the beans in that, add just the right amount of water, cover the pot, and cook them until the smoky meat had completely penetrated the beans. It was hard not to burn the beans. Too much water spoiled them. Patience. As they turned limp, dark, and delicious, I learned from her. These days of course we look down our noses at vegetables cooked until the life has gone out of them, but damn, they tasted good, and on the set in those first days, I understood that Ma might make beans the same way.

And all that patience that she taught me, I needed it during the long waits over the months and years of shooting. Waiting while lights were arranged, while the film was changed, while props were set up. In those first weeks, of course, I had no idea how to pace myself and tended to be ready at all times. I was stimulated by working on location—a set to inhabit, no wings, no backstage—it was *all stage*. We were making a movie, turning make-believe into something actual, and everything had an aura of romance to me. But as the season wore on, I needed patience with myself. I struggled with the fatigue of those early mornings and the long, long days and so much to learn. I had arrived in California broke and tired but paradoxically fit—I could do a back flip and perform a daunting monologue. But Hollywood was a different order of stress from Shakespeare and Company. People were constantly touching me, adjusting my hair, powder, lips, wardrobe. By the end of a twelve- or fourteen-hour day, I didn't want to be touched.

And that, coupled with the strain Tuie and I had begun to feel during Shakespeare and Company, took its toll on us.

The first week in Simi, the weather was steaming hot. I sweated inside my sponge rubber breasts and dark silk suit. My feet boiled in my new custom-made black boots. Fear gripped me—finally, I had a good job, but could I hold up under these conditions? Mike seemed unaffected; if anything, he thrived in the heat. It was only June, and I knew that heat would press on into July and August, increased by dry east winds in September. The little girl playing Nellie collapsed; ice packs were brought to apply to our director's neck. I moved slowly and held on. Whenever I was anxious, I tended to pull way inside myself, where I felt safe. Whitey powdered away the sweat on my face. When the weekend came, the weather cooled, and I learned that we'd been enduring an unusual heat wave, not typical weather for June, and I thought I would make it after all.

JUST AS MA WAS GLAD TO HAVE moved near a community with a church and school, so I was happy to see the arrival of other adult actors—colleagues. As the leading lady, I felt a responsibility to meet them graciously, to extend a hand and a smile as if I were the hostess of a party.

The episode that would open season one, "A Harvest of Friends," introduced the audience to the Ingalls and to Walnut Grove and all the townspeople as the Ingalls family arrive at Plum Creek. The show played up Pa's strengths as a hero figure of superhuman dedication and integrity. As an actor, Mike knew his strengths, too. He looked wonderful with his bare torso sweating as he worked, or when he did a slow burn to Mrs. Oleson's insults. He made the audience cheer when he stood up to the notion that he should've been in church instead of working in the field: "God understands farmers, Caroline." When this aired, I felt I could practically hear people across the country nodding and chiming in, "Damn right."

There were two father figures in the pioneer town. The civil authority was represented by Mr. Hansen (Karl Swenson), the owner of the mill and Pa's first employer. Our spiritual guide was Reverend Alden (Dabbs Greer), who led us in sermons with simple morals and singing "Bringing in the Sheaves." The school was held in the church by the pretty and compassionate teacher, Miss Beadle (Charlotte Stewart). Each of these characters was introduced in the book *By the Banks of Plum Creek*, but the Oleson family was created in the TV series offices. Mr. and Mrs. Oleson (Richard Bull and Katherine MacGregor) represented well-to-do parents with spoiled children, Nellie (Alison Arngrim) and Willie (Jonathan Gilbert), who were sharp contrasts to the Ingalls's plain thrift, hard work, and counting your blessings values. Mrs. Oleson was our villain, and Mr. Oleson was her upstanding, long-suffering husband, continually embarrassed by her bad behavior. Doc Baker (Kevin Hagen) completed the core of the characters of Walnut Grove, like a Chekhovian doctor with his fashionable buggy, romantic black hat, good manners, and educated charm. The actors, every one of them, were superb professionals.

Mr. Hansen was the first Walnut Grove character introduced. Karl Swensen looked exactly as he should for the older Swedish man with a tidy gray mustache and twinkly eyes. As the founder of the town, he carried authority, and Karl, as the most seasoned of us, and the most intellectual, was a natural. He had been working since the '30s on Broadway, on radio, and in films and TV and had had many long runs. Of all the wonderful supporting players, Karl was my favorite. In childhood, I fell in love with his voice when I listened to radio plays and the other programs he starred in. I was buoyed by Karl's days on the set. He was forever learning, was interested in everything, and I could always count on him for stimulating conversation. We had fun talking politics—probably because we agreed. The two of us were liberals in a sea of conservatism.

Of all the adult supporting characters, the one who most gratified the audience was Mrs. Oleson, played by Katherine

MacGregor. She had recently come out from New York and had all the vivacity and commitment required for a dedicated New York career. She was a large-boned, sexy brunette, and when we met, she said, "Call me Scotty." We hit it off immediately because we both liked to rehearse, and we both loved to laugh. We practiced our scenes together over and over and had special fun with our egg scenes. Scotty attacked her character with courage, unafraid to be disliked. I loved that about her. Sometimes an actor's desire for approval washes out the shadow side of her character, but Scotty never held back. She was definitely "Method," a devoted student of Sandy Meisner, a famous New York acting teacher who taught such stars as Jack Nicholson and Diane Keaton. And she was also a student of Stella Adler, who was famous among actors not only for her work with the Group Theatre, but for coming back from Russia after meeting with Stanislavski and viewing the work at the Moscow Art Theatre. From the ship docking in Manhattan, she shouted to her colleagues, "We've got it all wrong!" As Stella's student, Scotty was just one person removed from the high priest of 20th-century acting, Konstantin Stanislavski. Such stars as Marlon Brando, Montgomery Clift, and Kim Stanley practiced "the Method," and Marilyn Monroe had studied at the Actors Studio with Lee Strasberg. Al Pacino studied there. So had Scotty.

People loved to hate her. Whenever I was on the road promoting the show, people asked me about Mrs. Oleson. What was she *really* like? Really: Scotty was warm and boisterous and generous with a hearty, earthy laugh. She grew up in rural Colorado with a harsh mother, and I could imagine her as a ranch woman. Her tough exterior and brutal frankness masked the marshmallow tenderness of her vulnerable soul. Scotty's naturalistic delivery full of tics and starts so entranced the writers, they began to add the hesitations of speech to her dialogue. Soon we had the writers' pauses and hiccups, plus Scotty's own, creating a style the audience relished.

Richard Bull, who played Scotty's husband, was the quintessential actor—fully prepared, always excellent, with never a moment of friction. In "A Harvest of Friends," he established Mr. Oleson as someone who was straightforward, honest, and humble but couldn't keep his wife quiet. He was the perfect foil to Scotty. He had the virtues of modesty and humility, just as Mr. Oleson did, and never made a big deal of himself. He saw what went on but never got involved in the politics on set. Where Scotty was high-spirited, Dick was low-profile. I respected him, but he was such an introvert, we never got to know each other well. Once, when I published a column about women's roles, he said, "Who knew she was so deep?"

Dabbs Greer, who played the Reverend, was a large man from Missouri, like my Dad, with a voice softened by a slight Southern accent. No wonder he played so many ministers—he emanated the quality of simple kindness. His work was clean and specific and full. He was prompt, no nonsense, easily delivering in a timely manner. Whenever Dabbs was on set, I felt glad, he was so warm and gentlemanly and had such a light touch. He lived in Pasadena, where he took care of his elderly mother. He endeared himself to me when he told me I looked like Ingrid Bergman. I knew I didn't hold a candle to her, but when I was first thinking of becoming an actress, I read her biography and admired both her beauty and her mettle, so the compliment hit deep. Dabbs was frequently called on to deliver the moral message, to bring himself to tears over the latest local skirmish, and to sing countless renditions of "Bringing in the Sheaves." When he was introduced in "A Harvest of Friends," he had to be the heavy—making the families feel guilty because their husbands and fathers were busy in the fields rather than sitting in his pews. If someone had to admonish any of the Ingallses, he was certainly the softest and sweetest taskmaster we could have, our town's spiritual guide just as Karl's character was our secular leader. Together, they were the moral authority of Walnut Grove.

As Doc Baker, Kevin Hagen had romantic appeal hidden by his character's spectacles. Red-headed and tall, he was warm, and a graceful dancer. He was also something of a lady-killer. As Doc, his mellow voice, wise face, and bright blue eyes inspired confidence, and few of us could have guessed he was a dedicated single parent raising a young son.

Charlotte Stewart (Miss Beadle) and I were around the same age and had shared the counterculture of the '60s and '70s. Charlotte had qualified as a hippie in Topanga Canyon where she ran a boutique called Liquid Butterfly and wore long skirts. While she was doing that, I'd been strolling in my sandals and a long Indian dress on St. Mark's Place in Manhattan. We had danced to the same songs, worn the same peace symbols, protested the same war. Even before she completed her training at Pasadena Playhouse, she worked in Hollywood, most notably in David Lynch's *Eraserhead*, in which she played a delicate young ingénue with a monster baby. Charlotte brought youthful energy and kind charm to Miss Beadle and was patient with the children, though she could portray a steel spine. She invited Tuie and me to parties, and sometimes the three of us hung out together, so when I learned that Miss Beadle would not be in the show after four seasons, I was sad to lose touch. Happily, *Little House* reunions brought us back into each other's lives.

AFTER OUR FIRST MORNING IN TOWN, we all trooped up a dirt path to an old barn where long tables had been set up. The smell of animal droppings permeated the air as we carried our trays in and sat down. I retreated to the honey wagon for a short, air-conditioned rest where I could loosen my bodice. Then up, brush teeth, and off to the makeup trailer, where Larry and Whitey repaired the damage of sweat, lunch, and lying down. Before many days had passed, the caterers had moved the tables outdoors under some trees that gave blessed shade, but then the yellow jackets arrived, and I, who had run from bees when I was a girl, soon adapted, one hand nonchalantly fanning the air over my food as my fork moved determinedly from plate to mouth. If I didn't eat heartily, I knew in a couple of hours I'd be starving.

Once the caterers discovered if they hung a hunk of raw meat from a nearby branch the yellow jackets would buzz over there, so we forever had a flag of liver or steak flying high over our picnic. This, then, was glamorous Hollywood.

I often had the first shot after lunch. My close-up. I struggled to be alert in the heat and dust after a heavy meal. The high summer sun presented a lighting challenge for the cinematographer. Shadows from the desert sun overhead had to be counteracted with light at the level of the face and above. It took a raft of nine lights—each one made up of three rows of three flood lights mounted together in a metal frame on a tripod—and the dreaded "arc lights," placed about twenty feet back and actually *lit* to burn brightly onto the scene. Then add the lights to capture expression and eyes set close to the actor and my acting was reduced to pretending that I could *see*. Eventually, Missy told me to keep my eyes closed until the last possible moment, and that helped. If it happened to be a sad scene, tears were readily available. Imagine the heat and light on Ruthie Foster, my stand-in, who stood patiently while they adjusted all these lights, particularly on the days she played the postmistress in her 19th-century clothes. All the primary players had stand-ins, of similar coloring and height for the sake of the lighting. Ruthie was a curvaceous blonde, still in shape as a former dancer, and a sweet woman who chattered on in a friendly way. She was a real trouper; she'd been in vaudeville, earning her living from the time she was a teenager, and she was an invaluable asset to our company. Years after *Little House*, she was in the Palm Springs Revue dancing with other eighty-year-old showgirls, looking great.

After only one show's worth of these twelve-hour days in the hot sun, plus the added two hours of driving, I began to flag. I told Kent I was worried that driving the extra two hours was going to make the schedule too tiring, and he didn't hesitate. No need for negotiation, no need for an agent. From then on, he arranged for a driver to pick me up in a brown station wagon whenever we were shooting on location. My call was usually five thirty, and after the driver told me Faye Dunaway had a mattress in the back of her car, I began to bring a pillow so I could cat-nap on the way out to the ranch. One morning Mike was driving behind us, and when he saw what looked like an empty car, he was furious: *Those damned unions, featherbedding, sending a driver with no one.* When I sensed we were almost at the set, I lifted up my sleepy head, and Mike laughed. His ebullience was plentiful and authentic. This was his dream job.

At the end of each day, before the last shot, he announced, "This is the Playboy shot." That was the name of the bar where the *Bonanza* guys went after work, and the prop master had everybody's favorite booze available. After a day in the heat in Simi, I asked for a cold beer, and driving home, I drank it.

15. Too Good to Be True

"No one ever achieved anything from the smallest to the greatest unless the dream was dreamed first."
—*Missouri Ruralist* column, LAURA INGALLS WILDER

THAT SUMMER, WE WORKED EFFICIENTLY and well. Mike was continually telling jokes to keep the atmosphere light. He was quick, with high-flying ambition and more success behind him than most people have by the end of their careers. But the responsibility for this show was his, and it was formidable. As we shot, I began to understand why it took so many people to create a film. And why it took so long. We were racing toward the air date when Mike was forced to adapt to some big changes in personnel. Ed Friendly wanted the stories to be linked with ongoing plots, but Mike was opposed. They split, and not amicably, but Friendly had brought the project to Mike and owned the rights to the books, and I thought it must have stung to have no creative input. Mike told me, "It would never work. In syndication, the episodes can show up in random orders." After that, all final decisions were Mike's though he had the support of writer-producers like John Hawkins, whom he knew from *Bonanza*. And Kent, of course.

But Mike was the man: star, producer, often director, and writer, and for me, he was my acting partner, my "husband." He tried out guest directors, but while they were good, and we in the cast liked them, they were unable to please Mike. He had such a clear idea of what the show should be. One director, for instance, wanted me to play Caroline as a shy "country woman," but I saw her as more direct, and Mike was adamant. That director was gone. Early on, I asked Whitey to age my hands for a particular outdoor harvesting sequence. Mike stopped us. He said, "Do you know what your *face* would look like if your hands look like that? This is not realism," he explained. The style of the show, the people who would have staying power, all this shook out over that first season and soon the show boiled down to two directors and their teams. Mike worked with the cinematographer, Ted Voigtlander, and Miles as the assistant director, as they had on the pilot. The new team was director Bill Claxton, highly skilled "Buzzy" Boggs as cinematographer, and the gentlemanly, capable Maury Dexter as assistant director. Each team had a week to prepare and came in with all three in the picture, which made for great efficiency. But for Mike, who was acting during his prep week *and* meeting with writers, going to dailies of the shows he didn't direct, and overseeing every aspect, there was no break. Pacing himself was not an option.

The same seemed to be true for his family. When we returned to Sonora to shoot snatches of three or four shows with varied landscapes, Lynn and the two younger kids came along. One of the reasons that Mike liked TV series work was that he never had to go away for long stretches to shoot in distant locations. When we came in after the day's shooting, he'd jump into the pool and exuberantly with his kids. Then they'd all shower and go out for dinner at one of the family restaurants on the main drag of the little Western town. I heard Lynn call down from the second floor: "Mike—should I wash Shawna's hair?" as I headed for my room at the Gunn House next door. *Wow*, I thought, *even that she has to run by him.*

MIKE WAS DETERMINED TO DO EVERYTHING he could to make the show succeed. He had hired a great team, and added his own PR, Jay Bernstein, who was busy setting up press, and they were excited about a big cover story for the opening week. The in person promotional tour would fall to me. Production couldn't spare Mike for a day, let alone a week to visit affiliate stations. There were various markets that NBC wanted to push prior to the first episode airing right after Labor Day. Tuie was supportive, baking protein bars at home and packing them into my work bag to keep me going, but mostly I powered through one day after the next, grabbing a beer at the end of the day to relax. Didn't I deserve it?

One afternoon in August, as I headed for the exit doors, a work bag slung over my shoulder, Mike came up to me and said, "Tomorrow, you'll be going to the screening room to see 'Country Girls' during lunch so you can talk about it on the promo tour. We'll get you something to eat from the commissary."

I was tingling as I sat down in the cushy leather chair in my pioneer skirt. The lights came down. I'd seen none of our work since the pilot the previous March, and I was pleased to watch this touching episode, although I could see how I could have been better. Now, I realized, I not only had a lot to learn about how to act for the camera, how to sustain myself for the long hours and the long haul of a nine-month season, but I needed to learn how to do interviews with the press and appear on talk shows and local news shows.

I had heard of better-established actresses who refused to do PR, go out on tour, or do interviews, but I was mystified by that attitude. Wasn't it their show, too? I thought some people had odd ideas about what a real artist should or should not be willing to do and wondered if it was because they were painfully shy. One evening a friend of ours from the East Coast brought an actress I knew from New York to our home for dinner, and as she explained that she simply would "never do a *series*" (saying this word like it was spoiled meat), I could only nod. *Isn't she fortunate to be independently wealthy? She doesn't need to sign her life away for years.*

Before long, though, she was appearing regularly on one of the new evening soaps.

With two clips from "Country Girls," I was going to be hopping from city to city, one day in each, doing interviews and showing the scenes on local TV. I looked at my closet, and my heart sank. I had one good outfit. Before the premiere of the pilot at Paramount, I had gone to find something nice for a leading lady to wear. Driving by the windows of Holly's Harp on Sunset, I had yearned, so I went there. Her designs were typically chiffon gowns, graceful but off-beat, and when I learned our show "premiere" would be a 10:00 a.m. screening for families of cast and crew, I knew a gown would be ludicrous. Instead, I had bought a pretty, light-weight pantsuit in luscious green, well-cut and feminine. But one outfit could not get me through a tour of five cities.

After our moving expenses, we were financially embarrassed. Tuie's divorce was expensive and he was still seeking work as a screenwriter, and with my busy schedule, it never occurred to me to go clothes shopping, so now I had no wardrobe and no time.

Tuie's old friends, John and Sharkey Fink, had welcomed us when we first arrived in Hollywood. They were more fun and full of life than ten of their friends put together. John was an actor, but they had family money and were magnets for everyone they knew. Their *joie de vivre* made me think of Gerald and Sara Murphy, the Fitzgeralds' friends, whose story was captured in Calvin Tomkins's *Living Well Is the Best Revenge*. John and Sharkey lived in the Hollywood Hills above the Sunset Strip in the most charming home I had ever seen, Spanish-style, with a balcony off the living room that looked out over the city, and a gem-like pool. Their bedroom was painted whimsically, with air-brushed clouds near the high ceiling. Their den had a Moroccan bed in an alcove, with scads of tapestry pillows, perfect for opium dreams or, in our case, pot trances. When I started a women's rap group with a woman from New York, Sharkey was one of the first people I invited to join, and when I fretted in one of our meetings about nothing to wear on the tour, she opened her closet and said, "Take what you need." Sharkey had the most wonderful taste, and thanks to her, I was able to *look* like a TV star.

In 1974, before VCRs, before DVDs, the network provided me with two huge plastic cases containing video clips that I put in my suitcase along with Sharkey's clothes carefully packed in tissue paper to avoid wrinkling. Off I set on my five-day, five-city tour—which included Indianapolis I think, or maybe Chicago, New York, New Haven, Hartford, DC, and Miami. Honestly, it became a blur. I liked the people I met, the work came naturally to me, but the schedule was a bear. In each town the local affiliate station's head honcho or head of PR met me, and off we would go to dinner, where it was incumbent upon me to be charming. The next morning I'd rise early to get ready for the next day's rush. A typical day began with a breakfast interview with a newspaper reporter, attended also by the promotion chief of the affiliate station, before I was whisked from there to a radio station for a live interview, driven on to the local TV station for the lunchtime show, in a freezing cold, high-ceilinged studio with two or three cameras. I met and appeared with guests who had just written a book or invented a new gadget, and on and on went the schedule until the day ended, and I could have a drink. Then to the airport and on to the next town.

In Hartford, Connecticut, the promo man for the affiliate station—WHNB/TV30—was Howard Wry, a real pro. He and his wife picked me up at the airport in their own car, and we had dinner together in a typical American restaurant at my hotel where Howard laid out the schedule for the next day. He had arranged a reception in the afternoon, where I could be interviewed by a few outlets at once to save wear and tear. They left me to my presidential suite at the Sonesta Hotel, where I had lavish space that would serve for the reception the next day. Before the morning interview, Howard arrived with a photographer to get shots of me doing my hair and makeup, and in the afternoon, we videotaped promos to alert the local audience to watch *Little House*. I made these in each of the towns. At the reception, we had drinks, and I had photos taken with each of the reporters and local big wigs. Howard said goodbye there at the elevator, and the driver took me to the airport, where I ran into a long delay and had to run with my heavy tote across the tarmac through a summer rainstorm to a small Delta flight. The plane was seriously air-conditioned, I was a wet puppy, and getting a blanket from a snotty stewardess was a challenge. A deep fatigue settled over me—a mix of hunger and self-pity as my white wine spritzer of the cocktail party wore off—and I felt lonely.

The airport in DC was deserted when I finally arrived. I waited anxiously as I looked around for someone looking for me. Shades of arrivals in towns for plays where someone had "forgotten" to meet me rose in my memory, and I recalled a play in Atlanta, where I had signed on to replace another actress and arrived for the single afternoon's run-through with the company to find no one there. My stomach churned with hunger and worry, and somehow, I don't remember how, I got to the theatre. All those moments leave me, even today, feeling an edge when I arrive in a new place, uncertain if I'll be met as promised, and usually, relief—someone looking for me.

After a few days, I began to understand how Hollywood people wound up with entourages. I needed help, and I longed for a buffer—a way to get away from people without offending anyone. As soon as I was worn out or irritable, I feared I might snap at someone or say no to somebody, and my reputation would be changed forever; I'd be labeled as a "difficult" personality. This first trip was easier than most, because we weren't yet on the air, and if the hotel had a pool, I could take a quick swim, have a glass of wine while I got ready to meet whoever it was for dinner. When I had a break in the schedule, I ate in my room.

But it was later, after the show became huge, that airports were harder to get through since people wanted an autograph or time with me, and I had to do so much smiling. And naturally, everyone wanted to know about Mike. What was he really like? I could say without hesitation how talented and sensitive a director he was, and I surprised myself by discovering I had a gift for the gab since I sincerely believed we were doing good work. And I liked the attention. I won't deny that. But a part of me felt my soul was still in the theatre.

Monday morning, it was right back to the prairie and anticipation for our opening night. I was telling Larry and Whitey about the tour, about managing my own hair and makeup and missing them when Mike arrived with a copy of a popular fan magazine. He was thoroughly annoyed. "*This* I did not need a publicist to help me with!" The cover story he'd looked forward to presenting the show was instead a personal hatchet job. But there was more at stake than merely Mike's ego, and he knew it: If the audience took a dislike to him, they might reject the show, and all of his investment in time and money, his effort and plans for his career would be down the drain. He didn't say any of this. He merely got on with the day's work. But he fired Jay Bernstein that day. And I ached for Mike's disappointment.

THE FIRST SHOW AIRED ON SEPTEMBER 11, 1974, and overnight ratings from Nielsen were terrific. Even as we pushed on shooting the next episode, we held our breath for the week's ratings, and at the end of the week the *Wall Street Journal*'s Entertainment page declared, as if for a horse race, "The Winners Are!" with photos of Valerie Harper as Rhoda and me as Caroline! The week's ratings held up, too, and Mike laughed more than usual but kept up his brutal schedule. The article had not hurt the show. Still, it had not helped Mike's reputation.

In the fourth episode of that first season, Victor French returned to the fold, and we all were glad to see him back, as happy I think as little Laura was to see Mr. Edwards. In season two, his character would be given an instant family in the two-parter, "Remember Me," starring Patricia Neal.

On *Little House*, I had no time to let the words seep into my body as I had in rehearsals in the theatre—scripts often came in just before we shot them, with rewrites continuing until the scene was in the can. At home, I peeled potatoes or swept the floor while memorizing lines, trying to feel comfortable with a physical activity that often changed on the day we shot the scene. And some physical aspects couldn't be rehearsed ahead of time—dealing with a team of horses, inclement weather, or in my new show, our ninth, hitting a baseball.

Mike told me he had cast the son of his dear old friend Dan Blocker, "Hoss" on *Bonanza*, to play the lead with me in "School Mom." Mike had wept when he confided in me one afternoon the story of losing Dan without warning when he went into the hospital for surgery and died suddenly at only forty-three. I knew he had written an episode then in which Little Joe falls in love, marries, and loses his young wife, letting the whole company grieve. The man and the character had been deeply loved, and Mike created a way for the audience to grieve along with the *Bonanza* team. He had a special intuition that could put him on the wave-length of his audience.

So, when young Dirk Blocker, a sensitive actor at the beginning of a long career, arrived, everyone was already on his side.

The story opens as a snake spooks Miss Beadle's horse, and she is thrown dramatically from her buggy to the ground. The school board—Mr. Hansen, Doc Baker, and Mr. and Mrs. Oleson—asks Caroline to substitute while Miss Beadle recovers. On her first day, she is stunned at the Mercantile when her eggs have doubled in value, and Mrs. Oleson is honey-tongued. In the schoolroom, the Oleson kids have planted the notion that Ma isn't qualified, causing rebellion. She takes on a boy who seems to be the ringleader, asking, "What are you best at?" He says, "Baseball." And so she takes the whole bunch out to the schoolyard, where he hits a big one. She congratulates him; he challenges her to hit the ball. And she knocks it away, gaining the kids' respect.

But as soon as she gets the kids settled down to study, she walks right into the story's issue about a big boy named Abel who cannot read. When Caroline calls on Abel to read, all the kids laugh. Humiliated, he runs away. Laura says, "He's just dumb Abel," but Caroline learns from Miss Beadle that Abel simply hasn't had much schooling. Seeing that the boy's whole future is at stake, she persuades him to come back and finds a creative way to get all the kids in a learning game to help him to catch up. But Mrs. Oleson interrupts, insulting both Caroline and Abel. He runs again, and Caroline, whipsawed by her own anger, quits the job. In a touching scene, Abel shows her his appreciation, and when she realizes she has gotten through to him, they return to school together. In the end, Abel integrates into the class, Caroline earns the respect of the kids, and Miss Beadle returns. When Charles asks Caroline if she'll miss teaching, she hides how much she will, admitting, "Only a little."

Caroline, as a substitute teacher, lacked knowledge about her students that led to a crisis, and her perfectionism caused her to suffer when she realized she had made a mistake that could truly hurt another person, and I loved the script. I deeply identified.

Still, as usual that first season, we got the script close to the time for shooting, and I was nervous about how I would hit a home run with no time to practice. Again, I turned to my mother's book *Psycho-Cybernetics*, where I'd read about famous athletes who visualized plays over and over, seeing themselves succeeding. Actors do that, too. We "rehearse" in our imaginations. But hitting a baseball was another story. I was the kid in grammar school who was put out in right field, where, while other kids kept their eye on the ball, I did pirouettes. So now as Caroline, nervous about my ability even to hit the ball, I grabbed every second—eating breakfast, riding in the car, in line at the bank—to close my eyes and picture myself hitting that ball. Again. And again.

Mike and the crew had enviable camaraderie on Mondays—all about the game: "How 'bout them . . ."! For a while I tried to read the sports pages so I could at least follow their dialogue, if not participate, but that didn't last. I was not one of the boys. And they knew I was no jock. But the day of the baseball challenge scene, we gathered in the dirt in front of the school, and as the camera lined up for the shot, I walked around swinging the bat, loosening my shoulders, releasing my nerves with motion.

I imagine the crew was preparing to be patient, even to fake the shot, if necessary. But then came the pitch, and . . . *whack!* I knocked that ball home—*a crack shot, take that!* The best boy jumped back, the gaffer's head snapped sideways, eyebrows shot up like birds taking off, heads shaking as the director called, "Cut." The guys gave me a big hand, turned to each other and chuckled. I was as stunned as they were, but that hit earned me brotherhood, for the moment, just as it earned Caroline respect with the school kids. While the crew did the next setup, I was in my stride, connected to my breath, mind clear, and I knew I could keep hitting that ball out of the park as many times as we needed.

And working with Dirk was easy. He had unusual courage for such a young actor, to trust himself, to allow the thoughts and feelings to come and believe that they would communicate. Scotty and I thrived on our fights, playing our antagonism with relish. Mrs. Oleson was touchingly vulnerable when she had to humble herself in front of Caroline. That was the thing about Scotty's work: she had many layers. Mike and I had the fun of our late-night popcorn scenes. We usually shot them at the end of the day, when the kids had been released, their hours used up. Those scenes became regular opportunities for Ma and Pa to talk over the conflicts and reveal private moments. My sense of the intimacy was intensified, because my own family was crazy about popcorn. Dad used to make big kettles full; Mama would melt the butter, pour it on, and the whole lot would be put into big grocery bags for trips to the drive-in movies. Our prop man—first, Ron Chinique, and then Dean Wilson— made plenty for the crew, too, so it was family in the tiny bedroom in the Little House on the Paramount lot.

Ma's enthusiasm for teaching was obvious so in the end when she tells Pa she'll miss teaching "only a little" (since in those days she was expected to like staying home), I worried that we might be training a new batch of girls to deny their gifts in order to be "good." In interviews and at personal appearances, people often waxed nostalgic about the prairie world, but I focused on the *work*: washing the clothes in the creek, hauling the water to the house, heating it for baths, the gardening, the canning, the food prep with first in the fireplace, then a wood stove. Oh no, I would tell the interviewer: "There's never been a better time than now to be a woman. We have so many choices today." And still, even with all the appliances that make life easier, no matter what a woman chooses, if she has the need or the desire to be a mother *and* to work, it can be a strain, especially in this country where childcare can be hard to find, or to afford.

In my case, postponing motherhood never felt like a choice. It was a necessity. I had friends—other actresses—who were brave enough to go ahead and have babies while living as artists on the Lower East Side, but I couldn't face parenthood without more security. I worried I would delay too long. But I pushed aside my anxiety: I had a new script to learn. And I had passed a watershed moment—carrying a show, hitting a baseball.

MIKE SEEMED ABLE TO RUN ON FUMES. Until he couldn't. One weekend we were at home when the phone rang. Tuie answered and let me know it was John Hawkins, our producer. John never called me, so even as I answered, I sensed something was wrong.

"Mike's in the hospital, Karen. We're rewriting 'The Award' so you can play it."

"What's wrong?"

"Spinal meningitis. They've packed him in ice."

I got very quiet as John told me he thought Mike would be all right and went on to explain that I'd get new pages in the morning.

We'd barely gotten started, and everything was going so well, but now, with everyone else, I held my breath. Everything, in our *Little House* family and for Lynn and the kids, rested on Mike, and now he had crashed. *What would happen?*

The blue pages were messengered over to our place, and I set to work learning the show to be ready to start the next morning. In "The Award" Mary wants to compete in a history test to win a dictionary. Mike's absence is explained by Pa being away working in Mankato. Mary is so determined to win the contest that she goes out to the barn to continue studying at night. When she falls asleep, she knocks over the kerosene lantern and starts a fire. Caroline is awakened by the cows' and horses' reactions to the fire and rushes out, terrified, to find her child in danger along with the animals. Caroline beats out the fire, as the girls run back and forth to the creek for buckets of water to throw on it. Once the fire is out, Ma, overwrought, screams out a punishment: Mary will not be allowed to compete in the contest. And the suffering begins: Mary is ashamed of starting the fire and ruining Miss Beadle's history book and feels alienated from Ma. At the same time, she cannot stop studying, even though she is forbidden, and tries to dig herself out of her difficulties alone. Ma is worried that she has gone too far in her anger. Laura worries as she watches Mary prepare to take the test against Ma's wishes.

Despite my deep concern for Mike and his family, receiving this role on short notice was my oats. Like a racehorse trained to run, I stepped to the starting gate with a whinny and a spark in my eye. My years as a Broadway understudy, my time in summer stock doing a play a week, taught me how to rise to an occasion. Now I was on a familiar racecourse. And being the eldest child of an alcoholic—nerves refined in crisis—my spirit called, "Let me at it!"

We all worked with a quiet intensity, the danger to Mike an underground current that kept us on edge. Working with fire put me on high alert, too. It was "controlled" by our excellent special effects man, Luke Tillman, who explained to me exactly how this would work, but that was hay on fire, and the horse was actually frightened, and my body coursed with adrenaline. As Ma, I rarely got to cut loose physically and emotionally, but the scene provided me a cathartic moment. Bill Claxton, our steady alternate director, was patient as I asked if I could do the angry explosion with Mary again and again. Missy was outstanding in her portrayal of Mary's internal struggle and pitiful estrangement from Ma.

And when at last we heard that Mike's fever was down, and he was out of danger, we all took a deep breath. I was concerned about a scene that didn't feel quite right, and now that Mike was going to be okay, I felt I could mention it to John Hawkins. Tuie and I worked on the scene at home to make it flow better for Ma's character. Early the next morning, I brought our version in to John. He was a gruff guy who'd worked for years in Westerns, and I approached him warily. But John not only approved it, he seemed grateful for a solution.

In our revision of the scene, Ma brings her troubled mind to Reverend Alden for advice. She is torn about the stiff punishment she has doled out to Mary. Reverend Alden helps Caroline make peace with the fact that even though the punishment was an overreach, she needs to hold firm, so her daughters know her word stands. Mary doesn't take the test but instead uses the testing time to write out what happened and her need to make it right. Miss Beadle brings the paper to Caroline, who understands now just what Mary has been through and rushes to her to reconcile. The paradoxes inherent in parenting and the support of the community were themes that moved people. In *Little House,* the family was not alone. A lot of the institutions that historically provided support in this country no longer do so, and that is a loss I still feel. I think our audience felt it, too. Perhaps viewers identify with this loss even more now, as the show attracts its third generation on cable and video.

When Mike returned, he made a point of thanking me for my contribution to the script. He told me it had taken him years on

Bonanza before he was able to do that, but I knew he was just a kid when he started that show, while by the time I came to the *Little House* set, I had years of theatre work under my belt. Still, I was touched by his thanking me.

The meanness of the magazine article and Mike's hurt response, combined with his serious illness inspired me to do something to show him *our* appreciation. I wanted us to create a public acknowledgment, something that would speak to the Hollywood community. What did they know of Mike's professionalism? It needed to be declared publicly. It was and is customary for ads to run in the daily trade papers to call attention to good work. Often, during awards season, those papers are thick with ads. I went to the *Hollywood Reporter* and designed a full-page tribute. We all contributed to the cost. I think it was Kent who got the *Little House* artwork, and Missy's mom, Marian, kindly made the rounds for donations—asking for whatever people felt comfortable giving. The day the ad came out, I was bursting with pride. Mike barely acknowledged it, which was disappointing, but I know we all felt good about it. I suspected he was secretly pleased.

I imagine he was preoccupied with the two-part special he was writing and directing for the big climax of the season.

IT HAD BEEN A GREAT SEASON. We were riding high in the Nielsens; Mike seemed fully recovered, had made a beautiful two-parter for the end of season, and was happy with my work. I was relieved to have made it through the first, arduous season. Our last day of shooting happened to fall on my birthday, February 25th. At the wrap party, my *Little House* family had a cake with candles, and when I tried to blow them out, they sputtered and relit. *Ha ha,* a great joke watching me try and try, and my bewildered look around at each member of the crew searching for a clue. I had never seen such candles; I was a perfect victim. Mike's laughter was infectious, like bourbon and soda—warm, rippling, with a punch at the top—and he set everyone else laughing, too. Afterwards, he pulled me aside, wrapping his arm around me—his confidante, his colleague—and, leaning in close to my ear like a co-conspirator, said *sotto voce*: "Do you know how many people in this town wish they were doing what we're doing?"

I shook my head.

"Thousands. Thousands. Do you know how many pilots they shoot? We're the lucky ones, Karen. We're on the air!"

He was feeling high. The show was in the top ten, and the network had renewed it, easily and early. We all felt good about the work we were doing, his crew loved him, and we felt, truly, like one big happy family.

I had paid dues, but not the Hollywood kind. Unlike many actors, I had not shot six pilots while hoping year after year for a pickup. I hadn't been on the top like Mike, who then languished on the sidelines while others were taken seriously, and he was remembered as "just Little Joe," beloved once but over after *Bonanza* ended. I was happy for Mike, and for our success. I was glad to be working, grateful to have gotten a break. But this wasn't my dream. I squeezed his shoulder and smiled and nodded and hoped that this visibility on television would help me to achieve the goals I had for theatre, and maybe film roles. I hugged him and thanked him for my cake, and by the time I left that evening, I was lit up and relaxed, feeling affectionate toward all the cast and crew. These were dear people, and I felt real tenderness towards them. What could go wrong?

16. Towers and Walls

"Never bet your money on another man's game."
—*Farmer Boy*, LAURA INGALLS WILDER

TUIE HAD THE AIR OF A PROUD parent with a special birthday surprise for his child as he parked our old Volvo near the short street, its two parallel rows of garages tucked like small caves into the hill. He bustled me to a little campanile-like tower.

The antique elevator inside had two stops—below and above. He clanked the accordion door shut. Up we rode. He ushered me out to a secret neighborhood atop a knob-like hill where no cars could go. I was enchanted. To our left, the hill was a quilt of Heavenly Blue morning glories alongside a stairway. Directly in front of me was a white stucco apartment building I recognized from Robert Altman's film *The Long Goodbye*. I expected to see Altman's half-clothed young women lounging on the balcony. Here, above the Hollywood Bowl, we turned right, down a cement path past a motley collection of California-style homes, funky bungalows, small Spanish stuccos on either side bordered by overgrown cactuses, vines, and a monster of a century plant. About halfway down the path, I saw an imposing Spanish house on the right, and on the left, a Japanese-style house with carved overhangs on the roof above gray shingles—ours.

He led me through the crystal-bright entry and past the slightly shabby dining room straight to the living room. Grand. My eyes widened at the two-story windows across the entire back wall. I gazed out to a dizzying view of sky. A stunning room full of light. *I could live here?* I paused as I looked past the bowl to the Hollywood Freeway, but the place had a kind of worn-out glamour that seduced me. That house seemed ready for someone wonderful to call. Tuie escorted me up the carpeted stairs and along the loft-like hall that was open to the view.

There were two bedrooms, ours with windows on two walls, light visible all day long. A period bathroom with tub, separate shower, and a big, handsome pedestal sink linked to the other bedroom. We could have guests, too. He had done it again, found us digs with unusual charm. I was exhilarated, giddy. Let's see the kitchen! A red leather booth, kitsch and cozy for parties. And I would party there. There was even an indoor back porch, where we could put a washer and dryer if we had them—and we could move in right after our vacation.

We had planned a Hawaiian holiday with my parents. None of us had ever been. And I was so very tired.

When we were closing in on the end of the season, I admitted my fatigue to Mike, and he sent me to a doctor who had helped him. The doctor gave me shots, and I felt a rush right through my veins, into my sex organs. Supposedly these were vitamins, but as I look back, I think they must have contained speed. He gave me pills he said were for the pituitary. I didn't ask too many questions and started taking them. At first, I had more energy, but by the time we landed in Maui, my nerves were shredded. A buzzer for the seat belt sent me shrieking and jumping out of the car. Or I fell into a blue funk of depression and hid out in the bedroom.

Mom was shocked to learn that I was taking something without being sure what it was, so together we threw the pills into the toilet, and I seemed to improve. Swimming in warm water, the trade winds wafting pikake perfume, my parents' steadiness, all of these were healing. By the time we flew home, Tuie and I were full of hope, for our new home and for the new season. At least I told myself this was true. How weary Tuie was by then, I don't know. But surely, I thought, things would be better once we got home. I could rest, and we could relax with time together nesting up on High Tower Road.

OUR NEW HOUSE PROMISED STABILITY after that first year of patching it together, first one sublet and then a rental and cruising garage sales, buying a dead girl's clothes, bringing home awful plastic chairs from Western Avenue. Now, we celebrated every sign of rootedness. How Tuie had located the exclusive rental agent, I never knew. He seemed somehow to move smoothly through whatever world he needed to navigate, always knowing someone who knew the people he needed to know. There was something of the disenfranchised royal about him. It was no accident that he and I had boarded in the hippie farmhouse of a Russian prince in the English countryside, or that we had dined with the Earl of Warwick in an intimate dining room in his castle's armory, with a full knight's armor standing guard. No matter that we both were struggling artistically and financially, Tuie carried everything off with aplomb. He was perfectly at home with the old-world, fallen-from-grace aristocracy, as well as highly successful show biz folks, while my own deep sense of inadequacy with those people combined with alcohol often resulted in a sobbing scene when we got home. Or we would smoke grass and turn the whole thing into a joke. With bravado, I wore a see-through blouse to Warwick Castle. Tuie bought white garden gloves and we put those on to give them the "white glove treatment" upon arrival. When I got angry about anything, I used insight and sarcasm to put others down. *His friends.*

The spacious living room was empty but for a substantial carved table Tuie used as a desk. We each ordered a chair from a Scandinavian furniture store in Beverly Hills—his, a tall wing chair in brown corduroy and mine an overstuffed armchair with its own ottoman in white Haitian cotton. Not exactly a pair. I'd never ordered furniture. In fact, I'd retrieved most of mine from the streets of New York. Mom and Janey drove Larry's big truck down with the loveseat Mom had promised me so many years earlier, and it rounded out our living room seating arrangements. At an outlet that had markdowns on slightly dinged appliances, Tuie found a washer and dryer and somehow got them up to our hideaway on the hill. When people came to visit, the first thing I showed them was not the view; it was the washer and dryer, a long way from the Laundromat at First Avenue and Fifteenth Street. A long way from the brick wall my kitchen stared at from my third-floor apartment. A long way from the teeny bath and toilet barely walled off from the kitchen. Since we had begun to live together, we had been such nomads. The months we spent in England, we hopscotched to at least seven addresses. Since arriving in California, we had hung our hats in five different spots, most either borrowed or about to be torn down. I never acknowledged how difficult this had been for me—it came with the territory of being an actress, and my motto was "Travel light!" But the prospect of staying in one place for more than a year flooded me with relief.

On weekends, I planted flowers in front of the house, and a row of bright zinnias greeted me at the end of the workday. Near the front steps, I planted a mini-landscape of Irish moss and blue pansies to welcome our friends. One afternoon, I was watering these when I heard the pure soprano of Sleeping Beauty: "Someday my Prince will come . . ." I stood up and cocked my head. A recording? No. *A capella*. And I saw—in the vacant lot next door where an abundant garden bloomed—a small middle-aged woman singing. Meet Sleeping Beauty! We had definitely arrived in Hollywood. Our landlord, Philip Ahn, was a Korean actor we had probably seen playing an evil Japanese officer in World War II movies or a gangster in Chinatown intrigues. Life felt fun.

Both our mothers seemed to recognize that we had come to ground. His mother acknowledged our relationship by giving him her own engagement ring to give to me. I had never allowed myself to dream of a ring so exquisite—a deep-blue sapphire surrounded by tiny diamonds and set in platinum. My mom wanted to start me on a set of china. This was a ritual I had figured I would never have. And I lingered over the choices. She'd fretted for years over what gifts to give me—we were so different—but now that I could have nice things, she had found her solution to Christmas and birthday dilemmas. I chose a Limoges pattern called Anemone.

Off the dining room was a closet where we kept the liquor and the wine. John and Sharkey had introduced us to the wine merchant at Greenblatt's Deli, and we liked to go there to be advised about what to serve our guests. We began to pay attention to labels. Tuie was used to this kind of lifestyle, but it was all new to me—being taken to elegant restaurants for business lunches, where Tuie and I then took our friends. In my previous life, I scrimped and planned for months for a French meal, then splurged with fellow actors or roommates—an event. Now I was becoming familiar with delicious sauces, wine, and flaky desserts. I tried not to go overboard with the wine, but my tolerance was puzzlingly unpredictable. I made rules for myself: No drinking on an empty stomach. No drinking hard liquor. No mixing the grape and the grain. I used marijuana to even myself out. For a while it worked. I forgot that I'd been trying to get this right since college.

IT WAS TIME TO RENEGOTIATE MY contract before shooting began for season two. When my agent first described to me the seven-year contract with its built-in raises, I said, "But that's not what people get paid." (I was new to Hollywood, but I could read!) He explained that the first year would be low because I was unknown, but if the show succeeded, the following years would be renegotiated based on the series' popularity. We went to work with a "deal memo," standard operating procedure in Hollywood, where contracts were so long and complicated there was rarely time to finalize them before work began. So, okay. I'd heard that Joan Didion said that in Hollywood, the deal memo *is* the work of art. I was confident that my salary would be substantially more now that *Little House* was an established hit. We were still watching our monthly expenses and making do with only one car.

Deane Johnson, my distinguished attorney, and I went together to Mike's office to discuss my contract. It was hiatus, and the office was peaceful. Dressed in jeans and a pullover knit shirt that showed off his biceps and pecs, Mike sat behind his huge desk. Deane wore the expensive suit and tie that conveyed his position as the major partner of O'Melveny and Meyers, a powerful entertainment firm. The necessary small talk began with chat about vacations.

Mike loved the Hawaiian Islands and was glad we had gone there. His favorite place was the Kahala Hilton on Maui where he took his wife and kids every year. Deane told an amusing story about how Burt Reynolds had just come back from Maui, cutting his vacation short by almost two weeks, because it had made him so miserable. Mike didn't think that was funny, nor did he appreciate being reminded that he wasn't the biggest star around. In his own world, Mike was the golden boy with the looks, the gumption, and the talent—and a great head of hair. But Burt Reynolds was the biggest star in the world at the moment, and he was Deane's client.

Deane attempted to address my contract, but Mike diverted the conversation, refused all cues, let openers hang in the air, and without settling anything, we left.

Outside I turned to Deane: "What was that?" He said he didn't think Mike had handled himself very well. He would give him a call—maybe without me there, they could do business. And then for days and days, Mike didn't return Deane's calls. Eventually, he referred Deane to the network, and because Deane knew people at the higher echelons of the network, I figured he would settle things. But whoever it was he talked to was stubbornly uncooperative, and as the time came closer for us to return to work, I became more and more uneasy—*Do I go back to work?* I read in the trades about actors simply staying home in these situations until someone gave in and paid them. Deane didn't want me to take that route. He wanted me to be perfectly professional, and that approach made me more comfortable, too. When we went back to work, Mike decided to take this up with me personally, to help me to see reason.

"After all, there has to be some parity between you and the girls," he said.

Parity between me and the children? After all my years of training and personal sacrifice—not comparable to what the children brought to the table. My rapport with the kids was valuable—he wouldn't find that under every tree. Parity? No, I didn't buy that and felt frustrated that Mike wouldn't pay me what was appropriate. Another afternoon, when we were once again wrapping up the day's work after the kids had gone home, he sat down to explain to me that the network had done "testing," and I wasn't the audience's favorite character on the show, not even close. Therefore, "they" (NBC) didn't see the need to give me a substantial salary increase. My stomach lurched, but I didn't blink. No, I understood that Ma would not win a popularity contest, but she was an essential link in the show's success. "Uh huh," I said, "well, maybe you should let me go then." It wasn't a negotiating strategy. I felt my contribution was necessary, but part of me was willing to tear it all up—an angry nihilistic part of me who spoke up suddenly while maintaining an outwardly calm poise.

At the time, the trade papers were full of stories of the battle Sally Struthers was having with the Lear company over her desire to leave *All in the Family*, the number one show in the country. She had made a movie or two, and no doubt offers were arriving at her agent's office by the handfuls. But, of course, she wasn't available. Not available to become a movie star? Who could stand it? Sally was determined to leave the series. There was no signed contract, but certainly there was a deal memo. The case was on everyone's lips in TV land, and without ever mentioning it, it hung in the gloom over my late-afternoon, smoky conversation with Mike.

I drank more. My tolerance was slipping. Just get through this negotiation, I told myself. How long can it last? Hangovers became routine. In the night, I took B vitamins with spoonfuls of yoghurt to stave off the worst of them. Everything hurt. In the morning, I robotically walked to the freezer, put ice in a washrag, smashed it against the kitchen counter, and pressed it to my eyes, puffy and red. In Larry's chair, I sat stoically as he sprayed my head. It hurt all the way to the ends of the hairs. The brushes on the curlers were like needles on my sensitized scalp. The dryer was bad too, whirring heat around my ears. Whitey's Visine for my red eyes. I had heard tales of old stars who were drunks using something stronger for red eyes. But I guessed it had been outlawed. Anyway, I wasn't like them, I told myself. No. I was just going through a rough time. Trying to be pleasant. Not a morning person on a good day. And these were not good days.

AS AN EXPERIENCED HOLLYWOOD GUY, Mike cautioned me about the tough world of show biz life without a steady job. He actually said, "It's a jungle out there," but emotionally, I had withdrawn from him. I could see his manipulation. One day, out in the field, just as we were finishing a scene, and I was high-tailing it to an afternoon talk show, his usual peck to Caroline became a lengthy and deeply felt kiss. *Really? You'd really try that?*

Mike was the master of a small domain, a potentially hugely lucrative enterprise. The livelihoods of more than one hundred people depended on his success, so dealing with a stubborn leading lady must have been not just annoying but threatening to his whole scrupulously built construct. He knew one day you could be king of the hill, hail-fellow-well-met at the guard gate of the studio, everyone laughing at all your jokes, your advertising rates going up as the ratings rolled in, and you have only to glance for your

Ferrari to be brought to your side; the next day you can be out of a job, sitting by your Beverly Hills pool, wondering, "What's next?"

The campaign to bring me into line continued. One by one, scripts arrived from upstairs. We were getting them a little earlier than we had during the first season's mad scramble. My scenes dwindled as my contract remained unsettled. A typical scene would begin with a close-up of the coffee pot, my hand carrying it across the room, the camera panning with it and widening as I arrived at the table where Charles and, let's say, Reverend Alden were sitting. As the pot arrived in front of the men, my voice was heard saying, "More coffee, dear?" or, for variety, "More pie, Reverend?" Then the men had a discussion relevant to the theme of that episode. I walked back to the stove—off camera and out of the scene. In contract negotiations, I was asking for a minimum of two shows each season featuring Ma.

Adding to my frustration, Mike's plan for season two was to bring in stars he admired in order to boost our ratings. This meant the big roles went to Academy Award winners like Patricia Neal and Red Buttons. Our special, "Remember Me," starred the deeply affecting Patricia Neal as a dying mother and created a whole family for Mr. Edwards and Bonnie Bartlett as his wife. Bonnie, from Chicago, had that direct manner and brightness I associated with friends from there. I was glad to have her on our team.

As I held out for my money, Ma became the incredible shrinking woman. Watching Mike play his sensitive director role with guest stars while I was put on ice set off alarm bells inside me. We had been close collaborators, and I had thrived on our harmonious relationship, and on his approval. Being ignored and treated with contempt felt excruciating. It was all too familiar. I felt I was all over again the daughter of an alcoholic father who was patient and loving, then turned suddenly cruel, in the process shredding my self-esteem with his derision. Back then of course I didn't make the connection. Back then I only knew I was miserable and hoped that if I just kept up my professionalism, the conflict would be resolved.

It's only all these years later and looking back that I understand how easily I slipped into the role—be the good girl, play the part, and hope.

I prepared. I tried to pace myself. I even tried to stop drinking, but that didn't last a week. My drinking became seriously scary. Fits of rage—much of it directed at my loyal man—manifested in wine glasses thrown into the fireplace, screaming accusations. I have a flash of memory of kicking Tuie, once. I was baffled and self-justifying by turns. "You'd drink too if you were going through this," I'd charge.

When the script for "At the End of the Rainbow" came in, a fool's gold story in which Laura fantasized about the wonderful gifts she would buy for the family with all the "gold" she and her little friend had found, the girls and I looked forward to our fancy clothes and hairdos—out of calico and into white satin. We went to special fittings. Richalene had designed romantic dresses that could have come from a period French film set in the nineteenth century. I ran my hand over the thick satin and grinned when I tried on the wide brimmed hat with its white feather flourish. Whitey spent a long time giving me the glam makeup—false eyelashes and all. If anyone could do it, he could. Marilyn Monroe had relied on him for all her makeup, and when it came to publicity photos, she gave him complete discretion on what should be approved. When that show aired, I sat down anticipating looking great and hoping this would help me to get other kinds of roles. That stylish hat looked terrific, and its big feather fit well, but no one saw me. Mike had shot around me, cut out all the coverage of my face, left my "glam look" on the cutting room floor. The mortar on the brick wall I had run into was setting hard.

Had Mike stopped speaking to me then? Or was he just shutting me down creatively? It's hard for me to recall the precise order. And no wonder, as I drank more wine in the evenings, going over and over in my mind the unfairness of it all. I'd never handled ostracism well. As in all companies, people move away from the hen-pecked, and that's how it was with me on *Little House*. Karen was "changing." Karen was "difficult." Even Missy, with whom I had passed time off-camera playing backgammon, withdrew from me. Mike had a sharp tongue, and his barbs were well aimed. If you were on his list, his ridicule was infectious.

I was unaware then but learned later that at lunch, when he and the producers, writers, cinematographer, and postproduction people went to watch dailies, it was a free-fire zone. The men gathered in the comfy screening room and there our work, our faces—good takes, bad takes, ridiculous expressions alongside the noble—were writ large. Terrific fodder for Mike's cruel wit. There we would be skewered and pinned. Great bonding with the boys. The trouble was that when they came back to work with us, they had those words and images in their heads, and communal respect was diminished. As the summer wore on, my spirits fell lower and lower. Our late-afternoon collaborations turned into opportunities for humiliation.

There they are—the handsome couple, the perfect American parents, her muslin nightgown buttoned demurely at her throat, his nightshirt a soft, striped pink flannel. They sit in the tiny room, propped up in the small hand-hewn bed, eating popcorn, and calmly, sweetly, discuss the current script's issue, a flirt behind the words.

But pulling back, behind the camera, you saw the whole of the tiny room with its bare pine-board walls, the heavy, dark quilt covering the couple. Close to thirty people surrounded the simple scene, all men but one, crammed close together in order to see and do their jobs. The cameraman was on a cart with a seat, so he could be moved forward and back at the same time as the best boy pulled focus. The assistant director called for quiet and the thirty people moved in to do their work.

Since the room was so crowded, the star and the costar remained in the bed, captives while others set the scene. To pass the time while the prop man fetched more popcorn for everyone, Mike entertained his crew with jokes about the smelly, distasteful female anatomy—c-word jokes. A roomful of men guffawed, his eyes twinkled with mischief, and I was stuck in the center of that pool of light. I looked down, away, anywhere so as not to acknowledge and not to feel the embarrassment while everyone looked at us. Then "Action": We shot the adorable scene with camaraderie and such rapport, such . . . love. Our cameraman said, "We can do better," and then we shot it again. I rose above his bad boy behavior, a kind of school marm among a gang of rowdy boys, tolerant of my own humiliation. And "that's a print."

The camera was turned off, the men in their blue jeans backed off to the clicking and clacking of equipment, and it was on to the next scene while I dragged myself from under the quilt, split for the next change, hairdo, touch-up. And commenced to do all the close-ups for that day's work, one after another, with Mary at the script reading the kids' lines.

I had thought I was tough. Hadn't I survived being poor in New York? Hadn't I bounced back from scores of rejections at gobs of auditions? Hadn't I slapped the rear ends of taxis that cut me off when I was crossing the street? Hadn't I chased after flashers in the subway to intimidate them? But I was not tough. I couldn't let this treatment roll off my back. There were self-help books; Mama tried teaching me a meditation to help me to detach. I couldn't. Instead I was on high alert, in fight or flight mode without being able to do either. Mike had gotten rid of Ed Friendly, who had created *Rowan & Martin's Laugh-In* and owned the rights to the books, had brought Mike onto the project in the first place. *What did I have?* Perhaps fifty million people who believed I was Ma, and Deane Johnson, the most esteemed, gentlemanly attorney in Hollywood. And I had this: I knew I was not out of line. I wanted to be paid commensurate with what leading actors on top ten TV series in the mid-1970s were paid. No more. No less.

AN UNEXPECTED CALL CAME ON A weekend while Tuie and I were visiting my folks: an offer to play John Travolta's mother in the Movie of the Week, *The Boy in the Plastic Bubble*. Not an audition, an *offer*. I was elated. All three networks were producing original movies dealing with contemporary issues that aired during the two-hour prime time slot at nine o'clock. The producer knew my work from New York, and now I was on a successful series. This, then, was the snowball effect I had hoped for. *The Boy in the Plastic Bubble* would take me away from the *Little House* shooting schedule for just one day.

Mike refused. He "needed me" in Sonora, he said. I sat on a picnic blanket in a distant shot that Ruthie could easily have done in my place, furious, knowing I didn't need to be there and knowing there was nothing I could do about it. Back home I nursed my resentments, marinating them in alcohol and bursting into crying jags. I came into work in a blue mood. I didn't have the sense to hide my disappointment. I sulked, making things worse for myself and for those around me. The weeks dragged on and on, with no resolution.

After we had shot half the episodes for season two, a mini-hiatus gave us a chance to get away. Tuie brought me to the San Ysidro Ranch, where Jack and Jackie Kennedy had spent their honeymoon. Just below the Santa Ynez Mountains sat a ring of simply furnished cottages, each with a sitting room and bedroom, a perfect place, quiet and secluded. We left the car down by the office, and I delighted in the simple paths lined with native plants that smelled like home. An unadorned pool and two hidden tennis courts were out of sight just up the hill. An older man, who looked as if his ancestors might have built the Santa Barbara Mission, drove a golf cart around the circle of cottages to lay a fire in each fireplace. A truly restful place.

Suddenly, I was in the hospital. I didn't know how I got there. The nurse was helping me to walk from the bed to the toilet. Couldn't walk alone. Weak. Sick. On the toilet, I woke to realize I was at the Montecito resort. But everything had disintegrated. I remembered we had had a fancy dinner with wine and candlelight in the dining room. Our cottage. A bottle of Pernod. What was it that upset me? What did I think was wrong? I remember screaming and crying, my body bent over, anguish, blame. Why? I crept back to bed, ashamed and frightened. What was happening to me?

Back in Los Angeles, Tuie and I had begun to see a couples' therapist, and when we returned home, I mentioned the fear I had about alcohol to him. "Oh," he said, "you just use alcohol to get in touch with the daemonic," as if booze were a creative tool. When he said that, I felt relieved I didn't have to quit drinking. But I also felt dread circle my middle. *What to do about it then?*

One of Tuie's many contacts in Los Angeles was Cynthia Lovelace Sears, daughter of a successful investment adviser and mother of two appealing girls. Educated at an Eastern women's college, Cynthia seemed the epitome of grace and intellectual sophistication. She confessed that, as a student, high expectations placed on her writing talent had led to writer's block. She'd recently created a public radio show in which she interviewed many literary stars: Henry Miller, Lawrence Durrell, Twinka Thiebaud. She and I sparked each other's creativity. From the moment we met, we began to think of projects we could do together. Both of us were active in a women's consciousness-raising or "rap" group, where we explored women's self-abnegation, and the feminism we hoped would cure it. Perhaps because Cynthia's daughters were still in grammar school, she and I decided to create a board game based on *Little House*.

During the show's hiatus, we met regularly and created a prototype that was designed to be both educational and fun—and of course we thought we would make money, too. Mike liked it, but Ed Friendly still controlled all marketing connected with the show—dolls, toys, and yes games. And so that project collapsed, and Cynthia and I began to think about subjects for a Movie of the Week, subjects about women. I was hopeful that my perch on television could make our efforts on behalf of women's rights count.

I was thirty-two years old, and I had it all—engaged to a gifted screenwriter who was devoted to me, a plum role on a popular series, a loving family nearby at last. Tuie and I had so much to celebrate. And celebrate we did. But the violent twists in my moods were scary, and more and more I began to project my insecurities onto him, to blame him or to blame the battle over the contract, or, or, or. There was always something or someone to blame, and the more bewildered and out of control I felt, the more I clung to my rationalizations. And the more I drank.

By the end of season two, Tuie had to get away from my accusations, and my breakdowns. I don't know what preparations he had made before telling me. It was the weekend at home, and he broke off our engagement. I threw that exquisite ring at his feet, knowing I was behaving like a tragic character in a novel but unable to stop myself. That night, afraid to leave me alone, he called my mother and waited with me until the next morning when, with her train case, she arrived, and Tuie left for good. Mama took no sides. I imagine I was ashamed—I don't remember. I am sure I justified myself. My self-defense armor had a sharp sheen.

DURING WHAT I HOPED WOULD BE the final week of negotiations with NBC, I used all my self-control not to drink. After work, my agent, my lawyer, and I huddled at a small table in the bar of a favorite restaurant on the Sunset Strip. There they presented NBC's offer to me. It was a low offer, so I looked them square in the eye and said, "No. I don't want to do this anymore." They explained to me a show needed five seasons in order to go to syndication, and when I asked what that meant, Deane said, "You know how you see certain series on the air every night before prime time—five days a week—like *Dragnet* or *Lucy*? That's syndication. When a show's in syndication, you're no longer working, but you get paid based on the contract you negotiate now."

They showed me on paper how, over the years, the numbers would escalate.

"Five seasons," Deane said, "and you'll never have to work again."

My insides twisted around themselves at the thought of going back to work in that punishing silence, to the phony acting I pretended not to notice. The waiter checked to see if we wanted another round. I stayed with Perrier. I knew how to live simply, but my insecurity about money, heightened during the trying years in New York and London, rolled around in my mind. I didn't want to worry anymore about making the rent or panic if my car needed brakes. I didn't want to return to that life on First Avenue and the acrid smell in the hallway and the drug addict passed out in the vestibule beneath the broken mailboxes.

And so I wept. They had me. But I told them: I'll do it, but they have got to pay me more than this. A part of me thought, *Who do you think you are to hold out like this?* The other part said, *If this is what I have to do, then at least I'm going to be paid market price for it.* I dug in my heels. They conveyed my position to the network. The network fell silent. I went to work in limbo, not knowing what I was making or when it would be settled.

That summer, strife hung like a weight in the dusty air, the sky brilliant blue as we sheltered under the huge old oak in our made-up town, the millwheel turning on cue, splashing real water. Nearby, we could see the general store where it seemed to the audience that we could buy a sack of flour, but where the shelves were empty, and dark corners were favored by rattlers. I waited in the heat with the others and held my head high, despite the desperate need I felt to have the contract settled. Karl Swenson was balm to my nerves. He and I talked of books, and of current affairs, and he helped me through those days.

Then came an additional challenge. One day at the ranch, I was reading Edith Wharton's *The House of Mirth* when they called me to the scene in the barn. I got up from my director's chair and walked across the yard where the cow was chewing her cud and into the hot, stuffy barn. I've forgotten now the content of the scene, but I can't forget that I wasn't ready, and when the cue came for my part, words came out of my mouth, but the feeling wasn't there. I was as dry as the dirt where the chickens were pecking at corn. We completed the master. I assuaged my guilt over my less-than-stellar performance by telling myself I could improve it in the close-up. While the crew set up for the coverage, I tried to engage my emotions. Nothing. Brittle as the hay in the stalls. I was shut down.

I didn't know what had happened. There were no more distractions than usual: the camera, the lighting, the men standing close by. By then, I was accustomed to the ranch—the children's mothers, the animals, the visitors, the occasional reporter, airplanes overhead. These were normal. I was anxious about the unsettled contract, had never dreamed it would become such a sore issue and that Mike would turn so cold, but that was no excuse. I wanted to do good work, period. But suddenly that day, the emotional availability so necessary to an actor eluded me.

I was troubled as we moved on to the next scene. In acting I had found some security—instinct, training, experience had all come together. I knew how to do a scene. And then, not. My attempt at pacing myself had not worked. How was I going to find a way to survive the schedule and do my work regardless of the pressure or the tedium? Mike was a completely different style of actor from me. He banked on his star personality, and he joked around right up to "Action," and that kept him loose, as it does for many actors of his type. It was fun for the crew, as well. But I am a different sort of actor. I needed focus.

During the first season, I was tuned up and ready to go all through the long days for when I would hear "Karen, we're ready." During the coverage, if the scene wasn't demanding, I might read *Variety* or a little of the *Los Angeles Times*, but most of me belonged to what was next. For the second season, I knew that I couldn't keep myself on "high alert" for another nine months. It was too exhausting. I hoped to discover ways to relax between shots; I brought more absorbing books, and as I sat in the canvas director's chair amidst the dirt and farm animals, I let my mind go to a completely different world inside those books. But then came the day I was brought up short, my psychological state unprepared for the scene. Had I gone too far away? How to find some balance? I was in this for the long haul. We were going to run for years. How would I do it? I was really distressed. The fatigue had made me irritable, and I'd been cutting at home, of course, where it had done the most personal damage.

At home I poured myself a glass of wine and called Roy London to ask for help. Roy and I had been fast friends ever since our Broadway debut together in *The Gingham Dog*. Roy was a good-looking Jewish guy but not a leading-man type. He played the best friend or the roommate. Multitalented, he could paint and write as well as act—something of a prodigy, and with Joe Chaikin's Open Theatre Company, he had toured to Paris, where their performances were interrupted by the '68 revolution. Roy appeared in Antonioni's *Zabriskie Point*, was a founding member of the Circle Rep in New York and had written a play. He and Lanford broke up before Roy came out to California in a Lynn Redgrave vehicle at the Huntington Hartford Theatre. When we went out after the show, he told me he was ready to give Hollywood a try, and I invited him to stay in the extra bedroom on High Tower Road. He started going up for parts and soon was encouraged to stay in Los Angeles. After a few weeks, he moved down the path to a furnished room, signed up for driving lessons, but continued to take meals at my house. He wrote another play, produced it, and got a nice apartment in central Hollywood, which he furnished elegantly with little money, hanging a poster that proclaimed "Exactitude."

When someone asked Roy for acting lessons, he not only found his true calling, he changed hundreds of others' lives and careers. He started in the modest living room of a friend's apartment, where he could move the sparse furniture aside to do scene work. Roy was a brilliant teacher, developing techniques that ultimately empowered one actor after another. And after that day in the barn, I joined his class, grabbed hold of his teaching, and from then on, it didn't matter if all I was doing was serving scrambled eggs, my character was fully engaged. The series, with its long hours, short prep time, and political pressure, had forced me to up my game. It was Roy who helped me to do that.

Over the months in that friend's apartment, Roy elaborated on techniques he had learned from his studies in New York with Uta Hagen. The more he worked with us, the clearer and stronger his teaching became. Roy's students began to book the jobs. That ineffable quality that makes an actor fascinating on camera, I realized, was not simply the result of being born with "star quality." Roy taught people immediacy, excitement, how to be alive in the moment. He skipped over actors' nerves like a pebble on a pond, declaring, "Fear is a given. Then what do you do?"

The specifics of Roy's teaching are too subtle and myriad to describe, but a boiled-down example is this. Utilizing Stanislavski's technique as a template—employing an action for each beat of a scene—Roy taught us to imagine that I, the actor, wanted not an emotional response from my scene partner but a physical reaction so I could see instantly whether I had succeeded in my goal—whether that goal was wanting my partner to take off his hat, or to kiss me. "Keep trying to get what you want," Roy said. That effort created its own kaleidoscope of immediate feelings, small adjustments. He liked to ask provocative questions, quickly following with "Don't tell me the answer, but play it for that person." Roy inspired us to be vulnerable, to not know what we were going to do from moment to moment. This was analogous to my voice work, in which continuing to let go of the breath created spontaneous and original choices.

Casting directors started to notice Roy as the teacher whose students were booking the good parts. Michelle Pfeiffer was finding a challenge in Shakespeare in the Park in New York, and Roy flew in to help. Jeff Goldblum sent Geena Davis, who thanked Roy when she won her Academy Award for *The Accidental Tourist*. Brad

Pitt, one of Roy's students, made his smashing debut in *Thelma and Louise* (and the rest is history). Sharon Stone, nominated for an Academy Award, won the Best Actress Golden Globe for *Casino* and thanked Roy. As Hollywood buzzed, "Roy who?" students flocked to him.

But the series schedule made attending his class impossible, so I went to Roy for coaching. From then on, before beginning a movie or a play I consulted with Roy. As his friend, watching his life soar as he became the "coach to the stars" filled me with deep satisfaction. His zest for the work, his commitment to his actors and to process, was built on his firm belief in Truth, on not hiding. No arranging of one's feelings to look good or play it safe. Roy helped me, as he did so many others, to open the channel into the unexpected. His work was antithetical to cliché. Whatever obstacles I might face, he could help me find a way to make it *work for* the role. When later I was doing a play in which my so-called "best friend" wouldn't look at me in rehearsal, I complained to Roy, and he said, "Perfect. Then do everything you can to get her to look at you." Obstacles became opportunities, with Roy as midwife helping actors deliver vulnerability.

He also taught me what I brought into the room without trying: my type, my particular quality. Especially in Hollywood, knowing the roles that you are right for is important; few of us ever play roles far from type. But this has nothing to do with how we feel inside. As an ingenue, I had played nuns and kookie parts, even a prostitute. Roy helped me to realize my own wanton sophistication. An actor who is known for playing villains and tough guys—as Victor French was before Mr. Edwards—may in truth be a big softy. A man may be sexy and attractive to women although he is gay. During the studio days, there was a concerted effort to keep the public in the dark about any leading man's homosexuality, and aside from the personal torment of living in secrecy, the tragic consequences came home in Hollywood when Rock Hudson and others—Liberace, Nureyev—began to die from HIV without ever acknowledging they had AIDS. The stigma was stultifying. And their deaths were tragic and lonely. As the pandemic spread, more and more show business talents were struck down.

In the '80s, when Roy contracted AIDS, he swore me to secrecy, because if people knew, his work opportunities could dry up. His classes were packed, and he was about to break through as a director. I was relieved that the antiretroviral medicines seemed to be keeping the virus under control, and I kept his secret. I hoped he would beat this. But one day he called and told me the numbers on his tests had slipped. Dread crept up my spine. We had known so many talented people in our business who had died. One night at a fancy restaurant in Hollywood, Roy had introduced me to Larry Kramer, whose passionate play *The Normal Heart*[1] which had indicted both the New York City government and the Reagan administration for ignoring the disease, which made the tragic consequences worse.

When one day I called to schedule a visit with Roy in Los Angeles while I would be there on a break from shooting a film, his phone message said that he and his partner, Tim, were scouting locations. But no sooner did I get back to New Mexico, where I was filming *Wyatt Earp,* than Tim called to tell me Roy was in the hospital and didn't want anyone to know. I told Tim I had to leave for Kentucky, where I was joining Actors Theatre of Louisville. It was too late for me to get back to LA. I didn't know then that it was too late for Roy. He never left the hospital, and on August 8, 1993, he died at age fifty.

I like to remember Roy the way he was the afternoon he brought Tim over and we sat in my patio and had cold drinks. He had grown a full beard and let his head go bald; he had stopped dieting and was positively portly but in a great, dignified way, like a Sydney Greenstreet. He wore a white linen suit, elegant. They arrived in his BMW, the two of them happy and on their way back to their Hollywood penthouse from their getaway in Santa Barbara. And so in love.

Roy London lives on in me and in so many of his students' work. The audience sees him there, but I wish I could see him here. It was Roy's wisdom that enabled me, no matter what Mike threw at me, to give myself to "Ma," and to the audience.

17. Never Say Die

"Ambition is necessary to accomplishment. . . . To win anything, we must have the ambition to do so."
—*These Happy Golden Years*, LAURA INGALLS WILDER

WE WERE MORE THAN HALFWAY INTO the second season when Mike told me they had a special script in the works for Ma, and I hoped the thaw was coming. It was an adaptation of a story they had done on *Bonanza* for Little Joe. In "A Matter of Faith," Caroline gets a little scratch on her leg while she is helping to unload some wire from the wagon. Thinking nothing of it at the time, she continues with her work. The family is going away for a big country picnic, but Ma's obligation to bake pies for the church keeps her at home. The plan is for Reverend Alden to give her a ride to the picnic when he comes to pick up the pies. When the infection starts to take hold, she is alone. She applies rising dough to the wound, a natural remedy since yeast could act as an antibiotic and might have helped. But in this case the infection is already too deep. Thus begins a saga of pain, fever, and collapse. When Reverend Alden comes to pick up the pies—cooling on the porch—she's in desperate shape, unconscious, and can't rouse herself to call for help, and he assumes she's gone on with the family. While Charles and the girls frolic in the countryside, Ma becomes sicker, and in the climax, Caroline turns to her Bible for help. The verse "And if thy hand offend thee, cut it off..." seems the answer to her prayers. She takes the butcher knife in hand, steels herself for the cut, the camera blacks out.

This episode was heaven for me: make it physically demanding, pile on the pain and suffering, and let me at it. I was grateful for an episode that gave me a greater range than serving rabbit stew or getting the kids off to school. Transforming from happy, barefoot, baking woman to passing out in the mud in a rainstorm? *Yes, indeed. When do I start?*

Whitey arranged for us to have prosthetics made to show the advancing infection that would threaten Caroline's leg, and ultimately her life. He was unusually qualified to discuss this with designers because once, when he was working on a picture in the Caribbean, he'd gotten a minor wound to his hand that became infected, and in the tropical climate, the bacteria replicated virulently. His entire arm became swollen, gangrene began to set in, and he was flown home to be treated. Modern medicine saved his arm and his hand, but he knew if he hadn't been treated in time, he would have lost his arm, and his livelihood. Whitey understood viscerally that Caroline could lose her leg or her life.

He and I drove out to the North Valley to John Chambers' lab, where *Planet of the Apes* prosthetics had been created for the 1968 film. Chambers had received a special award from the Motion Picture Academy for that work, and a behind-the-scenes opportunity to see his studio excited me. His company worked in a big open, warehouse-like room with white walls. It was spotless. There they took a mold of my leg so they could create prosthetics that would fit seamlessly. We had three, in graduated sizes, made in order to show the advancing infection, and Whitey's artistry when it came to painting garish colors onto the molded swellings was remarkable. He knew how ugly and yet how colorful an infection could be. And each night at home I limped around so I could develop the physical progress of the infection—"living with" this debility hour after hour to achieve the effect I wanted. Bill Claxton was directing, and I was grateful because Bill was so sensitive to my need on occasion to pause to prepare for a scene.

What I brought to the role of Ma was the quality of purity of soul. Not that Karen Grassle was pure, but I had a deep-rooted longing for a spiritual connection and a true belief in wholeness. I'd laid aside my childhood obsession with Jesus, and I was no longer a Christian, but my commitment to my work was pure. By this time, anxiety over the contract and hurt by rejection combined with my hopeless strategy of killing emotional pain with alcohol and marijuana had gone a long way toward destroying my sense of self, but on occasion my soul seemed to flicker to life in service to a greater cause. I was fractured internally by anger, self-justification, and bitterness in those days, and I needed some of what Caroline Ingalls had—faith.

One afternoon, a week or so after we wrapped and moved on to another episode, Mike came to me while we were shooting some of my coverage of that day's work. He told me there were problems with "A Matter of Faith" and the next day, at lunch, he showed me the rough cut. It was disappointing, flat. Somehow, the camera had not captured what was there. It looked to me as if the scenes were all shot in a long shot, so the details of my work and Whitey's artistry remained nearly invisible. The distance made for a lack of involvement, and Mike was unhappy and wanted to reshoot some of the scenes. I was grateful.

He set a time, after all the kids had gone home, for us to do the work, and that afternoon felt like the old days: two colleagues working in harmony and creating something together. Our creative spirits did what we had been unable to do as human beings—we rose up and greeted each other, and as we worked, the respect and caring reminded each of us of why we liked each other and why we liked to work together.

When we were almost finished, as he and I walked toward the coffee table away from the crew, I thanked him. "I really appreciate your doing this."

"It had to be done," he said tersely.

"I've missed these times—working like this—together."

"Uh, me too." *A chink in the wall?*

I touched his arm and felt as if I might cry.

"I didn't know what to do," I said.

"It's my fault. I wouldn't talk."

"If something like that happens again, what should I do?"

"You can't do anything. I'm the boss. . . . It was my responsibility to address it."

I squeezed his shoulder, appreciating his acknowledgment, and said, "Thanks."

As we stood on the concrete floor of the dark stage talking, I could hear an almost audible sigh of relief from the crew, and arm in arm Mike and I returned to the set and completed the show.

Surely, I thought, *now he will settle my contract.*

But no. The standoff continued.

ALTHOUGH I FELT BETRAYED, I went on the next promo tour determined not to make our stalemate public. The trip was much harder, because of the lack of appreciation from Mike and the loss of Tuie, and by the time the limo picked me up in Philadelphia for *The Mike Douglas Show,* I was in a poisonous mood made up of one part loneliness, one part cynicism, and a big splash of low blood sugar. When the driver explained we needed to wait in order to pick up someone else, I was put out (*Me—wait? I'm tired. I need to get to the hotel, have a glass of wine, eat*). Fortunately, I didn't open my mouth.

We picked up a guy named Dave with a neat beard, compact body, and smart blue eyes who turned out to be a writer—a type I liked, but *whoops, a wedding band, so back off.* He was there to write for the week's cohost, the new network variety show star Jim Stafford, a country and western singer. I was to appear as a guest the next day when they taped.

Starving, I went straight to the hotel restaurant, and Dave joined me. His comedy team partner ambled in, looking for him. Tom was a tall, skinny guy with a neat Charlie Chaplin mustache and droll humor, and when I saw him, I thought, *I'm in trouble.* The next day after the taping, he asked me out for drinks and dinner. His neck was killing him, so I offered him a neck and shoulder massage. I left the hotel room the next morning before dawn to catch my plane, but not before we made love, and when I got home and told Mama how young he was, twenty-nine, she said, "Any port in the storm, huh?" But back in Los Angeles, ever after that, Tom would show up with good humor, offering to fix the screen door, or taking me out to hear comedy. He was sympathetic to my contract struggles, and a few months later, I helped him move his stuff to High Tower Road. In addition to an intense sex life, Tom and I shared deep affection, long work hours, and paid close attention to our industry, studying *Hill Street Blues*, and relaxing with *Saturday Night Live* in bed.

After Philadelphia, my tour went on to Minnesota and then Fort Worth, where the creative electricity Cynthia Lovelace Sears and I had generated found its subject. The head of the NBC affiliate station in Fort Worth remembered me from his station in New England the year before and had thoughtfully arranged an interview with a feminist reporter instead of the TV critic. Katie Sherrod, an investigative journalist, had just completed a series of original articles on wife beating for the *Fort Worth Star-Telegram*. She described to me what she had learned. Like most people at the time, I thought wife beating happened only among the poor or the ill-educated, but Katie enlightened me. She had talked with doctors' wives, a minister's wife, a cop's wife, and as she told me stories, I saw how television could expose it.

Frustration over the limits of Ma, fatigue from the relentless promo tour, all faded as I listened to Katie and felt a surge of energy to expose this long-hidden issue. Back home, I read Katie's series with my heart pounding. She had uncovered the horrid crime happening behind closed doors in homes of all kinds, all over the country. Cynthia agreed: This was the most compelling of the many subjects she and I had considered, so we began our project about battered women with passion. Coming from an alcoholic home, I was familiar with the anxiety, the fear of an explosive scene, the dread of waiting for the other shoe to drop. Tom was enthusiastic and gave us screenwriting tips. Besides being smart and talented, he was inhaling the practical side of the business.

In 1975, domestic violence was misunderstood and almost entirely hidden, and when Cynthia and I tried to do research, we found just one brief mention in a women's magazine about a shelter in England and one paragraph in *Newsweek*.[1] That was it. We knew we had to do what Katie Sherrod had done—original research. There were only two shelters for victims of domestic violence in all of the United States: one in St. Paul, Minnesota, and one nearby. We called Haven House in Pasadena and drove out to see the director and her assistant. They set up interviews with women in the shelter with the understanding that all their names would be kept confidential. We never knew their last names, and those women were incredibly generous in sharing their painful, personal stories as we recorded. Having had her own radio show interviewing authors on KPFK in Los Angeles, Cynthia was a skilled interviewer. And I had been attracted to journalism, doing research and talking to people about their lives. We were a good team, each of us drawing out the women in our own way, and their lives shaped our story.

We began the research and preliminary story construction during my off hours from the show. During the hiatus between seasons two and three, we worked intensely. Once back at work, I never knew when I'd be free, and since Cynthia was a single mom and needed to plan for time when we could work, I visited Kent to find out how he arranged the schedule. On a big cork bulletin board, colored strips represented every single scene for the episode about to be shot. Kent showed me how he could tell at a glance what equipment to order and which drivers, actors, and animals to call for each scene by looking at this board. His precision was one of the reasons the crew was so loyal to the show. Predictability was worth a lot because it saved money and contributed to a creative atmosphere. He showed me how to interpret the board so that I could let Cynthia know my availability. Whenever I got off work early or found a gap in the shooting schedule for my character, I raced to Cynthia's home. And we worked.

STEADY KENT, THE BALLAST FOR OUR boat, was also the person I went to about the tensions on the set. I thought perhaps he had to carry those extra pounds to absorb all the bombarding signals he was forever getting from every direction, while appearing calm at all times. Whatever internal pressures roiled him, to us he appeared unruffled and reliable. I asked him what I could do to break the logjam with Mike. Kent told me we should talk.

I explained, "He won't talk to me. It's awful." Kent knew he couldn't tell Mike what to do, but he also knew the situation was corrosive to the company's morale. He had watched my part being cut and knew what I was talking about when I said, "Look—it's got to be love or money. I'm not getting good scenes, so it will have to be money." And somehow, behind the scenes, he must have helped to resolve the standoff. He and Mike were not only a great team, they were friends, and I'm sure some secret masculine communication took place that most of us would never know, because suddenly one day Deane called me and announced I had won. NBC was coming through with a set of annual raises and required me, in turn, to sign the contract. My weekly salary more than doubled. A new schedule of salary increases was set through season seven, the last year of the contract. And equally important to me: I got guarantees of a certain number of shows featuring Ma each season—the work I needed to make this worthwhile for me as an artist. The relief, the triumph, and gratitude that the fight was over and we could move on were immense. At least, I thought we could move on.

I was under less stress and would have more resilience in the work with Cynthia, I thought. The basic structure of our movie, which we called *Battered*, had presented itself fairly early. We wanted interlocking stories from different classes of society. Developing the actual scenes and dialogue took more time, and exposure to the material was disturbing. Each of us began to have nightmares. Cynthia was an intelligent and talented writer with a steady, calm personality, and that was a good thing, because we drank plenty of white wine in our sessions.

But I was not steady, and fueled by double-duty workdays, swilling coffee and white wine, my mood swings became more and more erratic. One weekend, I went to UCLA to hear Del Martin on a panel. Del had written a book on wife beating that had been published by a small press, and I'd discovered it advertised in the classifieds in *Ms. Magazine*. I was eager to hear her and also to speak with her. Dr. Sharon Kaufman-Diamond, a psychiatrist with great insight about violence against women and how it permeated our culture, was another panelist, and I knew right away, she could help us immeasurably.

Within a few months, I followed up by calling her for professional help with my own life, which was becoming more and more bewildering to me. Without realizing it, the dedication to the project had led me to my own life raft. This is the beauty of synchronicity, which Cynthia and I also shared as we applied our whole selves to this film.

DURING SEASON THREE of *Little House*, we shot "Little Girl Lost," in which Carrie falls into an abandoned well. Mike was overwhelmed one day with my work and said he thought I could win an Emmy. He went to the phone to call NBC with this idea. I was buoyed by his support. Then nothing happened. Most of the other scripts developed during the previous months were minimal for Ma, but I did have some fun doing *Battle of the Network Stars* for ABC.

For a few weeks before the competition, I tried to get in shape. Walking up the hill (still smoking), swimming at the pool every night after filming when we shot over in Tucson. My old colleague, Bill Devane, was our NBC captain, and it was fun to be with other actors. I surprised myself when I beat Farrah Fawcett at tennis and Adrienne Barbeau from *Maude* at the obstacle course. The NBC team didn't win the competition that year, but we came back and won later. The producers provided limos for all of us, and after the competition, we all partied in our team trailers. I don't remember getting home. In the morning, I found my work bag set just inside the back door and the door closed. The driver had taken care of me. As Blanche says in *Streetcar*, "the kindness of strangers."

At the *Little House*, we had some genuine excitement when Johnny and June Carter Cash appeared on the show. June shared a story with me of such profound faith that I have never forgotten it. I knew they both had experience with alcoholism, and I wondered if she sensed my need, and soon I was working very hard with Dr. Kaufman-Diamond, who, as a medical doctor as well as a highly trained psychiatrist, began to take stock of my symptoms, physical as well as emotional.

Dr. Kaufman-Diamond had helped Cynthia and me as we developed our understanding of the battered wife syndrome. We had worked for months developing our characters and story.[2] We had decided the film would revolve around the stories of three couples. I would play the wife in the white, upper middle-class couple. We also sketched out a blue-collar older couple and a younger Black couple, starting out with little money and two small children. As we shared our ideas with experts, someone pointed out that one character was an "incipient alcoholic." I thought, *If he's alcoholic, then what about me?* The more I read and learned about the battering syndrome, the more I realized that I identified with both sides: the perpetrator's rage as well as the victim's pain.

One day as I was enthusiastically telling Mama about the progress Cynthia and I were making with our story, she told me her own mother had been beaten by her father. She had never mentioned this. I knew a lot about her life as a little girl, but I didn't know about the beatings. I wondered, though, if my mother had unconsciously chosen a husband who was an alcoholic because she was caught in a cycle of codependence and shame that she had absorbed as a little girl. My father never hit her, but psychologically Mama was hit again and again by his drinking.

And still, whenever Cynthia and I worked late, I drove home drunk along Sunset Boulevard, sailing around the curves, feeling the flow, heading for the High Tower Road house. On weeknights, by the time I got to the Sunset Strip, it was so late the place was deserted and in my tired, inebriated state, it seemed to me unnecessary to stop for red lights—stopping would only break my rhythm. I can only thank God that I never killed anyone.

Months into our work together, as my mood swings became more unpredictable, Cynthia grew understandably anxious about whether or not we would get a producer to sign on so that we could start getting paid. Fitting our work around her daughters' schooling and my shooting schedule was taking a toll on her. Many afternoons, the kids came home from school but had little time with their mom because we were working. Finally, I set up a meeting with Michael Jaffe, with whom I had worked on a Hallmark Special, and he made a development deal with us and NBC. We modestly believed we should turn our treatment over to a professional writer, but Jaffe said, "This is your story; you write it." At this point, I finally got the nerve to tell Mike I had a deal to do this film. At first, he was taken aback, but then he was supportive, offered to share the production process with me, and seemed proud when he told Teddy. I set out to learn more about the nuts and bolts of filmmaking. Teddy Voigtlander, our Emmy-winning cinematographer, shared his favorite book on cinematography, *The Five C's of Cinematography*. Mike let me come to dailies at lunch time, though when I discovered he made fun of the actors during these sessions, I stopped going because I didn't want his cruel jokes in my head later in the day, when I might be playing a scene with one of them.

Cynthia and I went to work writing. One of our techniques was to improvise the scenes into the tape recorder which we then transcribed. We each worked on different scenes before trading to rewrite. But suddenly Jaffe became anxious about getting a first draft. "It's fine if it's very rough—I just want to see *something*," he said, so we typed up our unfinished scenes and turned them in. That was a huge mistake and a hard lesson. Now *he* was convinced he needed a professional writer to get the script in shape. When we couldn't get the writer we wanted, he urged us to work with someone known for war pictures and macho subjects, because he liked the guy. Cynthia and I, humbled by our lack of experience, went along. Let's call him John Wayne. Our hero!

Part Five

Everything Flowers

"... for everything flowers, from within, of self-blessing;
though sometimes it is necessary
to reteach a thing its loveliness."
—"Saint Francis and the Sow," GALWAY KINNELL

18. Hitting Bottom

> "You know a person cannot live at a high pitch of emotion,
> the feelings become dulled by a natural, unconscious effort
> at self-preservation."
>
> —*The Selected Letters of Laura Ingalls Wilder*,
> WILLIAM ANDERSON, EDITOR

SOMETIMES CHANGE IS HURTLING DOWN the tracks, nothing will be the same, and although you've barely noticed the hum in the vibrating steel, it's coming nonetheless. This was my life at the beginning of season four, as I prepared to shoot an episode called "The Handyman." In this script, Pa suddenly has to go away for a job, just after demolishing our back wall to add on a real kitchen. As luck would have it, a wandering handyman shows up in town just in time to take on the job, live in the old sod house, and take meals with the family. The undercurrent was romance.

This was June 1977, and as I reflect back on this time, I feel as if two separate worlds were simultaneously spinning. By day I was optimistic: The contract was settled, Tom and I were looking for a house to buy together, a big PR firm was designing a campaign for a play I was going to do in LA—a play to prove my chops beyond the prairie—preproduction was underway for *Battered*, and I was about to begin an episode written for Ma. I planned to get in shape, get healthy. I told myself this as I carried my wine glass across the path to our neighbors' pool to exercise.

But by night I was sucked into the black hole: Chaotic, whirling emotions, sudden mood swings, anxious nightmares, and searing anger overcame me without warning. My journal was etched with despair. The I Ching warned not to "consume oneself like a flame." At one point I thought I was pregnant, and as I got sicker, my periods began to disappear. I adopted a cynical, superior humor, like the bumper sticker Tom gave me for my Volvo: "I'm mad as hell and I'm not going to take it anymore!" from the movie *Network* by Paddy Chayefsky. Privately I thought, *I need an exorcist, not a shrink.*

I CONTINUED TO WORK WITH Dr. Kaufman-Diamond. The first thing she had insisted on was that I demand the *Little House* company give me guaranteed time each week to see her, and Kent arranged that. She also insisted, "No more than two glasses of wine a night." I bought enormous goblets, arguing to myself that wine was my reward when a job went well, a balm when life was tough, a stimulant to keep going when I was tired, my sleeping draught at the end of a long day.

But Dr. Kaufman-Diamond zeroed in on my symptoms. She set up an appointment with a metabolic specialist to get to the bottom of my mood swings. When she confronted my self-obsession, I suddenly had a bracing view of myself. I'm amazed I didn't run from treatment, but some life-affirming force inside me kept me returning to her office week after week. I endured cascading humbling insights that conspired with a shred of hope that I could get better. She told me to cut out the self-pity at work. Playing the victim would, she said, only please the one doing the punishing. I switched up right away to a bright "Good morning."

All these years later I'm astonished that despite the depression, the long hours, double duty with Cynthia and Dr. Kaufman-Diamond, I felt upbeat because I had a delightful script to work on—a departure from the usual Ma. Just days before we were to begin, Susan Sukman, our casting director, came down to the set to tell me that a family tragedy had struck the star who was to play the handyman, but she had found someone new for the part.

"You'll really like him," she told me. "He's great looking, and he's going to be a star. His name is Gil Gerard." She was right on all counts. Within a few years Gil would be starring in his own series, *Buck Rogers*. He had that charisma many women find irresistible, and when he showed up on the set, even the little girls sat up and took notice. He was sweet and hard-working and endeared himself to all of us women—young and old. Like my dad, he was from the mid-South, and like my first husband, Leon, he had the soft edges and sensitivity that even high-testosterone men in the South often have. When our female hairdresser, Gladys Witten—she had been Marilyn Monroe's hair stylist—met him, she advised me, "He's for playing, not for marrying." I wondered, *How does she know? How do you tell?* I honestly had no idea.

When I was growing up, my dad was responsible and devoted to our family—in spite of his alcoholism. He paid the bills, was home most every night for dinner, helped with the dishes, and worked alongside Mama all day Sunday. I took their partnership for granted. My mother and I never discussed what made a good husband. In the '60s, my contemporaries and I had determined that our mothers' old-fashioned rules didn't apply, and we tossed out boundaries that had protected us as we matured—concern for reputation, fear of pregnancy, modesty—and launched the Sexual Revolution. When the Pill came along, the chief inhibitor disappeared. Young men had to do very little to lure us into bed. I remember discussing virginity with my freshman roommate at Cal, she and I concluding it was impractical. But I was unprepared for the men I met who didn't pay their own way, who fooled around, who didn't help with the chores.

What I hadn't counted on as a modern "liberated" woman was that my body would be so firmly connected to my heart and mind.

In college and on the Pill, I tried to have sex with someone and just walk away, but I could not easily compartmentalize my feelings from my actions. I might act free, but I became attached to the men I slept with and often quickly. I learned over the years that sex is so powerful a force for women (or at least for this woman), so bonding that taboos surrounding it can serve a critical function: protection until she knows clearly that the man to whom she is attracted is the partner she wants.

But I was dancing to songs like "Love the One You're With" and "Light My Fire," and I masked my true feelings with pot and alcohol. Eventually I, and so many others I knew who didn't say no, suffered heartbreak, sexually transmitted diseases, cheating husbands, and men who felt no responsibility to pay child support. Our "right to work" became our necessity as we struggled to take care of families on our own. As college-educated women, some of us began to wonder, what have we wrought?

While filming "The Handyman," I was still trying to separate my body from my soul and the erotic undercurrent of the plot was all too easy for me to play. While Caroline's boundaries were firm, my own were not, and Gil was distractingly attractive. Tom was working out of town, and so I danced with Gil to Fleetwood Mac, singing,

"Players only love you when they're playing . . .
When the rain washes you clean, you'll know." [1]

There was something I knew—but didn't want to know. Having a fling with Gil, humming along in my car to James Taylor's "Handyman," lying to Tom, and covering up my duplicity with white wine wasn't working. A head of steam was building up inside my core. I didn't suspect that my true desire was for stability, a husband who wanted a family, and children of my own. I didn't have a clue that I wanted what Caroline Ingalls actually had.

On the last day of filming "The Handyman," I arranged a buffet lunch for the crew to show my appreciation. Naturally, I ordered beer and wine along with sodas. It was meant to be a quasi-wrap party for the episode. We had only a few final scenes to shoot in the afternoon. By then, I had given up my strict rule never to drink while at work and occasionally had a "hair of the dog" drink during lunch. I was aware that I had to limit my intake, but I seldom knew anymore how much was too much.

That afternoon, long tables were set up alongside the interior set of the house and barn and spread with a simple lunch of cold cuts, pasta salads, bread, and condiments. And white wine. During the lunch hour, I played gracious hostess, pouring for others and having a glass myself. My attraction to Gil gave me an adrenaline rush, the work had gone well, and tension over my contract was in the past. All was right with my world. Wasn't it?

But when we went back to work, I kept wanting to return to the table for more wine. I moved farther from the table. I smoked a cigarette. I had my makeup touched up for the afternoon's work. I dropped Binaca on my tongue to change the taste. And still, my body felt as if a huge magnet was pulling me back to the table. The craving was interfering with my concentration. I walked outside, used the bathroom, took some deep breaths, and came back. The caterers had cleared the table and put leftovers on a small table near props. Never mind that we were back at work. No one could see. No one would know. I wasn't falling down. I wasn't dancing on the table. But my mind was focused on the wine bottle, and I suddenly saw I was utterly hooked. This time I had no one and nothing to blame. Except myself.

I shook it off. I had no time to reflect. As soon as we wrapped, I had to fly to the University of Wisconsin to be one of the main speakers at a women's conference. At the airport I was picked up and driven to a lovely small hotel near campus. The next day someone would pick me up to take me to the luncheon. The women attending the conference would be in workshops all morning, so I would have a little extra time to prepare my talk. I'd been making notes for weeks but hadn't finished writing it, and that night after dinner, under pressure to pull it together, I ordered a carafe of coffee and a bottle of white wine from room service and settled down to work. This seemed perfectly normal, but when the tray arrived with my drinks, a little voice inside whispered, "Enjoy this because it's almost over." I brushed that voice aside.

I dove into my subject, broadly, the fear of women and how it conspired to keep us an underclass. My talk was informed by such anthropological studies as *The Golden Bough* and *The Chalice and the Blade*, but the sources I was most excited about were Phyllis Chesler's *Women and Madness* and Jean Baker Miller's *Toward a New Psychology of Women*. Chesler's premise—that a sexist society makes women crazy—resonated. Without wishing to diminish her exquisite argument, in brief she had advanced the theory that, because the human fetus begins with two X chromosomes and only later develops masculinity, men had a cellular fear of falling back into their double-X chromosome femaleness. Therefore, they had to repress their own femininity and subjugate women.

In our research on battered women, Cynthia and I had noticed how acting victimized or showing weakness could frequently bring on more beatings. I was on a mission to arrest this pattern, excited about the potential of equality of women to advance freedom for both sexes. Baker Miller analyzed the way the lack of shared parenting landed resentment, fear, and anger on women. Steeped in feminist writings, with more material than I could possibly use, I wrote and wrote until late, leaving the three-by-five cards for the morning.

I took breakfast in my room, worked on the cards, and did my hair and makeup. I ironed my suit and dressed. I was dropped off at the conference center for the luncheon, but when I arrived, no one else was yet there. I learned the morning seminars and workshops were running late, so I waited at the bar, ordered a white wine spritzer—a ladylike drink—and studied my notes. Still, few people arrived, but someone from the conference assured me they would be there soon. *I sure hope they're right,* I thought. The longer I waited, the more butterflies flew in my stomach. *Oh—glass empty. Order another.* I'd always had stage fright before speaking engagements, and that day I felt unusually underprepared. *Hope this wine calms me down.*

Soon hundreds of women began to stream into the dining room, chatting in small groups, finding their friends, collecting at round tables of ten. Someone introduced me to my co-presenter, Caroline Bird, the author of the provocative book *The Two-Paycheck Marriage.* As I carried my third glass of white wine to the dais, Caroline and I struck up a lively conversation on the challenges of women earning more than their husbands or male partners and whether this subject might make a good Movie of the Week. The meal was the usual rubbery chicken and peas, but I was much too nervous to eat. In the sea of faces, I noticed one table where the group seemed decidedly unfriendly—they would look up, then lean in and whisper in a way that seemed hostile. This was my first experience with the antagonistic clique I later would become accustomed to seeing. It was the "Right to Life" crowd showing up to intimidate me at personal appearances. *Oh boy,* I thought, *wait 'til they hear what I have to say today.*

It was time. I stood, turned on my small Sony recorder and began. My talk focused on how a woman's sexual vitality expressed by her apparently magical power to create life, as well as her capacity to be multi-orgasmic, intimidated the male of the species. Man's need to identify his offspring and protect his property plus his lack of control stirred together were motivators for subjugation. I rolled on to the battle over women's right to procreate—or not. My talk was ambitious, and needless to say, a contrast to the image so many had of me as Ma. Some people had come to hear me spout Ma homilies, no doubt, but this was a feminist conference and I sensed the audience paying close attention.

Alas, I hadn't sufficiently boiled down my material or memorized. Rather, I relied on my notes, and excited as I was to make my points, I soon was droning on without realizing it. Suddenly I heard the click of my tape recorder turning off, which meant I had been talking for half an hour; I'd been asked for fifteen minutes. I flushed red, wrapped it up, and sat down, folding myself into the padded chair and wishing I could slide under the table. Applause, merely polite.

I couldn't have felt worse if I had stripped in front of them. I had disgraced myself among the women I respected. I was grateful my plane was leaving that afternoon, but now I had a raging hunger. I hadn't eaten lunch, so I insisted the unfortunate student who had to ferry me to the airport stop so I could get something to go. She wasn't sure where to stop, we had so little time, and there is no doubt I was being picky and impatient. She must have been relieved to see me checked in at the airport and out of her sight.

Once on the small plane making the short hop to Minneapolis where I looked forward to visiting Toni for the night, I leaned back and sighed. *Christ! I need a drink.* No problem. In those days, we were always offered alcohol when we flew. When my seatmate made a pass, I got up to confide this to the stewardess, and when she recognized me as a celebrity—the show was huge, and people were forever stopping me—she led me to the cockpit to meet the pilot. He and I were soon chatting away. I signed autographs for his kids.

Toni was waiting for me at the gate when I careened off the plane, but one look told her I was smashed. She drove me home to her cottage on a lake and fed me dinner. But no wine. She no longer drank. After dinner, as I stretched out on her couch, she began to talk to me about being an alcoholic. Toni was perhaps the one person in the world who could tell me—and who I could hear, "I'm an alcoholic, and I think you are, too." We had been drunk in the Berkeley Hills, stoned in Santa Barbara, and high in a London casino. She knew me. We had always had a unique understanding of each other and now, here was the disease, lurking. She named it. The only person on the planet who could say this to me and I would not argue.

She began to talk quietly about recovery, and the need to give up grass, too. If looks could kill, she'd have been exterminated. "But I can't get through this world without something!" I exclaimed. Despite being in intense psychotherapy—two to four hours a week by then—I couldn't imagine living without my "medicine." I had never been honest with my psychiatrist about how much I drank, and now with Toni, the walls were closing in. Still, her proposal—going to a self-help program—was out of the question.

I had an appointment the next day to meet with the director of the St. Paul shelter for battered women to get feedback on our script. Toni dropped me off at my appointment, and afterwards I caught a cab to the airport. On the plane, I discovered I had no cash (and this wasn't first class), and the stewardess wouldn't take a traveler's check for a drink. I turned my fury on the airline. Poor me. I sat and stewed throughout the long flight.

The next morning, I was sitting in bed, hung over and drinking coffee, when Tom said he had something he had to tell me. "When I'm working out of town," he said, "I don't feel this knot in my gut."

I sucked in my breath. I knew where he was going with this.

"I don't mean this as a threat," he said, "but when I get home, it's my stomach. I feel . . ."

He spoke slowly, even more thoughtfully than usual. I could feel his pain at having to tell me this life with me was terrible. I waited for him to finish, felt his hand lying gently on mine.

"It's this knot, in my gut," he said. "Like something awful . . ."

"I know, I know . . ." I said.

"I can't go on like this."

"No," I said. "You don't deserve this, Tom. You don't."

I had no answer for him or for myself. As he leaned in—concerned, still hopeful I could give him a magic solution—I looked at him and said, "The thing is, I can't promise you I'll get better. I've tried everything, and I'm no better. My psychiatrist is saying I may be hypo-manic—that's like manic-depressive."

Tom began to ask when, or why, or what, I'm not sure what he wanted to ask, but I slowly shook my head.

"I don't have any more excuses. Any more promises. I don't get better. I get worse," I said.

We both had tears in our eyes. I felt hopelessness envelop me.

We'd been getting ready to buy a home together, but could he still want to do that? After he went back to Utah, I continued to look on my own. Bereft, on nights when I was home alone, I found myself running upstairs, arriving on the landing only to wonder why I was there, running down again but not knowing what I wanted downstairs. I was having hot flashes and wondered if it was early menopause.

Thank heavens Roy was still alive then. I called him and asked him to meet me for dinner. We went to a little Italian place he had discovered. At first, I told him I wasn't drinking, but after a few minutes, we decided to split half a carafe. Half a carafe for the two of us was a joke. Years earlier, when Roy first came to California, he and I stopped at the wine merchant one Friday night to buy wine for weekend guests; I needed something better than the usual half gallons of Almaden Chablis I had at home. Someone in New York had sent Roy the recording of the then great new musical *A Chorus Line*, and back at my place we spun the record and danced our hearts out in a Bacchic celebration of show business—and we drank all the wine, all of it. So, ordering half a carafe to split was the epitome of denial. Naturally we followed it with a full carafe, and on a roll, we went to visit a friend and drank from his gallon of Almaden. Inspired, we tore off our clothes and dived into the apartment complex pool.

And suddenly, and without warning, my feelings were hurt. I pulled on my clothes, ran to my car, and drove home—quite a trick with one eye closed to keep from seeing double and both eyes spouting tears. I have no idea what Roy said to me that night. When I got home, I discovered that Molly was mad at having been left alone too long and had emptied the trash all over the kitchen floor. I swept and sobbed and sobbed and swept, a drama queen at her best, when Roy arrived. "What?" he asked. "What happened?" I talked in circles—worried about my partnership with Cynthia, paranoid that my attorney had heard something bad about me from our producer, afraid Tom would leave me. I wept, repeating over and over the tragic drumroll of events, experiences, people I imagined were destroying me. Roy was afraid to leave me alone that night, so he rushed home to get his clothes for an audition he had the next day and returned only to find me passed out in bed, a glass of wine unfinished on my nightstand.

The next morning, when I woke swollen with another god-awful hangover, I had only one thought: *I must never drink again.* That was five days after Toni told me I was an alcoholic. Five days since I'd heard that click. I knew I couldn't fight anymore. Surrender. *Whatever it takes, I must never take another drink.* In my mind, I imagined I would lose my lover, both my lovers, maybe my job, too. I thought, I'll never eat in another fancy restaurant or even have Mexican food. It was the end of pleasure. And still, even if all that were true, I was clear about one thing: no more drinking. I was finished. I called a recovery program to ask for help.

19. Sea Change

"This is now."

—*Little House in the Big Woods*, LAURA INGALLS WILDER

THE DAY AFTER MY SURRENDER, I had lunch with Deane Johnson, and he told me he had been planning to talk with me about my drinking. He'd heard some reports from Michael Jaffe, which embarrassed me, but he said that his best friend, William Holden, had been alcoholic and years earlier had gotten sober. Deane was enthusiastic about my plan.

I went to my appointment with Dr. Kaufman-Diamond and told her.

Otherwise I told no one. Afraid to fail. Afraid to jinx it.

For three or four mornings, I woke astonished to have another day without a hangover. Unsure of my ability to keep going, I confided only in my mother, my sister, and Roy.

Was it the third day when my neighbor asked me to go with her to the Valley to look for a refrigerator? At a loss, with a day free from shooting and feeling shaky and scared, I grabbed the chance not to be alone. I told my neighbor I was giving up alcohol and had gotten into a recovery program, and I learned that this news didn't shock her. She reminded me about the first time Tom and I had come to her home for dinner, and I'd spilled red wine all over my new cotton outfit and had to take off my flowing trousers to wash them. She and her husband hadn't minded since they'd had a secret agenda to get all four of us to take our pants off. But Tom and I demurred.

We headed north on a busy boulevard, passing rows of tacky commercial buildings. A billboard screamed its glamorous icy call for Russian vodka. Not even my drink, but my mouth watered. Day too hot, too bright. I dragged myself through showrooms of appliances, while my neighbor debated the insides of refrigerators, examined freezers. We rolled farther into this concrete valley of discount stores, car repair shops, and bars. Bars: their neon flashed brighter than the summer sun. I'd never liked bars, but that day every cell of my body yearned to enter one of those seedy, dark places, longed to sit at a long bar or in a padded booth where I could salve my wounded self. So, this was "craving." Until this moment of deciding to resist, I hadn't understood I had a craving. It had been like that on the set. On the plane. It was like that for at least two months. My nerves felt sand-papered. I sweated. I walked a tightrope.

PEOPLE SAY WHEN YOU FIRST GET clean and sober, it's wise not to make any other big changes, but that train was already speeding down the tracks. A few months earlier when Deane called to tell me my contract was settled, he asked, "What are you going to do with all that money?" and I told him I supposed I had better shelter some of it from income tax. Deane told me, "I wish I had fifty cents on the dollar today for every dollar I tried to shelter. The best investment I know of is to own your own home. You can write off the interest on your mortgage and build equity."

I shook my head at my own naïveté regarding anything having to do with money—and I was the daughter of a Realtor. But okay. Tom and I wanted to own our own home. He was a Midwestern guy with straightforward values, a guy who insisted he carry his own weight. We figured we could work out something so that each of us paid according to our incomes.

I had been going to open houses on Sundays, but it was hard alone, and with a hangover. Everything was so expensive. This was the year, 1977, when *Los Angeles* magazine ran a cover with an out-house on it and the caption: "What do you want for $200,000.00?" I was looking for small-paned windows, nooks and crannies, and I wasn't finding anything.

Then Bernie, my business manager, called about a house he thought I might like. It wasn't on the market yet, so on a Saturday morning, I drove to a serene part of Hollywood Boulevard I hadn't known existed, high above the Sunset Strip. The house sat on its adequate lot fenced off from a turreted, brown-shingled, grander neighbor on one side and protected by a cinder-block retaining wall from the granite hill on the other. The woman real estate agent, Bernie, and I walked through a high wooden gate, across the flag-stone patio to the front door. A weird entry. I turned up my nose: pass right by the swimming pool to reach the front door? *Southern California gauche. Not what I was looking for.*

And yet. And yet. The long and narrow living room had a brick fireplace all the way to the vaulted, beamed ceiling. The house was light and bright everywhere but the hall and bath-rooms. The master bedroom's sliding glass doors opened to a tiny garden and beyond to the lights of Hollywood and downtown. Down the hall was another bedroom, a roomy, cheerful kitchen, and a back porch for my washer and dryer, of which I was still inordinately proud. A small back bedroom—a maid's, I guessed—would be perfect for my office. As we walked out onto the patio, I admitted the patio and pool were nice, with a peaceful ambience presided over by a huge agave. And no one else had yet seen the place. (I later learned that my inside track was the affair my busi-ness manager was having with the attractive agent.) But the price was $180,000! Still, Bernie said I could afford to make an offer. I talked with Tom that night. And we did, but I had no idea that I was hurtling toward sobriety and would be fresh into withdrawal when escrow closed.

DURING MY FIRST DAYS OF SOBER LIFE, I was fearful of falling back into drunken despair, wild kicking rebellion, atomic anger. For at least two months, I looked at the world through pea-soup glasses, my nerves flailed like loose wires in air, my thermostat shot up, and I sweated it out. My blood sugar would catapult suddenly. I'd imagine people who were laughing clear across the studio were laughing at me. Told to drink a Coke, I tried it and felt better. Despite all the therapy, the physiology of my moods was mostly a mystery to me, and I realized I was truly a beginner. I knew I didn't know how not to drink. At recovery meetings, I heard it would get better. And I believed that. Mornings brought blessings—no hangover. No remorse.

But I was very shaky when it was time to pack and move. On a Friday afternoon, I rushed from work to the broker's office to sign escrow papers, sped up to High Tower Road to meet Roy, who was helping me pack. Tom was still in Utah. The moving boxes had not been delivered by the moving company, and the place was helter-skelter. I called the movers, and they said they would have to bring them Monday.

But Monday was moving day. I had the day off.

The man at the moving company did not see the urgency, and I began to complain through the phone about how I had to be out, this was my only time to pack, what did he expect me to do? I did my best to guilt-trip him, but he was unmoved. I inflicted some ear-scorching invective and hung up. A few minutes later the phone rang. I picked up in a panic. The moving man.

"What?" I asked.

"We can't move you. It doesn't seem like it's going to work out."

I was stunned. Then chastened. It was my own fault, and I knew it. That behavior had to stop. Over time I would learn that often the best consciousness raising came from the consequences of my own bad behavior. Roy let me cry on his shoulder, and then I got busy in the yellow pages looking for a mover. When I called Grizzly Bear Movers, butter wouldn't melt in my mouth. They brought the boxes right over. I had been saved, and I knew it. A crack in my armor. The bare beginnings of humility were seeping into me.

I wonder now why I thought I had to pack the whole house myself. I was on a top ten show; I had just received a raise and was making more money in a week than I had made the entire year before I got the show. But I was used to doing things myself; asking for help felt awkward. All weekend Roy and I packed as fast as we could. In each handbag, in every suitcase, in a carry-on or purse, Roy would find a corkscrew and ask—do you want this? No. No. No more corkscrews. No more rush to open the wine bottle.

Monday morning, Grizzly Bear Movers—enormous, friendly men—arrived. I was tame as a turtledove—they would have no trouble with me. Even as they took the long, arduous path uphill, loaded the rickety elevator, rode down, loaded the truck, returned and repeated, on and on, hour after hour, I did not utter one peep of complaint. I could have used a drink. And so could they, apparently, because when Roy and I finally drove over to the new house, the movers took a long time coming. They arrived, they unloaded, and after nine, Roy having gone home, I paid them, and they left. I walked around the empty house. I'd had all the walls painted white. An empty canvas. Quiet. Still. A new life beginning. Five days sober. I dropped my clothes on the flagstone and slipped into the pool and swam a slow breaststroke in the moonlight. I felt safe. And grateful.

The next day I returned to the old house to clean up. Tom was flying in and was to meet me there, but he was late, and full of resentment, I finished cleaning. When he arrived lit up with joy, I saw the plants in his trunk—his celebration of our new home—and I started screaming, "You went to a nursery! While I cleaned alone? I did the whole move! You were buying plants?"

I saw the happiness drain from his face. I began to cry and plead and tell him how sorry I was. "Sorry. Sorry. Sorry." That was his welcome to our new home. My "stop" button had burned out long ago, and it wasn't back just because I wasn't drinking. I had no more rationalizations, though. No excuses. I had no filter for the shame and powerlessness inside. I was horrified by my reactions, sorry, over and over. No one to blame now. Only Karen.

The next day Tom went to business appointments, and Mom and Dad came down to help me unpack. Dad brought his swim trunks and tried out the diving board. He hadn't been drinking, but I had beer in the fridge. It went with a move, didn't it? He drank a beer. Mom asked about Tom. Was that over?

I told her I no longer thought changing people was the answer. I was the constant in all the equations.

IN THE NEARLY EMPTY HOUSE, A SIMPLE routine developed. Most of the time Tom was working out of state. (No wonder.) At the end of the day, I'd return home in the still bright evening of Daylight Savings Time, attentively prepare a balanced meal while drinking apple juice from the wine glass I used to slurp from—some for the skillet, some for me had been my cuisine art—then off to the support group, back home to read, then sleep. Usually, I could sleep. Late that summer, during one of Tom's times home, I had this dream.

I am at a Hollywood party. Everyone is drinking and doing drugs. I know I mustn't, but I begin to drink and smoke dope—or is it cocaine? The scene grows dark. The snake of despair writhes in my gut. I pull away from my companion, hide in the closet, shrinking farther and farther in, hiding behind the clothes. My body implodes—it's terrifying, like dying. Remorse and hopelessness knock at my ribs. My heart is racing . . .

I woke in panic. Had I used? Had I had a drink? Slowly I could feel the true night. I was safe. I hadn't used any drugs or drunk anything. Weepy and trembling, I got up and walked down the dark hall to the kitchen. Like a good pupil, I followed the recipe I'd been given at the beginners' meeting: a mugful of milk splashed into the pan, add honey, warm gently, drink. The mug heated my hand. I held it to my solar plexus. I felt weak, as if I had no bones. Gradually, the milk's warmth, calcium, and sugar restored my equilibrium. I wrote down my dream, still feeling its power over me.

Sitting still in the dark morning, deeply relieved the dream wasn't true, I thought of my father—over seventy now. Maybe this getting sober business was too tough. Maybe he wouldn't be able to face it, no matter how much I wanted it for him. My warm milk gone, I sighed. Well, maybe sobriety is not for everyone. Soon it would be time to get up and go to work, and I was exhausted. I lay back down next to Tom to rest until the alarm.

The next morning's work went quickly. I got off before lunch, stretched my legs out of the dusty station wagon, said farewell to the union driver, and hoisted my work bag with script, newspaper, and snacks I hadn't needed at the ranch. Sprung! Free for the rest of the day. A swim, maybe a nap later. I let myself in through the tall wooden gate, walked across the flagstones, squinting at the pool flashing in the morning light, and there was Tom and some friends of his whom he was—what? collaborating on a project with? I can't recall except that he got rid of them seamlessly while I reached for— what? a cold drink, a glass of water? Always parched when I came in from that dry location—the dust so fine it found its way into my pores. We were standing in the white kitchen by the counter. No furnishings yet. No curtains to soften the angles. Just the telephone and the refrigerator.

"Your brother-in-law called." Something in Tom's manner froze me, my face upturned, waiting, waiting for the inevitable crash of the cymbal, the fact after which everything changes.

"It's your father, Karen. He died."

"What?" My incredulous, refusing mind. It must behave this way, though I knew it was true. He was gone. But what I couldn't believe and what burst out of me as I bent double, anguish throttling my cry: "But he didn't say good-bye."

Eyes closed, my head shook no. I grabbed the window sill. I was cornered there between the news and a window, the terrible telephone hung on the end of the white kitchen cabinet. I gasped, "Dear God, don't let me drink." It had been sixty-some days. *I don't know how to do this. I don't know how to live through this.* I reached for the phone, found the number, called a sober friend, told him, "I'm afraid I'll drink." The simple reply: you never have to drink again if you don't want to. I called for more support. Then I packed. Black wool designer dress—*good thing I bought that,* I thought dully. Tom drove me up to Ventura.

I learned that Dad's drinking had suddenly escalated. Janey told me he had been drunk during the day, and she had been furious at him. He and Mom had a terrible fight, and Mom went to Janey's house to spend the night. Dad disappeared. He was found dead in a room at a neighborhood motel, an empty bottle of vodka nearby. Police had to be called. Later an autopsy revealed the presence of sleeping pills.

AT THE NEW MALL, WE RODE up the escalator as if we had a destination. The stairs folded and disappeared into their braced tops. My head felt light, but my body carried sandbags of grief. What were we doing in this shopping center? Whose idea of a coping mechanism was this? On a good day I hated these places. But my sister, brother-in-law Larry, Mama, and I trooped along in motley formation. Janey held herself as tightly as a shell holds its oyster. My brother-in-law, our shepherd now, was bearing up. Mama was neatly dressed in her polyester-blend suit, her practical leather handbag on her arm. What use was that now? Now that he was gone? The trusty tissues in the side pocket, in case her widowhood should spill forth. Three females and a man, ever our configuration, for our whole lives. Only now Gene was gone. Daddy had finally taken himself out, as we always knew he would. And now he had kept the faith, kept his threat like a promise, deciding the end for himself, as if he had any control over anything at all.

What were we looking for in that sterile mall, its Muzak muting individuality? Did someone need something to wear to the funeral? Pantyhose? I can't imagine what our motive was, except—yes, to get out of the house. To get out, anywhere, from our house, the house where the molecules of the walls, carpet, dishes, maple side tables spoke, Gene, Gene. That big La-Z-Boy chair bought to relieve his back pain, smelling of his tobacco and his sweat. Untouchable now. It was too late for confrontations, too late for solutions, too late. And what a relief. Because the worst had happened. There was nothing to dread anymore. Except the next hour. Except getting through the night. Except tomorrow, dry as ashes.

Mom's neighbor brought a casserole. Someone dropped off a ham. Larry took me to Mayer's Funeral Home. Decisions were made: coffin, satin, open or shut. Mama, Janey, and I sat together at the kitchen table, still. The note told us the truth: "You don't deserve this." A scrap of paper. There on the family table, it looked inconsequential. Time in slo-mo. After this, what? Years of watchfulness, years of dread done. My sister's eyes were wide and deep. My mother's skin had crumpled like an old gum wrapper. She was grateful for one thing: Janey and I were old enough to see her side of the story. She would not lose us, too. No blame.

Tom had to return to Utah. I joined hundreds of locals in their Sunday clothes, the awful hush of the shaded chapel, and our little band of family behind the screened enclosure, me, Mama, Janey, Larry, manly and dutiful with their boys, bewildered in their little suits, silent not squirming on the smooth pew, while Mama, stricken, looked at the program, looked out through the mesh to see who was there. I noticed the big horseshoe of flowers sent from the show. The minister hadn't known Daddy, so he kept it short, but when his friends stood up to eulogize, they could barely talk, so deep their loss, men choked with tears. The pianist played a medley of old favorites of his, and she got so carried away with the chance to perform that her renditions went on and on.

Janey and I began to steal glances at each other, our sense of real time abruptly back, our hands folded in our laps. I thought we might giggle, wishing for the hook. Finally, the pianist wrapped it up, the benedictions droned, and we rose, moved through water to the casket—how cold his face and his frozen expression, which his never was, couldn't be—and out toward the open door, where we clasped each other and sobbed, our bodies rippling against each other in an embrace as close as we would ever know. Blowing our noses and returning to responsible roles, turning aside and giving support to our mourning mother, the restless grandchildren in the too bright sunlight.

A WEEK LATER, I HAD TO go to Tucson with *Little House*. Already fragile in my new sobriety, with shock and grief piled on, I felt vulnerable and bereft as I arrived at the desk of the Hilton. My new sober friend had left a message at the desk: "Welcome to Tucson." Sober support. Maybe I would be all right. In the morning, in the makeup trailer, Mike made a joke about suicide. It cut me. Did he know? Was it on purpose? I was dumbstruck. I did my best not to react. If he knew, it was too cruel, and I didn't want to give him the satisfaction of seeing my grief. If not, then it was just coincidence, and I needed to let it go. When not needed in a scene, I walked far up a dirt road on a hill in the desert. Clyde, our transportation captain, came and kindly drove me back for the next shot. Scotty invited me to eat dinner in her room, away from the noisy bar restaurant where the crew was imbibing. Kindness was saving me.

Too soon, I was playing *The President's Mistress* in an NBC movie starring the marvelous Beau Bridges. Into the Hollywood apartment where my character has been murdered, the crew rolled a body bag on a gurney. My job was to climb into it and be zipped closed. I eyed it with dismay. It must have been like this. When they took Dad away from that room. A gurney. A bag. Two guys. I climbed in, closed my eyes. They zipped me up. I hung onto myself deep in my center. Then they rolled me out of the apartment. They got the shot. Unable to breathe, I ran downstairs to the smoking room.

The next blow was a call from Gil with bad news: "Go on antibiotics, you've been exposed to gonorrhea." God, what else? I would have to tell Tom. I had no defense. I was reduced to just one goal: don't take a drink. Before I left Ventura after the funeral, I dreamed that Tom was leaving me. In the dream I understood. It was all too much. He was worn out. I didn't act out: "I understand," I said. "You've been wonderful." Actually, it took a while longer, a month or two, but I was calm as I'd been in the dream. Surrendered. I repeated my line from the dream. "I understand. You've been wonderful."

JAFFE CALLED TO SAY THAT HE was taking a new screenplay to the network—it was based on the one Cynthia and I had worked on for over a year. We learned that on the sly, our coach, John Wayne, had been writing his own version. When Cynthia and I read his script, we realized that not only had he stolen our subject and our characters, he had approached the subject with a slimy tone suggesting that beating women was sexy—even to the victims. We were appalled, but Jaffe was firm—this was the script he believed he could get made at NBC. That Friday afternoon he would send the script over to the vice president in charge of movies, a woman.

As I listened to him, I was outraged, but I could hear the voices of all the women we had talked with giving me courage. I muttered a prayer and telephoned the VP, Deena Kramer, and told her of our concerns: We had the trust and confidence of our research subjects and would definitely not allow our names to be attached to this John Wayne version. She asked me to send over our script.

Thank heavens, weeks before, Tom had insisted that we not leave it unfinished. "Write the ending. Even if you're not crazy about it. Finish it!" and I had stayed up most of that night doing just that. So, when Ms. Kramer requested it, I went to my files, dug out the finished script, and trembling from the rush of adrenaline, I had it copied and messengered over to her.

The network set up a meeting.

On the day of our appointment, Cynthia arrived at my place looking dazzling. We were not surprised to find our outfits were color-coordinated though we had not spoken of what we would wear. We had that kind of synchronicity, and we both were ready for a fight. But we were nervous, too. We were two good girls who had gone behind the boss's back and over his head. Still, as we drove to Burbank, we reminded each other that it was necessary: Our integrity was on the line. We owed this to all those women who had trusted us. Our script would either succeed or fail, but whatever happened, we couldn't be involved with the script Jaffe wanted to produce.

When we walked into the waiting room of the VP's office, we saw Jaffe and John Wayne seated on soft ivory couches. We greeted them coolly, with polite smiles, and a few minutes later all four of us were called into the VP's office. Once we all were seated, Kramer picked up their script, shot them a piercing look, and said, "Gentlemen, you have no idea what it is to be a member of a class in jeopardy." They looked stricken. Cynthia's eyes flicked to mine—we had won. Sweet, sweet vindication.

Jaffe was annoyed with us for going over his head but wanted to complete his deal. And so, John Wayne rode out of town. A week or two later, Deena Kramer gave us her notes, and Cynthia and I went to work to make it all it could be. Having lost, Jaffe handled himself with grace and humility, trusting our instincts, giving us approval of the director and cast, a true coup. Unlike most writers, suddenly we had a full, creative experience.

The caliber of actors who wanted to perform in the film stunned those who had been skeptical, but I knew actors would recognize a juicy character when they read it. Mike Farrell from *M*A*S*H* signed on to play my husband. Joan Blondell and Howard Duff, who had been movie stars when we were kids, signed on to play the older, blue-collar couple. LeVar Burton, very hot coming off *Roots*, and the excellent Chip Fields would play the younger couple. The immensely talented Diana Scarwid was cast as Joan Blondell's doomed daughter, bitter and broken-hearted. My darling old friend Fred Gordon won the part of her abusive husband. And Ketty Lester, who I admired from *Little House*, would be tough and compassionate as the nurse who saves the young Black wife. Our sensitive director, Peter Werner, had just won an Academy Award for his short fiction film. What a team.

20. *Woman's Work*

> "I don't know but sometimes I believe in women's rights.
> If women were voting and making laws, I believe they'd
> have better sense."
> —*These Happy Golden Years*, LAURA INGALLS WILDER

IT WAS TIME TO SHOOT *BATTERED*. By the fall of 1978 the
worst of the grief was past. On the first day of principal photography,
our cinematographer, John Bailey (not yet famous), was setting up
the shot at a classic house in central Hollywood, and I was so excited
I wasn't sure how to contain myself. I did yoga on the lawn, rolled
up and down to release the overpowering enthusiasm bursting out
of me. Those scenes we had so long visualized in our living rooms
were coming to life, words we had created were being spoken aloud,
and when I heard, "That's a print," and knew those words and those
movements were recorded, I was delirious! This creation that had
lived inside for so long, now existed outside of me. And we never
had to rewrite that scene again.

Battered was scheduled to air that fall right after *Little House*,
a time slot that guaranteed great ratings. When I went out on
my annual promo tour that September, NBC's New York office,
seeing an opportunity, set up meetings for me and Chip Fields in

Washington, DC. At that precise time, Congresswoman Barbara Mikulski and her House committee were writing H.R. 12299 to support victims of domestic violence. I arrived in DC tired at the end of a long day but excited and honored to meet that evening with the brilliant congresswoman, who had also been a social worker, and the rest of the committee in a small conference room buried in the basement of the Capitol Building.

I briefed the committee on our research and the vital importance of each community creating its own shelter system. For example, I told them, in a small Appalachian town where everyone knows everyone, an institutional place for women would be too dangerous. To this day, the locations of shelters for battered women are secret to protect the inhabitants from enraged partners. The committee listened. They wrote the legislation so that towns and cities not only would be unfettered by national requirements but also could receive grants based on the specific needs of their community.

Chip Fields arrived the next day, and she and I began our work. After a radio interview, Chip remarked, "You're such a lady!" I laughed and said, "Yeah, I suffer from terminal politeness!" Those years of research had taught me how trapped a woman could be by the good girl syndrome: Trapped into not speaking your mind, trapped into taking responsibility for other people's moods, trapped into trying to fix everything. My character in *Battered*.

Our film was shown in a screening room just off the halls of Congress to help the committee garner support for their bill. After the screening, Chip and I took questions, and we were gratified when Representative Mikulski and her colleagues succeeded in establishing the first national support for shelters. That moment was groundbreaking, and all these years later, seeing the support that has grown—California has a surcharge on drivers' licenses that supports shelters—I still feel proud.

Chip and I headed back to Hollywood, looking forward to the night our film would air, but when we returned, I was shocked to learn that Mike had prevented the showing in the scheduled slot—he told the network the audience might confuse my character in the film with Ma, and *Battered* was moved to a less propitious time. While Cynthia threw a party for the principals, I felt too vulnerable to join, so I invited a few friends over to watch with me in my still-empty living room; with only the loveseat Mom had given me, the sound was hollow.

The film garnered a hugely positive response, and when Cynthia and I learned it was being used as a training film for police in New York State, we were especially heartened. Prior to that time, many police encounters with domestic violence cases often resulted in injury or death to the officer, but our film provided a platform for discussion about better ways to approach volatile couples. Within a few years, California alone had twenty shelters, where in 1975, there had been one. I was invited to all the major talk shows to describe the problem, to clear up the impression that if a victim didn't "just leave," another beating was her own fault. We exposed the way the syndrome undermined a woman's autonomy and self-esteem and how the police and judicial systems contributed to that powerlessness. Our film led to other films that tackled the subject, and consciousness about wife beating changed completely. When in 1984, Farrah Fawcett won an Emmy for her portrayal in *The Burning Bed*, in which a battered wife, driven to desperation, burns up her husband in their bed, her star wattage helped still more people begin to understand. These were special years in television, a time when the networks mounted movies weekly that addressed important, hidden social issues. As a nation, it seemed, we were hungering for the exposure of the shadow side. And still, the idealized world depicted on *Little House* continued to thrive.

In Hollywood, I invited twenty actresses to join me in helping the ever-increasing number of shelters to raise funds. We were Stars for Shelters, each actress going to a different community to appear at a fundraiser for the shelter. Some, like Katherine Helmond, continued to take an interest even after our first foray, and whenever she was appearing out of town, she would contact the local shelter to offer to help. Proud as I am of the work we did to bring the problem to people's attention, today's preponderance of shelters and the fact that they are always full demonstrates we still have a long way to go to eradicate violence against women.

I REGRET DEEPLY THAT DAD NEVER got to see *Battered* realized and that he barely knew me sober. After his death, Mom and Janey and I did twelve weeks of intense grief work with my psychiatrist. Words we had never spoken, fights we had tried to forget, revelations of what it had been like living in our house opened us up to each other, creating opportunities for us to be and feel connected. In my new house, I furnished the guest room with a French iron bed and Pierre Deux fabrics, so Mama could sleep over comfortably. We three had fun sharing the perks of my success: booking a day at a spa, shopping at Saks for new outfits, eating lunch at a French restaurant. When I was the cohost on the *John Davidson Show*, I invited them to come. To surprise them, I had taken my grandmother's unassembled quilt pieces that all our lives Mama had kept on a high shelf in a closet and arranged to have them joined together, then quilted with tiny hand stitches—one for Mama and one for Janey. While we were on the air, I presented the quilts to them, and the studio audience applauded my mother and sister's surprise and delight. We were stitching ourselves together.

And for the next five years, the Hollywood Boulevard house gave me a supportive base. From the spare, bare home, I built my recovery. I didn't just change my lifestyle: My entire focus moved to health. My fear of drinking made me willing to try all the suggestions sober people described. I began each day with a simple spiritual reading. At meetings I washed ashtrays—to be of service without having to talk. At work, people wondered aloud if I'd joined a gym. I had fun exploring design shops on Melrose Avenue and began to spend some of the money I was earning, and little by little, my house got furnished. Some days were even easy. I bought a soft yellow Mercedes Benz 450SL as a reward for all the hard work—and now I had a garage I could park it in. After *Battered* aired, exciting opportunities for writing and developing new work came my way. I had forged a new life—lonely but real.

By 1978, my health was improving. I had a new sober pal, Constance, who I had met when I first went to a meeting. I'd crept into the crowded hall, where people milled around, drinking coffee and talking animatedly. *Were there really so many alcoholics in Los Angeles?* Many seats were already taken, and I scanned the back section of the room for a seat not too far from the aisle. I excused myself as I picked past people's knees and sat next to a clean-looking young woman with a head full of light brown curls. She wore a blue-and-white striped oxford shirt with the collar turned up and looked "safe" to me. Not so the disheveled guy just behind her. At the end of the meeting, I stuck out my hand and introduced myself by my first name. I had seen others do this, and I was trying hard to do what they did.

"Are you an alcoholic?" she asked pertly.

"Yes. Uh, yes, I am."

"You don't look like an alcoholic," she said. (*Was she kidding?*)

"You don't look like an alcoholic, either," I answered.

"Are you going to do this?"

"Yes. Yes. I've got to."

"Well, I have to, too. I'm allergic," she declared. (*But of course. We all are.*)

I saw her next a short time later at a small Hollywood party, where many people were sneaking into the bathroom to snort coke. She and I practically grabbed hold of each other, and she smiled shyly at our little miracle. After that we began to meet for meetings and share our stories. At the end of a workday, instead of having a glass of wine, I called her. I called her when I panicked and thought maybe pills would be a solution. Constance knew better.

We became close quickly. When we met, she didn't know about my work, and I rested in the anonymity, but a magazine cover photo in the supermarket changed that, and at the next meeting, she teased me by bringing it along. She was both shy and friendly, like a puppy. She had grown up in the tonier neighborhoods of Los Angeles and had many famous friends. Through her I met a number of the strong actresses I had admired in movies. Carrie Fisher, the surprisingly strong heroine of *Star Wars,* had been her neighbor, and Constance said she recognized her brilliance even when they were kids. Candice Bergen, Constance's close pal in high school, lit up the screen like a bolt of lightning when she appeared in *The Group*, the popular movie based on Mary McCarthy's novel. I loved that film about the "modern" young women of their time, especially the work of the actress Joan Hackett, the dazzling brunette. Constance introduced me to her at an obscure Middle Eastern restaurant hidden behind shops on Melrose Avenue. She seemed exotic and fascinating to me— like a European diva. I felt quite awkward and shy meeting these dynamic women, but sometimes I could present myself as someone working on *Battered* and feel that gave me a calling card. Despite being sober, I hadn't cured years of self-criticism and wondered if it was possible to be accepted among these creative women I so admired. Television was still treated as the country cousin to the movies and looked down upon by many in Hollywood, and our show was not "hip" like *M*A*S*H.*

But my life began to whirl with opportunities to act, to create new work, and to serve others. Learning to navigate offers was tricky. As an actor who had been through lean times, I dared not say no, but I wrote a note to myself and put it on the bulletin board in my office: "I'll think about it." Instead of wearing myself to a nub with all the yeses, I learned to delay, so I could actually think about it. I couldn't do it all, and I knew my appetite for more could leave me exhausted.

Looking back at my calendar and telephone log from this period, I'm astonished at the number of bases I ran. I had a great, capable assistant, Geoff Calnan, and many days when I came in from shooting at the studio, I showered and changed into one of the designer outfits Constance had helped me find, then Geoff handed me a slip of paper with an address, and off I'd go in my spiffy yellow Mercedes "to take a meeting." I scooted to afternoon talk shows, accepted awards in San Francisco and Atlanta, took meetings with potential subjects for Movies of the Week or with producers for whom I could create new material. On Sundays, I frequently grabbed five changes and drove to NBC to shoot a week's worth of Hollywood Squares. I was on an adrenaline rush and found inside me a live wire that hadn't been activated since the FSM. The gal who had rushed to high school with Sara Sue to fix the student government kicked in. A chance to make a difference revved my motor.

When I received a call from Representative George Miller's office letting me know that the national bill for battered women's shelters had passed, I felt proud, and when the Dinah Shore show asked me to debate the Equal Rights Amendment with Phyllis Schlafly, I said bring her on. I used Schlafly's own heroes like President Eisenhower to defeat her specious arguments. For years she had been one of my bêtes noires, because of her campaign to stoke the fear that the ERA would take away women's privileges—such as the right to be a housewife. And even decades later, at ninety, Schlafly was speaking out to keep transgender people out of bathrooms that match their gender identity. Some of her old predictions have come to pass, and we are none the worse for it. Nor will we be when the transgender community achieves acceptance. The only thing that keeps a woman from being able to be a housewife if she wants to is an economy that requires her to contribute to the family budget.

IN 1979, FOR THE HIATUS, I decided to fulfill a lifelong fantasy and rent a place in Malibu for the break. I imagined walking Molly on the beach and having a quiet, reflective time. But then an offer came to do the independent feature *Harry's War*, shooting in Utah, and off I went. Did I have a speaking engagement in Oakland to help raise funds for a shelter for battered women? Good, I could also contact some old friends in Berkeley, and with luck clean up some messes from my drinking days, then rush back to Utah to finish the film. I felt an unstoppable drive to take advantage of every opportunity, to grab every chance while I had it. I was also fueled by the thrill of feeling that I belonged, that what I had to say mattered. And getting a chance to know all those actors and producers I admired drove me, too.

Constance was excited to tell me that Joan Hackett was giving a party for the Equal Rights Amendment. She volunteered her home in the canyon above Beverly Hills for the first consciousness-raising fundraiser for the ERA. The open house took place on a sunny (what else?) Sunday at Joan's—all beige and glass—opening onto a wide deck overlooking the canyon. We were twenty-five women and one or two men—actors, writers, and producers. Cheryl Ladd waved hello, and I congratulated her on taking over Farrah Fawcett's part on *Charlie's Angels*.

Joan introduced Virginia Carter, the writer-producer from Norman Lear's organization, who lit the spark that started the Hollywood ERA movement. Norman Lear and his partner, Bud Yorkin, of Tandem Productions had enlightened the American TV audience with politically astute, hilarious shows like *All in the Family, Maude,* and *Mary Hartmann, Mary Hartmann*. Virginia, a patrician woman with a no-nonsense style and utterly unadorned, began her speech that day by telling us the history of the ERA, the brainchild of Alice Paul,[1] and first introduced in Congress in 1923. Virginia read the one-sentence text:

"Equality of rights under the law shall not be denied or abridged by the United States or by any state on account of sex."

Obvious, you'd think. But, she explained, it had been introduced in Congress every single year since then and finally, fifty years later, in 1972, it passed by the two-thirds majority of both

Houses. Then, it had seven years to be ratified by at least thirty-eight states, and now, we needed just three more. Virginia's moral outrage that we Americans had been living without this right (for all these years) was contagious. We had fewer than two years to get the job done! We had to push this bill through so women could at last gain our full legal status. Virginia was straightforward but passionate, making her pitch for action and, finally, for money. We got out our checkbooks, and thus began the crackling chain reaction of the Hollywood ERA movement, exponentially expanding with every event. Less than a year after that gathering, there was a huge march in Century City and a rally where thousands of women and their children cheered. More stars were scheduled to speak than there were hours and stage to hold us. The media responded to all the names, and coverage was tremendous. We began to help out in other states. One Friday after work I flew to Colorado to be the celebrity attraction for an ERA march in Denver and spoke to a vital crowd of women and their children on Saturday, then returned home in time for work Monday morning. When Colorado ratified, I celebrated without a drink.

IN CALIFORNIA, WE NEEDED A BIG event and I joined the committee to plan a showy luncheon with speakers and entertainment. The sharp, witty, and well-organized Mike Donlan and I joined forces to organize the location and catering. The Bonaventure Hotel was the newest, most original landmark in Los Angeles. Every movie and TV show wanted to shoot the shiny, silvery columns that formed the building. When I dashed into the lobby, I saw Mike in his IBM pinstripes and tie. He gave the impression of being much more straight-laced than he turned out to be and working together for this cause was the beginning of a special friendship. When we learned we had to wait for our appointment, he kept me company while I had a snack in the coffee shop. (I was still learning to take care of my wildly fluctuating blood sugar. Still unable to get up in time to eat properly.) We discovered we had much in common, including a wry sense of humor, and the subtext of our partnership was the natural affinity that the gay world had with the women's movement. Our meeting with the events manager was propitious: We had knocked on the door just as the Bonaventure was building its reputation. We anticipated three hundred-plus people, many celebrities; this would be good press for the hotel. We made an excellent deal, and Mike and I took this back to the committee. Months of evening meetings, ego-driven promises of "I can get you Helen Reddy" topped with "I can get you Barbra"—so credulous me was convinced our turnout would be huge. But as so often happens with good causes, many of the names that were mentioned did not commit and ticket sales were arduous. The most dedicated volunteers finally bought packets and gave them to friends so we could fill the tables.

On the day of the luncheon, the ballroom looked inviting. The curtains shone. The flowers were original and arrived on time. Raquel Welch showed up looking utterly chic and treating everyone with warmth. We waited nervously, and Governor Brown was led in just in time, spoke, and was rushed out by Gray Davis. The entertainment went on too long (after all, this was the entertainment world). The sparkle died; guests drifted out. Mike and I looked at each other, shrugged, and went on because the cause was worth it.

The pinnacle of these fundraisers was at Marlo Thomas's estate in Bel Air. As I drove into the parklike grounds above Westwood, I reflected on how Marlo had been leading the pack in the movement for equality. She and Gloria Steinem had shared the podium at a dinner Cynthia and I attended when we were writing *Battered*. Marlo was the main speaker at the fundraiser at Renée Taylor and Joe Bologna's Beverly Hills home. Unassuming and gracious, she sat at our table that day while she waited for the chairperson to take her to her place. And now she had offered her home. I handed the keys to my new Mercedes to the valet and tried not to let my jaw drop when I saw the stunning mass of trees obscuring the house. I walked, amazed, through the lush landscaping, unbelievably green for Southern California, down a path that led away from the ivy-covered mansion, reminiscent of an English castle. I joined the celebrities, publicists, reporters, and guests. Bella Abzug was set to speak, and our expectations for the fundraising auction were high. We expected two hundred well-heeled people from the industry, including Jane Fonda, Robert Altman, Norman Lear, and Shirley MacLaine.

Hors d'oeuvres were served by uniformed caterers—often actors supplementing their income—while people schmoozed over drinks. By that time, I was able to greet many actors and actresses from our previous work, and I felt grateful to all these people for giving their day off to the ERA. We all knew the point was getting the votes in the state legislatures, where the amendment had to be ratified in order to be added to the Constitution. And now we had less than a year to go. The funds we raised went to support these efforts.

By the time the auction was in full swing, some of our guests were pretty high. Robert Altman (whose work I was crazy about) took himself to the podium and announced that he would give all the profits from his next picture to the ERA,[2] and "Now, can we get back to the party?" That stuck a pin in the balloon, and the fundraising sputtered out. Many people drifted off to their cars. Forty of us stuck around for the commemorative photo. I was proud to be a part of this group of talented, dedicated people.

AS MY BIRTHDAY APPROACHED, I WAS working as compulsively as ever, I had a new boyfriend, and he and I decided for my birthday to take a trip to a solar eclipse weekend being held at the Big Sky Ski Resort, which Walter Cronkite had built in Montana. I was no skier. As a young person, I couldn't afford it, and as an actor, I simply couldn't risk breaking my leg; indeed, many Equity contracts forbade skiing. Still, I looked forward to the trip, but then an urgent call came from the Hollywood ERA Committee: There was a movement afoot to rescind the ERA in South Dakota, which had ratified it in 1973. Would I go to call on members of the state legislature? I was a natural for this state because the Ingalls family had had a home in the Dakotas, and the vote was imminent. We couldn't let votes start moving backwards. We were so close.

I wanted to go, but I needed a breather, a complete change, so feeling flush, I arranged for us to fly in a private plane from Montana after the eclipse to reach South Dakota in time for the legislative debate. The freedom to hire a private plane—I'd fallen in love with them when we flew in the Gold Country to save time—and to feel virtuous at the same time was irresistible. I could practically be in two places at the same time, and so the night before the eclipse, in the sharp, cold Montana air, my boyfriend and I walked to listen to a lecture about the eclipse.

The next morning dawned cloudy. Meteorologists were keeping a close eye on the weather and the clock, with the pressure on to deliver the "show" we had all come to see. Organizers were communicating every few minutes with meteorologists stationed in the field and ham radio operators looking for an opening in the cloud cover. As with the ERA, we all knew if we didn't catch it now, it would be a long time before another chance came along, and so, in Wild West pursuit, we followed the big buses as they sped along the open highway, changed course and drove down a country road, then switched back to another, speeding across the open prairie. When I saw antelopes on the patchy snow, I shrieked with delight and belted out, "Oh give me a home where the buffalo roam . . ." The world was white, frozen white and edged in tan dead grasses. The sky was, as advertised, enormous. Finally, we all came to a stop beside an open field, and everyone piled out and looked up—sun! Eclipse aficionados took out their cameras, special lenses, tripods, and telescopes with sun filters and set up all over the field.

A hush swept over the group sprinkled there below the white gleaming. As the shadow moved across the sun, all the Earth seemed to tense and draw itself tightly together. The birds went still, and deep quiet descended. The Earth seemed to be holding its breath as the shadow completely shrouded our sun. An eerie light lit up the prairie—a twilight like no other—all mauve gray and vibrating. A gasp, it seemed. The primitive me sensed what ancient peoples must have felt at such moments—simple terror as if a god had died. It lasted only minutes, and then a sliver of sun reappeared, and the shadow moved away and disappeared. The Earth exhaled, and joyful incomprehensible voicings, birds, rustlings rose on that Montana plain, and I understood why people traveled the world to catch another and another. I comprehended why Stonehenge, why the Great Pyramid, why all those massive stones had been moved, for to be able to plan for such an enormous and terrifying event would have given people confidence that the world was not ending.

Then on to the airport and the fight for the ERA. I was aquiver with adrenaline: This was my idea of living—rushing from one intoxicating once-in-a-lifetime event to another, no longer jacking myself up or calming myself down with alcohol or grass. Instead, I felt high on life. And I felt so privileged.

We landed in South Dakota on time, but at the state house in Pierre, we found the legislators had retired to an eatery. The local organizers whisked us to the bar-restaurant where we could approach the lawmakers and persuade them to hold on tight. One of our talking points was that the wage for women at the time was 59 cents on the dollar for men. And forty years later, we still have not accomplished equality, not even a penny a year of improvement. I think of the vast sums saved by companies over all these years, saved at the expense of women. Of course, wages have been flat when adjusted for inflation, so it doesn't take a mathematician to figure out that the profits have not gone to the middle class, not to families. And not to women.

But back then, in the dimly lit restaurant, our eyes were full of light, and we argued with facts and with humor, with passion, even flirting to try to keep the ERA ratified. But specious arguments against the ERA had begun to fill people with fear: Men and women sharing the same bathrooms! Gays having rights! Women sent to the front lines! All these scenarios, I believe, masked the real fear: women's autonomy. And in the end, we came up three states short.

I WAS ACTIVELY ON THE LOOKOUT for material oriented to women's issues to produce with NBC, and one day a friend brought me a spec script, a charming whodunit. The female private investigator was amused, offbeat, and independent like the writer. I loved the idea of starring in a lighter Movie of the Week. I met with Chris Abbott at La Scala Boutique one mid-afternoon when the restaurant's red-upholstered booths were nearly deserted. An attractive blonde with enormous blue eyes, Chris was married, living in the Valley, and making her play to break into television. With theatre as our common background, and her marvelous sense of humor, we hit it off right away, and I took her script to NBC. The network didn't buy it, but I kept looking for the right project, keeping Chris in mind.

She wanted to write for *Little House* and worked up some ideas to pitch. After five or six seasons, a new writer was challenged to master all the established details and come up with a story we hadn't already done. We had worked our way through stories that the books provided and craved new material like a cotton gin craves cotton, and I'd grown hopeful that *Little House* could contribute to the fight for women's equality.

Chris and I began work behind the scenes to come up with stories accenting Caroline's character, and advancing a woman's perspective. We sat on my patio and brainstormed clandestinely. Having won my contract, I was still in the doghouse with Mike, so I couldn't present the scripts myself. But Chris could. One of our ideas was to write a script focused on a woman's right to vote. *Little House* took place in the second half of the 19th century when Susan B. Anthony had traveled the country to promote this right, and her correspondence with Elizabeth Cady Stanton for women's suffrage was inspiring, so Chris and I focused on that. By 1980, we had come up with a prairie *Lysistrata* based on the classical Greek comedy in which the women refuse to have sex until the men end the war. In our story, a charming comedy called "Oleson vs. Oleson," a woman comes to town to present a petition for women's property rights. When the men of Walnut Grove refuse to sign it, the women decamp to Nellie's Restaurant and refuse to go home until the men sign. Most of the men are overwhelmed by "women's work."

In the story, Mrs. Oleson and Caroline join forces. Camaraderie among the female characters is like a big slumber party, the men are comically incompetent, and in the end, the women win. It was funny and relevant. After it aired in season seven, I was pleased to receive a call from Valerie Harper congratulating me—"I knew you must have been behind it." I didn't share a story credit, because I didn't want Mike's antipathy toward me to hurt the project. Soon Chris was hired permanently on *Little House*—finally, a woman writer on staff. A coup! She brought a warmth and wit to the material that frequently reflected a woman's point of view.

Then she and I set about writing a film based on the book *Those Wonderful Women in Their Flying Machines* about the WASPs who flew during World War II .[3] We couldn't get it made. At the time, even Goldie Hawn couldn't get Rosie the Riveter made. Nevertheless, Chris had broken through to the benefit of other women writers and our audience.[4]

21. Buried Desire

> "There are a lot of decisions we make in this life we wish
> we didn't have to."
> "But it's not right."
> "That's easy to say when it's not left up to you."
> —"Remember Me," Part 2, *Little House on the Prairie*,
> MICHAEL LANDON

AT FIRST, THEY WERE JUST STANDING and talking a little longer than he talked to anybody else. Then she loaned him *My Mother, My Self*, Nancy Friday's probing book exploring her relationship with her mother—fitting since, as his work so often revealed, Mike had been wounded by his mother. Then they began to walk farther away from the action, engrossed in conversation, and in each other. It was awkward as hell for us in the company. Everyone saw. Everyone looked away.

Missy had grown taller, and a new stand-in who could relate to a young teenager had been found: Cindy Clerico was a nice young woman, eighteen, and her tiny, slim body looked great in the tight jeans that had been made popular by *Charlie's Angels*. She wore cute, colorful tops, and when Mike began to arrive jubilant at the makeup table, crowing about the benefits of bee pollen for the aging male,

Whitey found a way to laugh with him without actually acknowledging what was going on. But Whitey had been around.

Mike's open discussion of his revived libido distressed me. I didn't want to think about his penis. I knew his wife. I had been in her home. She had been kind to me. And I thought about their children—there were still three at home, I thought—and younger than Cindy. This, after doing everything his way. Not dancing. Going to the spa right after childbirth. Living with his long work hours. All the business entertaining. Christmas Eve alone with the kids, while he gambled at the office. I remembered her at the People's Choice Awards, holding herself tight, trying to be pleasant to Tom and me while Mike was loaded. She and the kids had reminded me that night of Janey and me at some of the Grassle family celebrations. And now this?

It all blew up. Lynn followed him, I guess, to their secret hideaway, a bottle of vodka was thrown, the tabloids got wind of it, and it was a painful mess. Mr. Perfect Family Man moved on. Soon Cindy showed up in a Porsche, having become a "makeup artist." Mike and Cindy got a place in Malibu. Before the divorce was done, Cindy turned up pregnant. (That bee pollen was really something.) They married in 1983.

Series work is hard on marriages. In those days, the cast and crew had to commit to nine months a year of twelve-hour or longer days for a one-hour drama. In our company, I recall at least four divorces in key positions within a few years. Kenny Hunter, our tall, quiet, gray-haired cameraman, used to call his wife every lunch break when we were at the studio. I'd return from the commissary, and there he'd be, standing in the pay phone booth outside the stage, visiting with his wife, keeping their communication open, keeping the marriage alive.

Little House **HAD BEEN A RELIABLE** lead-in to strong ratings for NBC's Monday night lineup. Instead of waiting for our contracts to run out in season seven, the network opened negotiations during season six to extend for two more years. I was already digging deep to give my best work despite fatigue with the whole enterprise. I was trying to be grateful, a worker among workers, and steer clear of gossipy cliques. But two more seasons? I was reluctant, though I did see that the show provided a foundation for all the other projects I was developing. Still, I wanted my freedom, but then they made me an offer I couldn't refuse. I signed on for seasons seven and eight, promising myself that I would go no further.

One night at dusk I drove with my sober boyfriend back to Hollywood from a family holiday. Shadows slid slowly down the golden hills. Traffic dragged. Celebrations in Ventura often ended this way, with a slow slog home, but I wouldn't have thought of not showing up for Mom. But after two years with this man, we were not yet engaged, and had less and less to say to each other. His darling three-year-old daughter spent many weekends with us; truthfully, I was more in love with her than I was with him. In the car in front of us, silhouettes of a couple and a small child were framed for the long ride, and the image activated my longing. Unavoidable. A deep blue mood descended.

Once home, I crawled into bed and turned out the light, but grief shot up like a punch to the gut. Long-denied yearning for my own child was on me like a wrestler on a foe. Sobbing had its way with me. Sitting up was no use. I tried to stand but that was no use either, I was bent with it. Couldn't catch my breath. Hyperventilating. He got me up and walking, but I could not regulate my breath. He brought a paper bag from the kitchen, and I blew into it like a neurotic Goldie Hawn character. Finally, the breath slowed; I washed my face and lay down to rest. I resolved to call my older, wiser friend from the support group in the morning. I didn't sleep.

In the morning, as soon as was polite, I called Shirley, and she invited me to come right over. Self-consciously, I told her what had happened. Now I knew what I wanted: I wanted a family. I wanted a baby. I had put it off for so long. "Well," she said, "now we know what your will is—we'll have to see what God's will is."

She asked if I was hungry. I was starving. She explained that when we don't sleep much, we need to eat more. *Oh.* There was so much to learn about how to ride these new, sober waves. She fixed me a meatloaf sandwich with plenty of mayo. And after that, I couldn't stop wondering how much I had hidden from myself. It was too much to absorb, and I realized I had to turn over what would happen next to God. That man I had spent two years with went his way, and again I was crushed. But I went on with my work, the inner work: More surrendering to the unknown, more trying to trust that something beneficent was operating in the universe. Mom believed it. Shirley believed it. Maybe I could, again.

By that time, Ma had five children, and the child actors were turning into teenagers and running with faster crowds than I wished for them. Their childhoods would not come again. And I would not be able to have children forever. I'd already shot a show in which Ma passed into early menopause. Cindy brought their newborn to the studio for us all to see. Those tiny fingers made me gasp, and my insides heaved with longing.

My mind became plagued with the memory of my early pregnancy. At twenty, during the apprenticeship at the Workshop, I had just moved in with JoAnne Akalaitis and her roommates in San Francisco. Before we went looking for a bigger place, I slept on the cot in the living room. One warm night, I was writing in my journal when a thought suddenly electrified me: How long since I'd had my period? I counted. Leafed through my journal. I was more than a week late. I was never late. Early sometimes, but never late. Heart pounding, I counted again. I really was late. My breasts had swollen as they did each month, but this was not the usual. This was the other. The dreaded. I was pregnant. I knew it. *My God, what will I do?*

I got up and dressed. I went out walking. *Where to go, what to do?* I knew I could not have a baby. But abortion was frightening, and illegal. A woman I knew had been through one and had described a nightmare. *How to do it?* Up over the hill and down to the marina, walking and walking. Illegal abortions were dangerous,

could be fatal. *Who could I tell? Who could help me find a doctor?*
I needed the counsel of a more experienced person. There was a
successful novelist I had dated, a grown-up. *Go now.* Through the
tunnel with cars whizzing past, loud, to his apartment in North
Beach. I climbed the stairs. *What if he was in bed with someone?
How embarrassing. Besides, I didn't know him all that well. It wasn't
his problem.* I stood paralyzed outside his door, then trudged back
to our flat.

Shame isolated me from my roommates, my coworkers. JoAnne
never disclosed personal feelings. I admired her but was ashamed
to move in and be a problem. In the morning, I walked the few
blocks to Bob La Vigne's apartment, where Rob was living in a
spare bedroom. Bob was a good friend, older and sophisticated,
but Rob and I didn't go to him either. Instead, we hatched a plan
to cause a miscarriage. I began to take high doses of quinine that
made my head buzz and my ears ring. Rob and I would meet in our
neighborhood park, where he counted as I pounded my lower back
against the grassy hill. Nothing came of this. I was a healthy twenty
year old. My anxiety was like a scream suppressed.

I told Toni. She knew someone with a name of a doctor in
Tijuana. Rob called. It would cost $350 cash. Nearly four months
of living expenses. Where would it come from? Rob said he'd get it.
He kept hoping I would miscarry. I continued my quinine—taking
a break only for my performances—and then pumping it back in.

We met with Toni to talk over the plan. She leveled with me.
"Karen, you don't have time to wait. What's he doing?" Rob had
been dragging his feet for over a month.

"It's the money. He doesn't want to tell anyone, I guess."

"Where is he anyway?"

"He's coming."

"He has to get it. It's his baby. Listen, I'll take you if he won't."

There was a knock at the door. He arrived, beautiful and
bedraggled in worn out pants, and Toni gave it to him straight: "It
has to be now. No more than two weeks from today."

He borrowed the money from his brother's friend, and we booked the operation and the flights. After my matinee on Sunday, Mother's Day, we took a bus to the airport. In the pocket of my corduroy coat was the Mother's Day card I had neglected to send. I found a pay phone and called collect. Mother was so annoyed she almost didn't accept the call. I apologized. Again, too little and too late. I hung up, feeling very bad about myself. We waited, tense and depressed.

"Karen!" I cringed as I turned and smiled—a friend from high school on her way back to college in San Diego after a weekend in San Francisco—and she was on our flight. What was I doing there? "Meeting a friend," I lied. Rob and I felt so guilty and nervous, we were sure she would guess our reason if she knew we were going to San Diego. As he went to change our flight, I "caught up" with her, then cheerfully waved good-bye.

Eventually, we left for San Diego and drank on the plane. We took a cab to a motel near the border and checked in. Had to lie at the desk. Seeing "Mr. and Mrs." I felt diminished—he'd never said anything about marrying me. In the room, we had beer and perfunctory sex. He told me, "Someday you will meet someone and want to get married, and when you do, don't tell him about this." I began to cry. Furious, I shattered a glass against the tub in the bathroom.

The next morning, we crossed the border, got a taxi, and gave the driver the address. The driver knew what was up right away and wanted a payoff. Frightened, we denied everything. Got out. Walked around. Finally, got another cab and had it drop us near but not at the doctor's office where we climbed the stairs, relieved the place was clean. The nurse wore a spotless uniform. But she hushed us as she hustled us into another room, then finally into the doctor's office. He didn't want to take me because the first taxi driver had tried to blackmail him. We hadn't realized it, but he was breaking the law here, too. He wanted more money. We hadn't any. He decided to take what we had.

Then they shooed us out, whispering, and told us to come back in a couple of hours. I had had nothing to eat or drink that morning because of the operation. Outside it was hot and dry and dirty. A little boy was selling slices of watermelon on the street. I never wanted a piece of fruit so badly in my life. I swallowed. We walked in miserable silence. We found ourselves at the jai alai stadium and went in. It was cool, and we watched practice. The young men slung the ball at the far wall with incredible speed, then caught it in the big skin bag and slung it back again. The languorous tock-tock rhythm soothed us.

That sound recalled another time in Tijuana, a family vacation only six years before, when I still felt like a child. We had been to the jai alai games. We bought souvenirs—silly straw hats with palm trees and donkeys on top and pretty, painted Mexican dancing skirts decorated with sequins. I spent my savings on a big silver bracelet. A drunken sailor tried to grab me on the packed street, and my dad just laughed it off. I was thirteen and humiliated, betrayed by the man who was supposed to be my protector. But that same father took me to a doctor in Ventura when he saw how in love I was with Vince. He told the doctor I was "engaged to be married" but wanted to finish college, so I needed birth control. Privately, Dad told me if I ever told my mother about this, he'd deny it, and the doctor fitted me with a diaphragm and gave me some spermicidal cream. If only I'd used it consistently, I wouldn't be in this fix now.

Stupid, I thought, on top of everything else. Or was it something more pernicious—self-destructive, Freud's death-wish? I suspected it was.

Finally, it was time to go back to the doctor's office. We climbed the stairs. I was weak with hunger and fear. The nurse took us to a little dressing room with a locker. In gestures, I was told to put on a cloth gown and put my clothes in the little locker. I did. But I forgot my watch, the one that my parents had given me for high school graduation. I started to open the locker again, but the nurse came in: They were ready. I handed the watch to Rob, who was nervous and seemed annoyed with me. Then they took me away. We entered a small, white room. I got up on the table and put my legs in the cold steel stirrups. They gave me sodium pentothal, and I began to cry. The last thing I remember was staring at the polished wooden crucifix on the wall and praying not to die.

They brought me back into the dressing room and had me get into a clean single bed. I passed out again immediately. Rob got me up, tried to get me dressed, and put the watch back on. He was anxious to get the hell out of there, but the nurse came in and stopped him, she put me back in the bed, and I was allowed to sleep for a few hours. They didn't want us to leave before dark. Then they sneaked us out, and we caught a taxi to the border. The border guards challenged us; we had no souvenirs. They were conspiratorially suggestive, but they couldn't prove anything, and we played innocent. On the bus to the airport, I leaned my head against Rob's shoulder and fell asleep, but he pushed me up, told me it was "bad form."

I spent the night and the next day with Toni in Berkeley. She fed me, took care of me, and walked me to the bus when it was time to get back to San Francisco for the evening performance. Then I pulled my grief tight around me like a big black cloak. Guilt rode my back like those monster monkeys from *The Wizard of Oz*.

TEN YEARS LATER, IN 1972, I was pregnant again. After almost a decade on the Pill, I had given it up because of the serious side effects reported in Barbara Seaman's book *The Doctors' Case Against the Pill*: stroke, paralysis, even death. I asked my gynecologist for something safer. He discouraged me from going off the Pill, but I was adamant: "They're experimenting on our bodies! If men got pregnant, we'd have something safer. After all, we've been to the moon."

"The Pill is the moon," he replied and fitted me with a diaphragm and cream.

In Los Angeles to look for work that summer, I began an affair, nothing serious, and I got pregnant. New York had legalized abortion. I rushed back there as fast as I could. What a change in environment for women! I could have my own doctor, a real hospital with a supportive staff. Dr. Paulson helped me to work through my conflicting feelings about a decision in which there had been no good choice. At the hospital, I paid the flat fee in advance, and a date was set.

On the morning of the abortion appointment, Fred swooped like a great mythical bird into my apartment and scooped me up and off to the hospital. When I checked in at the window at the hospital, I was surprised to be greeted warmly. No judgment. I was directed to a room I'd share with three other women. We were scheduled for tests early and surgery later. We were treated with care and respect. In the elevator on the way to get some blood work, a friendly nurse asked me what I'd been using for birth control. I told her the diaphragm. She said, "That's why you're here—it's only 85 percent effective." I told her I'd given up the Pill.

"Why?"

I explained, and she understood and suggested I consider the IUD. Afterwards I felt grief but not guilt. Not shame. As I made the appointment for an IUD, I was sad I still couldn't include a baby in my life, and back in my rent-controlled apartment, I gratefully accepted another contract standing by for *Butterflies* on Broadway and had no doubt about whether I had made the right choice. It was my only choice. I was grateful to the State of New York for making this as painless and as safe as possible. Anti-choice advocates use grief as an argument against ending a pregnancy, and yes, there is heartbreak, but it is nothing compared to the heartbreak of an unwanted child, the deprivations of poverty and abandonment by mothers who can't handle motherhood. Living through this decision consciously was an experience in living through a time when there were no easy choices and the decision deepened me, made me a better vessel for expressing the human struggle.

WHEN WE STARTED *LITTLE HOUSE*, I'D thought I was moving toward marriage, stability, and family. But with my depression, rage, and alcoholism, I lost two good men, first Tuie then Tom. Sober, I couldn't blame anyone and had to face myself. One night, after a quiet dinner, I headed up the hill outside my house in Hollywood for a walk. It hadn't been that long ago, that tough time in New York—just a few years, but everything had changed. The dry night air seemed to wrap itself around my shoulders. In that moment, I no longer felt alone. An overwhelming wonder came over my mind—spacious and bright. I was truly sober. Now I believed it. Maybe I could have a child. Not just play a mother on TV. Now I could trust myself—maybe now. Maybe it wasn't too late.

22. *New Acts*

"Success gets to be a habit, like anything else a fellow keeps on doing."
—*By the Shores of Silver Lake*, LAURA INGALLS WILDER

HOW TO FIND A HUSBAND? I had no idea how to find out if a man was serious or a good candidate. With the sexual revolution, dating had disappeared. Most men expected sex, and many had lost the knack of pursuit. I recalled my own attitude in the '60s, when Dr. Paulson tried to talk to me about containing my sexual desire, recalled that liberated me had known better, but now, willing to reexamine my behavior, I saw that my old ways hadn't helped me achieve what I wanted. I wasn't getting any younger, and my biological clock wasn't just ticking—it was racing.

That season I got married a lot. A part on *Love Boat* gave me a romantic happy ending. When I arrived to shoot it, I was amazed to be sitting in the makeup room alongside a star I had seen in many musicals at the Ventura Theatre: Jane Powell. Then off to costumes to get into the swimsuit. The top didn't please the costumer, and she pulled out one falsie after another. I did my best to become a mannikin while she stuffed first one sponge, then another cotton pad into my top. They knew my breasts were small when they hired me. The previous week I'd had to wear the swimsuit into the producer's office to get the nod of approval during the costume fitting, and now, nearly time to rehearse the scene by the swimming pool, I couldn't imagine what would satisfy the costumer. Every week, the show opened with the introduction of the guest star couples of the week being greeted by the regulars while some young, sexy people lounged around the pool. The camera lingered on female body parts. The idea was to catch as many audience eyes as possible in the first few seconds while also working to keep the wholesome tone of the show.

The old Berkeley feminist was not outraged, because I knew the score and being able to get out of my prairie skirt and play a comedic romantic lead was great. No one in Hollywood remembered that I'd played comedy on Broadway. But these "beauty aids" that might keep the director waiting were making me nervous. Soon I would be free from my *Little House* contract, and I knew I needed to demonstrate my comedy chops. Still dissatisfied, the costumer sent an assistant to find more falsies—different shapes, crescents, pillow-pads—and I began to take deeper breaths. I thought, *Aren't we in Hollywood? Isn't this the place where they do this successfully all the time?* The assistant director knocked at the trailer door—they were ready for me.

She let me go to rehearsal with instructions to "come right back afterward."

The falsies were not going to get me down. For years, I had craned my head to look whenever I passed the 20th Century Fox lot, and now I was here, seeing the roofs of the old New York street set I'd seen at matinees so long ago. Though the lot was much reduced, with vast amounts of the land sold off to create Century City, it still buoyed me to drive onto its manicured grounds, and I loved being made up with more pizzazz to play my kookie/clever character. I sped out to greet Joe Namath and rehearse our pool scene.

Joe, the football hero, was such a cute guy, with blue eyes as intense as Paul Newman's. No wonder Hollywood had come calling. Many athletes were given chances for a second career in the movies. Merlin Olsen on our show, who wound up with his own series, *Father Murphy*, had a dual career as sports announcer and series star, besides owning the Porsche dealership that had been his insurance policy in case he got hurt too seriously to play ball. His success as an actor was due less to his acting than to his simple decency, a presence built of equal parts confidence and humility that he projected on TV.

Joe seemed shy; we rehearsed our scene, and I scooted back to the swimsuit challenge, to the prodding and prying. Finally, we ran out of time, and I was pronounced passable. I went off to play the scene, pushed up as far as I could go, a reminder of my first Equity job, when our costume designer had cleverly built up my costume with a padded bra to give me the fleshy rounds that would look so alluring in a low-cut period dress. Then I accented my cleavage with rouge and highlighted the breast tissue, so it looked bigger under the lights. At the opening night the general manager said to the costumer, a pal of mine, "She was good, but you should have padded her," and we howled with laughter. So, it was no news to me that I didn't have a lot to push up, but I'd accepted my breasts as they were, even grew to appreciate them, and as Twiggy replaced Marilyn as the ideal, I'd begun to feel more and more comfortable even dressed in tight tops, even braless.

Our *Love Boat* director had deep roots in comedy, and even had a vaudeville show opening that weekend. He and I communicated perfectly, and I had a lot of fun with my character, who pretended to be superficial but had a cunning plan to get Joe to marry her. When lunch was called, Joe disappeared, as did the pretty blond extra who was my stand-in. But they were back in time for the scene after lunch.

And back on *Little House*, Mike and I got remarried, as if reflecting my preoccupation. Simultaneously, a few suitors appeared. I consulted a woman older and wiser than I in the recovery group about what do, and she told me to stay out of bed. Say good night at the door. Take time to get to know who he is. She told me to be sure to give myself time. Despite my desire to be as free as any man, I knew that after sex I lost all objectivity. I began to date differently than I ever had and I was frank about my intentions. I was looking for someone I wanted to share my life with, and who wanted to share his with me.

One man actually said, "You don't expect me to court you?" I left him behind just as I was leaving behind old behaviors that hadn't served me. Another seemed to feel he suffered too much when asked to wait for sex. Not promising. A sober pal of mine, a writer for the *LA Times* and *TV Guide*, was invited to a party for "successful singles" and invited me to join her. We both were three-plus years sober and ready for romance with someone who would not be intimidated by our success. I wore my new Armani pants and silk shirt, and off we went to a house in Santa Monica, the home of a woman photographer. The crowd was young middle-aged, dressed "business casual," and voluble.

There we met a businessman named Allen Radford, a friend of the hostess, who presented himself as a man who'd been transformed by a weekend workshop in which he learned to understand "unconditional love." My friend later referred to him slyly as "Mr. Unconditional Love," mocking his facile SoCal enlightenment. But Allen's enthusiasm was disarming. He was a large, strong man with lively blue eyes, who already had made it and lost everything in a bankruptcy, for which he admitted full responsibility. A week or so later, he called to meet me for a walk, and I told him I was looking for a partner to share my life. He grinned: "So you want to play hardball!" It turned out that after years of easy bedding, he relished the challenge of courtship. He admitted his own longing for companionship.

On our second date, Allen took me to C. C. Brown's ice cream parlor on Hollywood Boulevard. I had sweet memories from the summer when Karen Ewing and I had studied at the ballet studio next door, and I still loved the parlor's black-and-white checkered floor. And I loved ice cream. Good date. But would he want children? He already had three.

I asked.

"Only if my wife does," he said.

It was not an enthusiastic response, but it was an open one. I hadn't met his kids, but he was an involved father, and so I decided to see him again. He said he would call in a few days, but it was weeks before he called. Valentine's Day. I picked up the phone, and he asked, "Will you be my valentine?"

"No," I said.

"You won't?"

"No. You don't get a valentine by calling in the afternoon and expecting a date."

"Well, would you like to go to La Jolla this weekend?"

"No, I'm not free."

"Oh. Okay, I'll call you in a few days."

"I've heard that before."

"I said that before?"

"Look, you don't have to say that. But if you do, I expect you to follow up."

"Got it. I'll call you in a few days."

Not long after, on our way to a screening at the Writers Guild, he announced his serious intentions. I told him it wouldn't work. "You'd steamroll me."

And so, he reined himself in, courted me with patience, tenderly described his children, and his self-disclosure about his business mistakes gave me confidence that he was trustworthy. In back of his recently acquired fixer-upper, he was starting over in the garage with two employees, slowly paying off his creditors.

He started sending me gigantic bouquets. I had never seen such beautiful flowers outside of 19th-century paintings—fresh roses, carnations, alstroemeria, stock, and stunning stargazer lilies whose aroma filled my rooms. I'd rarely been spoiled, and his gesture made me buoyant. Still, I took a wait-and-see attitude.

On mornings when I didn't have to be at work until ten, Allen met me for breakfast. He took me to so many French dinners, I began to need to diet. When he invited me to go to La Jolla for the weekend, he was willing to let me have the spare bedroom. He was patient, and so was I, for once. We both knew the stakes were high. We were not young, we were scared, but we finally managed to get engaged, and the next night we danced at an art fundraiser for Barnsdall Park, the beautiful Frank Lloyd Wright property. He surprised me by being a terrific dancer, light on his feet. That night we seemed to dance on air.

More and more I pulled my focus from *Little House*. Both Allen and I were active with our careers, and I got to know his sweet boys, ages nine and fifteen, and his lovely ten-year-old daughter. He was rebuilding his career as a commercial real estate developer, and I was developing a movie about a different mother—Mother Earth.[1] When the *Little House* scripts didn't involve Ma much, instead of feeling disappointed, I saw opportunity to focus on my personal life and new projects—and I had my guarantee of two Ma episodes to look forward to. I didn't want to stop acting, but I wanted to be a mother, and I looked forward to a variety of roles—parts in which I could transform—in theatre, TV, or movies, once I was free from the series schedule. I let the network know that season eight would definitely be my last.

In all long-running series, new settings, new plots are needed. In season five (1978), Matt Labyorteaux, who had played Charles as a little boy in an earlier episode, was brought back to play the rapscallion orphan Albert, who the family takes in when they move to Mankato for a change of pace with "city life." Matt's knowing laugh and smart charm brought a new dynamic to the Ingalls family. He and Laura were natural co-conspirators. Mary's blindness had taken her away first to study at the blind school; eventually, she fell in love with her teacher, married, and had a baby.

In season seven, we were back in Walnut Grove. Ma's success running the restaurant in the hotel that Charles managed in Mankato led to Nellie's Restaurant in Walnut Grove. Mary was rarely in the stories, Laura was being rushed into courtship with Almanzo, and the Ingallses soon needed more kids. My darling Grace was still a baby. Carrie's character had not been developed. A sagging feeling came over the set. Not only had some of our favorite crew members and actors died, some of the stories had become a real stretch. Between a blind school fire burning up Alice Garvey and Mary's baby, and then a rape script, we seemed to have lost our way. At the end of that season, a two-parter called "The Lost Ones" introduced Melissa Francis as Cassandra and Jason Bateman as James, and the Ingallses adopted them to fill the house back up with kids.[2] Though the kids were talented and as cute as could be, I was reluctant to get too close because I knew it would be for just one season. Besides, my heart was engaged with Allen's kids.

During that eighth and final season, the cast and crew learned that NBC had bought an idea for a new show. A huge sigh of relief from the crew—steady work! *Little House: A New Beginning* would star Melissa Gilbert and Dean Butler as the Wilders. I was glad for them and looked forward to my own departure, but first I anticipated a rich role for Ma, my contract honored. Instead, when the last possible script appeared, it was about the kids, and only at the very end of the episode did Ma deliver the story of "Stone Soup," an old folk tale in which a starving town survives when each person contributes their one small bit of food to the pot with a stone in it. A good moral, but that was no kind of a role, and that was a slap in the face. (Was this retribution for leaving?) In my drinking days, I had used liquid courage and confronted people who angered me. As a sober person, I discovered I was a coward.

I "screwed my courage to the sticking place," as Lady Macbeth says, and at the end of the work day, with the page of my contract that spelled out my guarantee tucked into Ma's apron pocket and the script for "Stone Soup" in my hands, I went to talk to Mike. I kept my voice calm. I looked him directly in the eyes. "This script does not fulfill my contract," I said.

"If you count the words, it's a big part."

"You know as well as I do what a good part is."

"Well, talk to the network."

"I'm talking to you. This is your show."

"Go ahead and sue. Any judge will say this is a big part."

"You have not fulfilled my contract."

"You can sue."

"I want you to keep your commitment."

Then silence. We stood looking at each other.

"Talk to the network."

A small disbelieving shake of my head, I held myself tall, turned on my heel, and walked to my dressing room as he called to my back, "You're not a nice person!" I'd achieved nothing but my self-respect, and as I stripped off the skirt, unbuttoned the blouse, unlaced the black boots, I shook, and adrenaline coursed through my body.

I drove to Constance's apartment, rage and powerlessness bubbling up in hot wracking sobs. Mike's flagrant disrespect rendered me vulnerable to all the old regressive thoughts—I'm broken, I'll never get satisfaction, achieve happiness. But an understanding friend, getting something nourishing to eat, a support meeting, these would help me cope with emotional storms. And so for the last of that last year's episodes, Jason Bateman starred in a two-part special with Mike in which Charles insists on a miracle to save his boy after a fatal gunshot wound. And he is resurrected.

That was how we ended eight years.

THAT YEAR, THE ANNUAL WRAP PARTY would be bigger since it was the final party for our show, and once I was able to gain perspective, I made plans for how to wish the new show good luck. I invited Allen and his kids to come to the wrap party and had a big cake designed to depict both the iconic Little House, and the house that would be Melissa and Dean's in the new show. "From our House to Yours, All the Best! Love, Ma," the cake said, and I had it delivered to the studio to be shared by all. I imagined a presentation full of good wishes. But when I arrived at the party, I felt everyone's coolness toward me. I understood. I had been instrumental in breaking up the successful run when I gave my notice a year earlier. Our kids had grown up, and it seemed they couldn't hire a new Ma.

The party was a sad affair on the same old stage. While these parties had never been the best celebrations, there was a special pall over this one—*Little House* as it had been was over. We had all worked hard to make a show we were proud of, but now everyone seemed sad. There was a band. The lights were dim. And to me the atmosphere felt murky. The concrete floor was unforgiving to heels. Allen had hired a limo, his kids got a kick of being "inside Hollywood," and he smoothly led me in a dance. We were happy, but when I found the cake I had had delivered shoved into a dark corner, I realized my gesture had not been well received, and knew my only choice was to let it go. Victor got terribly drunk and made a sloppy, maudlin speech about how great Mike and the crew were, and Allen and I shared a look and decided it was time to leave. I gave a last hug to "my children," had a poignant goodbye with Matt Labyorteaux; we gathered Allen's kids and waltzed out of there.

A FEW MONTHS LATER, IN APRIL, Allen and I married in the garden of our cherished friends, Carl and Kathleen Little, with only family and a few friends present. We celebrated with our wider circle at the Riviera Country Club, including some of my *Little House* family, then took off for a honeymoon in Italy. We were showered with good fortune. For the time being, we moved into my house on Hollywood Boulevard, and when all three kids were there, it was like a big slumber party. We planned to take time to find our family home where all the kids would be comfortable, including room for the hoped-for baby and the big Thanksgiving feasts Allen loved hosting for his four-generation extended family. We both were excited about finding a place to fulfill our dreams of family life, entertaining friends, and—as he joked—big enough to satisfy his ego.

And after about a year, we finally found it. One Thursday morning I was driving along Sunset Boulevard to my women's group and noticed a big, old Spanish house set back from the street. I sighed at its simple but elegant proportions and thought, *Why can't we find a place like that?* After lunch, as I headed back to Hollywood, I saw an open house sign on the lawn. I whipped a U-turn, pulled up in front, parked, and jumped out of the car. As I walked into the entry hall, I saw an enormous living room on the left and dining room to the right. Was it too formal? But just behind the living room was a library with mahogany bookshelves that drew me in and took my breath away. Behind the dining room was a symmetrical butler's pantry and a kitchen that looked as if it had not been fixed up since the house was built in 1930. Knowing Allen's love of designing kitchens, this seemed an enhancement. I hurried back to the front hall and up the broad staircase. The master bedroom had a door that connected to the nursery—at least I imagined it as the nursery. I was so excited, I had to stop and use the toilet.

On Saturday I took Allen to see it. Though it needed an overhaul, the proportion and good bones were there, and after we walked up the graceful staircase to the large bedrooms, down the back stairs to the kitchen, and out to the huge backyard—the lot was nearly an acre—Allen invited the man from the bank to join him on the lawn under a magnolia tree. He began to negotiate immediately. I was astonished. *Looks like we're buying a house.*

MANY MONTHS LATER, AFTER A sweltering La Niña summer with Allen's kids piled in with us in temporary quarters, our contractor gave us the go-ahead to move into our home. The complex renovation was not complete, but the house was functional, and I felt a thrum in my blood as I coordinated the move that would consolidate our lives—his stuff, my stuff, kid stuff—into one permanent space. I was sweating alongside the movers when Allen pulled up in the driveway with our favorite sandwiches from the Italian deli. The kids and I came out and the five of us plopped down on the grassy swell of the side yard under the jacaranda tree for our picnic.

Lavender blossoms floated about us, and the breeze from the Pacific puffed coolness. The white butcher paper crinkled as we pulled open the wrappers and ate hungrily. Behind me, I sensed the derelict rose garden—bushes brown, leaves crisp and spotted. Mama would help me recover it, I knew. Whiffs of ambrosia from the tree. A stillness. The air sparkled with potential. Joy bubbled up in my center as I chewed. Allen and I smiled at each other. We were blessed, and we knew it. We had joined our lives and were about to settle in this home as a family. I was forty. It felt like it had taken me a whole lifetime to get here. What came easily and naturally for some had come hard for me. *Now,* a thought whispered, *I will have a family and a child of my own.* I was soufflé light and as grounded as a cow with her calves suckling. If this were a novel, a dark cloud might obscure the scene. We might shudder in the chill. Or perhaps a sudden hailstorm would send us dashing into the incomplete indoors.

But this is memoir. We sat there, innocently happy.

Afterword

> "The snug log house looked just as it always had. It did not
> seem to know they were going away."
> —*Little House in the Big Woods*, LAURA INGALLS WILDER

ONE AFTERNOON WHILE I WAS READING in our library, the
phone rang. The room had restored beautifully: The mahogany
cabinets had acquired a luster and held my books behind glass-
paned doors. The green walls we'd copied from the Russian Tea
Room in New York set off Allen's old leather sofa near the fireplace.
How I love this room, I thought as I got up to answer. It was Mike. I
was truly surprised. It had been more than a year since our stinging
goodbye. But he told me they were doing a special, and he wanted
me to be in it. He could have just sent an offer through my agent,
but he had picked up the phone, and I appreciated the gesture.

"Of course, I'll be glad to be in it," I told him.

When the script arrived, it was clear that this was to be the last
Little House—ever. *Little House: A New Beginning* had not caught
on and was canceled after only one season. We could have gone on
doing specials like *The Waltons* did, but Mike had made a radical
choice, and I read the script with astonishment. The plot involved
a "bad guy" who'd schemed to take over the town, and now the

townspeople, rather than let him have it, decided to blow it up. That's right—blow up Walnut Grove!

"I've heard of cutting off your nose . . . but what did he want to spite?" I wondered aloud to Allen.

At the end, the entire cast would be assembled to witness "The Last Farewell"—boom, boom. Well, not the entire cast, because Scotty refused to appear. Her bitterness over Mike's lack of appreciation had bled so deeply into her spirit that she couldn't bear to be there. And Karl Swenson, gone—I remembered supper in his Swedish cabin on a hill above Laguna. He passed quietly after completing the starring role when Mr. Hansen died.

AT THE RANCH, I RUSHED TO hug Dabbs then Kevin. Here, too, was Dick Bull, who flew in from Chicago, where he and his wife had settled for the lively theatre scene. Much of our crew was still intact, though Larry was gone, and Whitey had retired and moved out of state. During the weeks of shooting, we took full advantage of opportunities to catch up. And then we came to the last scene. It had to be shot last, for there would be no Walnut Grove afterward.

There was a heavy, mournful atmosphere as I took my place with my fellow actors, looked around at our fine crew, watched Luke Tillman wire up the biggest special effects the show would ever see. It was easy to cry for the ending of something that had been deeply rewarding, with all its ups and downs: the chance to work consistently, the dear fellow workers, our children no longer children, a real finale. I was sad but not bitter. I had worked hard to heal the hurts I had carried when I left. Now I could simply be there. We stood in a line, a regiment at the last battle. They blasted those buildings to smithereens. Then "dismissed." More hugs, tears, goodbyes as we dispersed, took off our prairie clothes, descended from the honey wagons, and climbed into the brown Ford to be ferried to the parking lot and away.

FIVE YEARS LATER, IN 1990, I wrote to Mike to let him know what I was up to, and he wrote back, saying, "Give me a call so we can talk about the old days—before we both forget them!" When I called, I heard about his family: By then, he and Cindy had two small children, Jennifer and Sean. As we visited, I asked him how Victor had died. He'd been a regular on Mike's latest hit show, *Highway to Heaven*. "Drank himself to death," Mike said, as casually as if he were saying that Vic had missed the bus. The obits said lung cancer, but Mike knew better. Another big, gifted guy killed by alcoholism.

Less than a year later, Mike received the terrible diagnosis of pancreatic cancer. He handled the death sentence like a mensch. He was much too famous to keep the story within his family and closest friends. He brought it out in his own style, letting the public know what he was dealing with and the choices he was making while consulting with Cindy through it all. He joked on *The Tonight Show* that he was doing only one press interview—*Life* magazine—because life was what he wanted. In that first-person article, Mike said, "I've abused my body over the years . . . I drank too much. I also smoked too many cigarettes and ate a lot of the wrong things. And if you do that, even if you think you're too strong to get anything, somehow you're going to pay." In the article Mike was transparent—telling people what he was trying, what he hoped would help, without claiming to have any answers.

He showed balance and humility in his last, short months.

He was gone on July 1, 1991.

IT WAS NEARLY FIFTEEN YEARS LATER when an out-of-the-blue call from Kent came, inviting me to a reunion in Los Angeles. I had settled in the East Bay across from San Francisco, near my birthplace. We had lost another favorite crew member, and Kent had had a rough go with his health and knew it was time. Due to the unexpected longevity of the show, many of us in the cast had been brought together over the years at various Laura Ingalls Wilder museums, nostalgic TV shows, and fan reunions. Our kids had transcended child stardom to become remarkable people. Our ranks had thinned, but like old army buddies, we cherished being together, even at funerals. I jumped at the chance to see people from the crew and staff I hadn't connected with in all these years. My annual letters had gradually ceased, as addresses had changed, and I moved from place to place. I was glad I wasn't in a play and was free to go.

"It'll be lunch since we're all getting older," Kent said.

On the short flight from my nearby airport in Oakland to LAX, I tapped my feet when the plane was delayed; at the car rental office I willed the line to move, move, jumped in the car, and sped out to the country club in the valley where Kent and Susan had settled. I rushed into the big dining room, which was packed with tables of ten, scanned the room for Kent. Everybody was already seated. I spotted Mike's grown kids, poised and handsome. Ah! Hal Burton, Jack Lilley!

I saw Maury Dexter's white hair and found a seat at an adjacent table. The cast table was already full, and besides, I'd seen them all recently, but who knew when I would get to see the crew again? Matt Labyorteaux was at Maury's table. He and I grinned at each other. I approached Maury gently from behind so as not to startle him. "Maury?"

"Karen Grassle! I have to stand up." A big hug. "Karen, I have to tell you, what you put up with, when I think of what was slung at you, what a talent, what a lady. When I watch those videos, what you were able to do—with all the mistreatment coming at you— you showed such character—what a great talent."

I began to cry big gloppy tears about two sentences in, embraced him, thanked him.

But he went on: "I was hoping you'd be here today so I could tell you this. I wish I'd told you a long time ago. You—you went to your dressing room and never let it hurt your work . . ."

"Oh Maury, I thought people didn't see. Didn't realize . . . you were all so, so—"

His words—he went on—salved years of isolation and bound up old wounds. My tears so quick to spring up and pour out proved to me how deeply I'd needed this acknowledgment of my struggle, and for the rest of the day—amidst loving greetings with dear, long-missed fellow workers, the embarrassment at not recognizing some people, the posed photos—all this passed in a halo of grace after that brief exchange with Maury. I read a tribute I'd written to Kent, embraced my colleagues and my "children," and returned home, feeling a deep calm that not even Los Angeles International Airport could touch.

Acknowledgments

MEMORY CALLED AND I FOLLOWED. First to a class given at OLLI, Berkeley by the brilliant teacher Deborah Lichtman. Deborah's notes and insights on my early drafts guided and motivated me. She inspired a group of us to form our own circle where we have continued to write and support each other's work.

My heartfelt gratitude to the Addison Street Writers Circle—Sue Ezekiel, Ruth Hanham, Eleanor Lew, Vivian Pisano, Kate Pope, Anna Rabkin, Martina Reaves, Maryly Snow, and Linda Sondheimer. We have been meeting weekly for more than a decade, persevering in our writing, sustaining and heartening each individual's efforts. We have given feedback with more insight as the years have passed. My memoir was developed in this safe, but invigorating atmosphere.

For reading early versions of the manuscript and offering their insights, I want to thank our Circle most especially, as well as the discerning feedback of the late Toni Clark, Lawrence Thornton, Fred Gordon, Kent Wolfe, Diana Gould, Karen McLellan, Molly Barnes, Suzanne Courtmanche, John Argue, and William Vandegrift. Early members of ASWC, Kris Albert, Margo Dashiell, Doris Fine, Marga Riddle, and Steve Murtagh, encouraged my process as well.

My deep gratitude to my astute, insightful, and fast editor, Amy Friedman. Other editors and professionals who read the book include Victoria Nelson, who offered invaluable notes, and Adam

Reed of the Joy Harris Agency, and Mitchell Waters of Brandt and Hochman, who believed in the book's future.

My son, Zach Radford, has been a source of encouragement and support throughout the long years of this process, and rescued me when I was technically challenged. Many friends gave me emotional support, including Carol Cook, Gigi Gamble, Trish Kiefer, Amy Perry, Colleen Stein, and Deborah Efron. Some also connected me with their contacts in the publishing world, notably Alison Arngrim, Lynn Atkison, Molly Barnes, and William Anderson.

For permissions to quote from authors, I am indebted to Noel Silverman at the Laura Ingalls Wilder Trust, Jeanne McLellan, Tara Weikum, and Peter London at HarperCollins. LeeAnn Platner at NBCUniversal provided permission for me to quote from the *Little House on the Prairie* series.

For their confidence in the book and creative work to bring it to fruition, I am grateful to Brooke Warner and the staff at She Writes Press. Megan Beatie has given her enthusiastic P.R. expertise to lend wings to this project.

I am indebted to Elissa Rabellino for final proof-reading, Beth Wright for early copy-editing, and practical assistance from Aliya Charney, Karina Gomez, and Julie Faherty. Stalwart support through research and myriad essential tasks came from my assistant, Jamie Valle.

About the Author

KAREN GRASSLE, known around the world for her iconic role as Ma on *Little House on the Prairie,* grew up in Ventura, California. Raised by hardworking, loving people, undercut by the alcoholism of her father, Karen graduated from UC Berkeley and attended the London Academy of Music and Dramatic Art on a Fulbright. She went on to a career in New York as well as in theatres all over the US. She co-wrote and starred in the TV film, *Battered,* and is known for her advocacy on behalf of equality for women. In the last fifteen years, she has appeared in many plays locally and out of state, as well as in three indie films. She resides in the San Francisco Bay Area and takes pleasure in her relationship with her son, Zach Radford, and in gardening.

Endnotes

Bright Lights, Prairie Dust

Chapter 4—Duet
1. W.B. Yeats, "Among School Children," *Collected Poems of W.B. Yeats*, Macmillan and Co., 1952.

Chapter 5—Undertow
1. T.S. Eliot, "The Lovesong of J. Alfred Prufock," *The Complete Poems and Plays 1909–1950*, Harcourt Brace Jovanovich, 1971.

Chapter 7—Art and Death
1. Henry Hewes, *The Saturday Review*, August 26, 1961.
2. Herbert Blau's papers would grow into his book, *The Impossible Theatre: A Manifesto*, Collier Books, 1965.
3. www.americantheatre.org/2015/06/16/going-national-how-americas-regional-theatre-movement-changed-the-game/

Chapter 8—Waking Up in Berkeley
1. Michael Lerner was nominated for an Academy Award in *Barton Fink*, 1991.

2. Jo Freeman, *At Berkeley in the Sixties: The Education of an Activist, 1961–1965,* Bloomington: Indiana University Press, 2004, 220–21.
3. Barry Kraft would become the esteemed Shakespearean dramaturg for the Oregon Shakespeare Festival, acting in all of the canon.

Chapter 9—Practice

1. *Marat/Sade*, Peter Weiss, 1963.
2. Swoozie Kurtz made her Broadway debut in 1975, has won one Primetime Emmy and two Tony awards, and is currently in a recurring role in *Grace and Frankie*, Netflix.
3. The next spring, David Warner became a star in the film *Morgan*, which also introduced Vanessa Redgrave to an international audience. He went on to win an Emmy in 1981.
4. Janet Suzman, Oscar nominee for Best Supporting Actress for *Nicholas and Alexandra* (1971), was a LAMDA graduate.
5. Paul Scofield, considered to be one of the greatest Shakespearean performers, won both a Tony and an Oscar for his portrayal of Sir Thomas More in *A Man for All Seasons*. Also during his career, which spanned six decades, Scofield won an Emmy and a BAFTA.
6. Roshan Seth played Pandit Nehru in Richard Attenborough's brilliant 1982 bio-pic *Gandhi*.
7. Shunryu Suzuki Roshi (1904–1971) was a Zen monk and teacher and the founder of San Francisco Zen Center and Tassajara Zen Mountain Center.
8. Later, when Lynn and I became friends while working in Boston and on Broadway in *Sweet Sue*, by A. R. Gurney (1986-87), she shared that a London critic had so wildly praised her—describing with eloquence how "she hung the laundry"—that she could never again hang the laundry without feeling self-conscious and, therefore, gave up reading reviews forever—or at least until after any show she was in closed.

Chapter 10—An Actor's Life for Me

1. Joanne Akalaitis went on to become an award-winning director of Off-Broadway plays and was a founder of Mabou Mines, the avant-garde theatre company.

2. Philip Glass became a world-renowned composer known for creating a new musical style, called "minimalist" by critics, and was especially famous for his operas, including *Einstein on the Beach*.

Chapter 11—Eating the Big Apple

1. Mark Crowley, *The Boys in the Band*, Off-Broadway, 1968, published by Farrar, Straus and Giroux that year.

2. Actors take note: It was only five years later that Cicely triumphed in *The Autobiography of Miss Jane Pittman*.

3. Kristin Linklater, *Freeing the Natural Voice* (Drama Publishers/ Quite Specific Media, 1976) was developed during these workshops, in which Meg Wilbur, my acting and teaching colleague, took and transcribed notes.

Chapter 12—Hooray for Hollywood

1. Eileen Heckart was a Broadway star whose career spanned nearly sixty years. In 1972, she won the Best Supporting Actress Oscar for *Butterflies Are Free*, a role she originated on Broadway.

Chapter 13—Having It All

1. *Entertainment Weekly* would later call Jeannie Epper "the greatest stunt woman that ever lived." October, 2007.

2. On television series, the producer credit usually goes to writers. As the years went by, Kent McCray would become a producer of the show based on his invaluable contributions.

Chapter 14—"We're Home"

1. T.S. Eliot, "Little Gidding," "Four Quartets," *T.S. Eliot: The Complete Poems and Plays 1909–1950*, Harcourt, Brace, Jovanovich, 1971.

Chapter 16—Towers and Walls

1. Larry Kramer's, *The Normal Heart* premiered Off-Broadway at the Public Theater in April 1985 and had a revival production on Broadway in 2011.

Chapter 17—Never Say Die

1, Erin Pizzey opened the first shelter for victims of domestic violence in Great Britain in 1971.
2. For Cynthia's article about our collaboration, see *Working It Out: 23 Women Writers, Artists, Scientists, and Scholars Talk About Their Lives and Work*, edited by Sara Ruddick and Daniela Daniels, Pantheon, 1977.

Chapter 18—Hitting Bottom

1. Fleetwood Mac, "Dreams," *Rumours*, Warner Bros. Records, 1977.
2. Caroline Bird, *The Two-Paycheck Marriage: How Women at Work Are Changing Life in America: An In-Depth Report on the Great Revolution of Our Times*, Rawson, Wade Publishers, 1979.

Chapter 20—Woman's Work

1. Alice Paul, 1885–1977. For more information see the Alice Paul Institute: www.alicepaul.org.
2. Unfortunately, Altman's picture came out and bombed. So much for his fundraising largesse.
3. Sally Van Wagenen Keil, *Those Wonderful Women in their Flying Machines*, Four Directions Press, 1979.
4. After *Little House*, Chris Abbott went on to a highly successful career in television, producing *Magnum, P.I.*, *Diagnosis Murder*, and other series, as well as creating her own excellent though short-lived series that dealt with race relations in the 19th century.

Chapter 22—New Acts

1. Based on *Morgana's Fault*, a novel by Susan Ries Lukas, Stereopticon, 1975.

2. Melissa Francis went on to Harvard and to head *Melissa and Money* and *Outnumbered* on Fox-TV. Jason Bateman is a director of and actor in major motion pictures as well as on Broadway, where I admired his brilliant work as the pedophile in *August, Osage County,* 2007. Current: *Ozark*, Netflix.

Permissions

Quotes from *The Selected Letters of Laura Ingalls Wilder*, edited by William Anderson (Copyright © 2016 by William Anderson, Letters © 2016 Little House Heritage Trust) are used by permission of HarperCollins Publishers. Introduction, annotation, footnotes, explanatory text, photograph captions (© 2016 William Anderson) are used by permission of HarperCollins Publishers.

Selected text excerpts from *These Happy Golden Years* by Laura Ingalls Wilder, Illustrated By: Garth Williams. TEXT COPYRIGHT 1943, 1971 Little House Heritage Trust. Used by permission of HarperCollins Publishers.

Two (2) selected text excerpts from *Farmer Boy* by Laura Ingalls Wilder, Illustrated By: Garth Williams. TEXT COPYRIGHT 1933, 1961 Little House Heritage Trust. Used by permission of HarperCollins Publishers.

Two (2) selected text excerpts from *Little House in the Big Woods* by Laura Ingalls Wilder, Illustrated By: Garth Williams. TEXT COPYRIGHT 1932, 1960 Little House Heritage Trust. Used by permission of HarperCollins Publishers.

SELECTED TITLES FROM SHE WRITES PRESS

She Writes Press is an independent publishing company founded to serve women writers everywhere. Visit us at www.shewritespress.com.

Home Free: Adventures of a Child of the Sixties by Rifka Kreiter. $16.95, 978-1-63152-176-8. A memoir of a young woman's passionate quest for liberation—one that leads her out of the darkness of a fraught childhood and through Manhattan nightclubs, broken love affairs, and virtually all the political and spiritual movements of the sixties.

All the Ghosts Dance Free: A Memoir by Terry Cameron Baldwin. $16.95, 978-1-63152-822-4. A poetic memoir that explores the legacy of alcoholism and teen suicide in one woman's life—and her efforts to create an authentic existence in the face of that legacy.

The Coconut Latitudes: Secrets, Storms, and Survival in the Caribbean by Rita Gardner. $16.95, 978-1-63152-901-6. A haunting, lyrical memoir about a dysfunctional family's experiences in a reality far from the envisioned Eden—and the terrible cost of keeping secrets.

Where Have I Been All My Life? A Journey Toward Love and Wholeness by Cheryl Rice. $16.95, 978-1-63152-917-7. Rice's universally relatable story of how her mother's sudden death launched her on a journey into the deepest parts of grief—and, ultimately, toward love and wholeness.

Notes from the Bottom of the World by Suzanne Adam. $16.95, 978-1-63152-415-8. In this heartfelt collection of sixty-three personal essays, Adam considers how her American past and move to Chile have shaped her life and enriched her worldview, and explores with insight questions on aging, women's roles, spiritual life, friendship, love, and writers who inspire.